Dionysos Rising

Dionysos Rising

The Birth of Cultural Revolution
Out of the Spirit of Music

E. Michael Jones

Fidelity Press
South Bend, Indiana
2012

Cover by Michael Murphy Design, Inc.

Copyright 2012 Fidelity Press, South Bend, IN
All Rights Reserved
ISBN 978-0-929891-10-1
Printed in the United States of America

Contents

Chapter 1
Richard Wagner — 7
Chromaticism, Adultery, and the Beginning
of Our Cultural Revolution

Chapter 2
Friedrich Nietzsche — 47
Transvaluation of All Values as the Prosecution
of the Cultural War

Chapter 3
Arnold Schönberg — 91
Craving the Law and the Totalitarian Reaction

Chapter 4
Sympathy for the Devil — 125
Theodor Adorno, Aleister Crowley, Mick Jagger

Bibliography — 171

Index — 175

Chapter 1

Richard Wagner
Chromaticism, Adultery, and the Beginning of Our Cultural Revolution

> The man that hath no music in himself,
> Nor is not moved with concord of sweet sounds,
> Is fit for treasons, stratagems, and spoils;
> The motions of his spirit are dull as night,
> And his affections dark as Erebus.
> Let no such man be trusted. Mark the music.
> —William Shakespeare
> *The Merchant of Venice*, V, i, 82-88

> And a man who has not "music" in him is apt to disintegrate states; since music is equally suggestive of personal love or political concord.
> —G. Wilson Knight
> *The Shakespearean Tempest*

> And the music will correspond to their minds, for as their minds are perverted from the natural state, so there are perverted modes and highly strung and unnaturally colored melodies. A man receives pleasure from what is natural to him. . . .
> —Aristotle
> *Politics*

The so-called Revolution of 1848 did not arrive in Dresden until the spring of 1849—that May to be exact—when the king of Saxony fled from his capital to a nearby fortified castle and appealed to the Prussians to restore order to his troubled kingdom. The Saxon soldiers were caught in the middle of all this, since Prussia was after all a foreign country. Where they to stand and fight the invaders shoulder to shoulder with the Saxon insurrectionists, or were they to obey the wishes of the king and fight with the Prussian army against their fellow Saxons?

Since he was both a native Saxon and an aspiring insurrectionist, Richard Wagner found the former alternative the more appealing and, as was often his wont, acted on it with dispatch. Wagner was the director of Dresden's orchestra, a position Kurt Mazur was to find similarly politically charged 140 years later, when the masses took to the streets in Dresden once again to revolt, this time against the revolution, not for it. In addition to his musical duties at the time, Wagner had also taken over the editorship of his friend August Röckel's *Volksblätter*, a revolutionary broadside that threatened to cease publication when Röckel had to leave the country on short notice. Wagner went to the *Volksblätter*'s printer and ordered their biggest sheets printed in their largest type with the question, "Are you with us in opposing foreign troops?" [1]

The question was directed at the Saxon army, to whom the fliers were to be distributed. Unfortunately, the fliers got hung on the barricades instead, never making it to the troops for whom they were intended. Their chief effect, as Wagner later was ruefully to surmise, was simply to provide evidence against him when the state charged him with high treason.

Wagner seems to have left evidence enough to allow even the most obtuse judge or jury to convict him. In addition to the singularly ineffective revolutionary fliers, there was the letter to Röckel calling him back from exile in Bohemia and urging him to take part in the fight. The letter was found on Röckel's person when that unfortunate person was apprehended during the first few days of the insurrection. Then there was the matter of an order placed with Herr Oehme, the brass founder, who testified later that Röckel and Wagner had come to him prior to Easter 1849, instructing him to make a number of hand grenades, which were destined actually for another insurrection in Prague. When Röckel came to trial, he claimed that Wagner alone had placed the order, a claim that, if intended to produce leniency, was singularly ineffective. If it was intended to incriminate Wagner, it was a work of supererogation. Wagner was quite capable of producing self-incriminating evidence all by himself.

On April 8, 1849, Wagner waxed rhapsodic over the Goddess of Revolution stalking the land, issuing threats of the following sort:

> I shall destroy the existing order of things that divides united mankind into hostile nations, into powerful and weak, into privileged and deprived, into rich and poor, for its sole effect is to render us all unhappy. I shall destroy the order of things that makes millions the slaves of a few and those few the slaves of their own power. I shall destroy this order of things that divorces enjoyment from labor, makes labor a burden and enjoyment a vice, makes one person wretched by reason of deprivation and another by reason of affluence. I shall destroy this order of things that consumes men's energies in the service of dominion by the dead.... [2]

These were strong words for a woman, even if she was a goddess, and even stronger words for Dresden's *Kapellmeister*, words bound to bring him into contact with others who were as perfervid as he in their desire to destroy "this order of things."

One such man was a certain "Dr. Schwartz," a man in his thirties, with thick black hair and beard, whom Wagner found "colossal and possessing a primitive freshness and power" [3] that he found, if not irresistible, then at least attractive.

"Dr. Schwartz" was, in reality, the Russian aristocrat and anarchist Mikhail Bakunin, who, in spite of being wanted by the local police, had taken an apartment in Wagner's neighborhood and had taken as well to coming to the rehearsals Wagner was conducting of Beethoven's Ninth Symphony, which was to be performed on Palm Sunday of that year. Bakunin was so taken with Wagner's rendition of Beethoven that he could not restrain himself. After one rehearsal he rushed up to the conductor and assured the bewildered Wagner that even if all of the world's music were going to be lost in the coming revolutionary holocaust, they (Bakunin and Wagner) should do everything within their power to see that Beethoven's Ninth was preserved.

A few weeks later, it looked as if Bakunin's prophecy was about to come true. On May 7, Wagner spent the night in the steeple of the *Kreuzkirche* reporting on the movements of the Prussian troops and dodging sniper fire. Around eleven o'clock he watched as the old opera house went up in flames and burned as only an old wooden building stuffed with linen could. It was, he said later, describing the terrible droning of the bells and the constant ricocheting of the Prussian bullets against the steeple walls, "one of the strangest nights of my life." [4] And it was followed by one of the most beautiful days of the year. He was awakened, in proper romantic fashion, by a nightingale. On Sunday, May 8, as Wagner was hurrying through a Dresden now caught in the crossfire of revolutionary struggle, one of the insurrectionists, who had evidently attended his performance of Beethoven's Ninth, exclaimed that "one of joy's divine sparks had just ignited that firetrap and burned it to the ground."[5] He was referring to the opera house, and the news filled Wagner with mixed feelings. "The report of this Pathos, which came upon me so unexpectedly, had a strangely empowering and liberating effect." [6]

The short-lived revolution in Dresden had an even more pronounced and liberating effect on Bakunin, who could now walk the streets freely, examining the barricades and smoking his cigar. What he saw left him unimpressed. Bakunin felt that the revolutionary guards had virtually no chance of defending their hastily erected barricades against the more disciplined Prussian troops. He spent the first few days of the revolution walking around the barricades, enjoying what he probably thought was a temporary freedom, and making fun of what he considered the amateurish attempts of the defenders.

Wagner tried to interest him in his music but quickly came to the conclusion that the only thing the black-haired Russian anarchist was interested in was destruction. "This destruction of every civilization was his enthusiastically pursued goal, and the only amusement he entertained with any cheerfulness was putting all his energies behind achieving this goal." [7]

Shortly after the abortive attempt to distribute the fliers to the Saxon troops, Wagner offered to read Bakunin his poem on the Niebelung saga, which eventually became the four-opera Ring Cycle. But Bakunin was not interested, perhaps with good reason; the revolution might have come and gone during the reading of this extensive work. Undeterred, Wagner went on to describe a work that he was planning based on the four Gospels. Jesus of Nazareth was "a tragedy," which Wagner was planning to have performed on "the ideal stage of the future," presumably at some time after the nascent revolution had achieved its reforms.[8] Bakunin, for his part, showed only a little more interest in this project than in the Niebelung poem. He confined himself to certain *a priori* artistic suggestions, without giving Wagner the chance to show him his actual work. Bakunin wished him well but was hardly willing to get involved in the details of the libretto. He had, however, a few suggestions. For starters, Wagner should portray the Christ as weak. Bakunin then had some musical suggestions as well: the music should confine itself to variations on certain texts being sung by the various choral voices. The tenors were to sing "Behead him," the sopranos, "Hang him," and the basso continuos (sic), "Fire! Fire!" [9]

As a librettist and musician, Bakunin was clearly ahead of his time. His Jesus of Nazareth is not difficult for us to imagine, for we have had the dubious advantage of over a century's worth of cultural revolution to draw on, cultural revolution *ad nauseam*, so much so that our imagination is hardly challenged to compose the libretto out of the bits and pieces of a culture that has surpassed itself in its desire for destruction and self-immolation. Bakunin's Jesus sounds like a cross between Martin Scorcese and John Cage.

Wagner, however, was having a more difficult time imagining the sort of music that should accompany that kind of text. ("You won't need any instruments then," Bakunin had told Wagner, referring to the period following the revolution and at the same time giving a rather prophetic look at the state of music one hundred years later.)[10] The reason for this was simple enough. That sort of music had not been invented yet. In fact, it would take over a hundred years to come into existence, and only as the result of music Wagner had yet to write. That music would come out of Wagner's revolutionary mind-set, but not in a way that was immediately apparent to Wagner at the time. That Wagner had his heart set on a political revolution was obvious to everyone who knew him, from the people who read his revolutionary broadsides in the *Volksblätter* to the authorities who gathered enough evidence against him to put him on the Saxon wanted posters. The artist was poised to fulfill his new role even if that entailed being without instruments and opera house: one ingredient, however, was lacking: the revolution itself.

By the evening of Sunday, May 7, it had become clear to Wagner that the position of the insurrection was as untenable as his own in his role as its forward observer in the steeple of the *Kreuzkirche*. What had been "a relatively peaceful" observation post was coming under increasingly accurate and heavy fire, to the point where "unarmed men were out of place." [11] In addition, Wagner's wife had let him know that her anxiety about his well-being had reached the breaking point and that it was time for him to come home. Wagner left Dresden by foot on Monday, May 8, a beautiful spring day, he informs us. After meeting up with his wife at a village outside Dresden, the two of them traveled by a circuitous route, necessitated by the refugees and reinforcements clogging the roads, to his sister and brother-in-law's house in Chemnitz.

Wagner returned to Dresden a few days later. But the journey was for the most part a fool's errand. He had heard that the barricades had held, but this was only because the Prussian troops had decided not to make a frontal assault. They had decided instead to go around the barricades by breaking through the walls of the neighboring houses and then to head toward the city hall, which was the seat of the provisional government.

Bakunin, whom Wagner found lying on a mattress smoking a cigar, was trying to buck up the courage of a violinist who would cringe every time a shell exploded in the vicinity. "You're not playing the violin here," he said. "You would have been better off if you were, Musician!"[12] Bakunin's plan was to fill the *Rathaus* with all of their available powder and then blow it up when the Prussian troops broke through. He was prevented from fulfilling his plan by the fact that those opposed to it simply made off with the available explosives. Wagner saw Bakunin and Heubner, the leader of the provisional government, as both rode away armed but in full retreat from the debacle in Dresden. Bakunin was put in charge of the retreat, and among the first victims of his compulsion to destroy were the trees that lined the Maximillians-Allee. Bakunin had them cut down and made into a defense work against possible cavalry attack on the flanks of the retreating troops. Bakunin found the lamentation of the residents of the Allee over their trees particularly amusing, even to the point of mocking their pronunciation of the "beautiful trees" that had fallen to Bakunin's horticultural anarchism. The owner of the coach Bakunin was riding in, expressed fears for his property, prompting a similar outburst of scorn on Bakunin's part. "The tears of the Philistine," Wagner remembers Bakunin saying, "are nectar for the gods."[13]

As impressive as Wagner found Bakunin and his methods, his bohemian panache, and his animal magnetism, he was forced to admit that the revolution had failed and to flee for his life. It was to be another twelve years before Wagner, the quintessential German composer, would set foot on German soil again, and then it was only as a result of strenuous efforts on the part of a whole host of European luminaries, including the Empress Eugenie. Wagner fled first to Weimar with future father-in-law and fellow composer Franz Liszt. When a wanted poster with his picture on it appeared in Weimar, Wagner decided it was time to leave the Germanophone world altogether. His original destination was Paris. After being convinced, however, that the direct way there was too dangerous, he decided to leave the German-speaking countries by way of Switzerland with the help of an expired passport formerly belonging to a Swabian professor.

Wagner's attitude toward revolution during this period is fraught with ambivalence. On the one hand, we have his letter to his wife written in mid-May, immediately after the resistance of the communal guards in Dresden had collapsed. "The Dresden revolution and its whole outcome," he wrote,

> have now taught me that I am anything but a true revolutionary: the very failure of the insurrection has shown me that a truly victorious revolutionary must proceed entirely without scruple. He cannot afford to think of wife and child, hearth and home. His sole endeavor must be destruction, and had the noble Heubner been prepared to act thus at Freiburgh or Chemnitz, the revolution would have continued victorious.[14]

Martin Gregor-Dellin cites this part of the letter as proof that Wagner had not recanted his previous revolutionary beliefs. His argument is not very convincing, especially in light of the more frequently cited subsequent part of the same letter in which Wagner makes plain that

> people of our sort are not destined for this terrible task. We are revolutionaries only in order to *build* on fresh soil; it is *re-creation* that attracts us, not *destruction*, which is why we are not the people whom fate requires. These will arise from the very lowest dregs of society; we and our hearts can have nothing in common with them. You see? *Thus do I bid farewell to revolution. . . .*[15]

On the other hand, in late July Wagner was holed up in Zurich, hard at work on his essay "Art and Revolution." He begins by quoting approvingly Carlyle's description of the French Revolution as "the breaking out of universal mankind into Anarchy" and tells the reader, "I believed in the Revolution, and in its unrestrainable necessity, with certainly no greater immoderation than Carlyle."[16]

The two passages are not simply contradictory; they are dialectical in a way that a Hegelian like Marx would have appreciated, even though the later Marx expressed more annoyance than anything else when the name of Wagner came up, as it frequently did, in conversation. The public essay on revolution is not simply a reaffirmation of the revolution Wagner had repudiated in private to his wife. It is a reaffirmation of a revolution that Wagner was in the process of subtly redefining.

Perhaps his experience in Dresden of the destruction-bent, but ultimately ineffectual, Bakunin was enough to convince Wagner not only that he did not have the stomach for what it took to succeed at revolution, but also, of the fact that the revolutionary urge for universal destruction was overrated as well. All that the ruthless and overpowering Bakunin could manage out of Dresden was a few smirking aphorisms and extensive arboricide. The so-called man of action, bent on destruction, treated Wagner's musical ideas with a barely concealed contempt. Only the actual performance of the music from *The Flying Dutchman* seems to have made an impression on him in much the same way that Beethoven's Ninth had. But for all that, what had Bakunin and his less ruthless fellow insurrectionists accomplished? Bakunin's thirst for universal destruction had left little more than a few dead trees in its wake. The Prussians had restored the Saxon king, and Wagner, Röckel, von Biberstein, and the rest of the revolutionary leadership ended up either in jail or in exile. Judging from what he had to say in *Art and*

Revolution, Wagner was as committed as ever to the overthrow of existing conditions. However, the scope of his rebellion had changed. His desire for change now went deeper than the political process in terms of its end and beyond the political process, beyond even revolutionary politics, in terms of the means to bring that revolutionary change about. In the aftermath of 1849, Wagner went from being a failed political revolutionary to being an enormously successful revolutionary musician.

The publication of the ostensibly so radical *Art and Revolution* was in reality the beginning of a turn inward that would be consummated some years later. Wagner was still for revolution, but the terms of the revolution had changed from the political to the cultural. In the redefining of his vocation he put himself in a position to have much more far-reaching consequences on the society he hoped to revolutionize.

Art and Revolution was a revolutionary document, but one characterized by a retreat from the political. Written under the influence of Proudhon and Feuerbach, it purported to lay the blame for the current state of affairs at the feet of a socio-political system. Even in doing this, however, it kept refocusing on prepolitical conditions that had more to do with the human condition than they did with the abuses extant under any particular political system. In the modern age, there are revolutions, and there are revolutions, and virtually all of them are an incongruous mixture of *ressentiment* against the human condition as represented by a particular political institution. The revolutionary agendum espoused by both Wagner and Bakunin was so politically diffuse that no political reform could have accomplished it. As a result, it is only natural that its political death would only release its revolutionary soul into freer flights of fantasy, where its disembodied soul was free to posit conditions that it was safe to say could never find incorporation in any political system anywhere.

In other words, the events of 1848 had proved to be a powerful incitement to a revolution that was essentially metaphysical in its scope. That there were political conditions that acted as a catalyst is undeniable. However, the catalyst came and went. The political failed to become the proper vehicle for these revolutionary aspirations, just as it had failed over half a century before in France. So out of the ashes of political debacle arose—smoke-like, genie-like, phoenix-like—the soul of the cultural revolution that would come to be known as Modernity.

And what were its deepest aspirations? Then as now, liberation. When Gustav Kietz visited Wagner's wife shortly after the Prussian troops had withdrawn from Dresden and Wagner himself had escaped into the beginning of his twelve-year exile from Germany, he recounted being disconcerted by the squawking of the Wagner's parrot, who would punctuate her sob-filled story with cries of "Richard! Liberty!"

Liberty, indeed! Even a parrot can say it. But freedom from what? Wagner was burdened by debts, by an unhappy marriage, by a career that seemed stalled in the provinces, but most of all, as "Art and Revolution" makes clear, by a system of social values that seemed to drain the color out of life. This value system was known as Christianity, which he describes as something that

> adjusts the ills of an honourless, useless, and sorrowful existence of mankind on earth, by the miraculous love of God; who had not—as the noble Greek supposed—created man for a happy and self-conscious life upon this earth, but had here imprisoned him in a loathsome dungeon: so as, in reward for the self-contempt that prisoned him therein, to prepare him for a posthumous state of endless comfort and inactive ecstasy. . . . therefore the poor wretch who, in the enjoyment of his natural powers, made this life his own possession must suffer after death the eternal torments of hell! Naught was required of mankind but *Faith*—that is to say the confession of its miserable plight, and the giving up of all spontaneous attempt to escape from out this misery; for the *undeserved Grace of God* was alone to set it free.[17]

As the final and partially italicized passage makes clear, Wagner was talking about Christianity in its Protestant, specifically Lutheran, redaction. Wagner had a life-long love/hate relationship with Christianity, and part of that struggle was the attempt to identify himself with either its Protestant or its Catholic expression. He was raised at the heart of Lutheranism; the Vatican and the Wartburg are two symbolic poles at the center of his crucial opera *Tannhäuser*; and in composing *Parsifal* he sought out the advice of a Bavarian Catholic priest. The Christianity that Wagner found so repugnant is the essentially Protestant version that was the social underpinning of the high noon of capitalism in northern Europe and England where "God is become Industry, which keeps the poor Christian worker alive only until celestial market conditions bring about the gracious necessity of releasing him into a better world."[18]

Given this view of things, it is not difficult to see Wagner hoping, like Marx, to bring about a change in human relations by bringing about a change in the socio-economic structure. The man Wagner denominates as Christian is someone characterized by superficialities. His head is crowned "with the halo of Christian hypocrisy, decorate his breast with the soulless tokens of dead feudal orders: and ye have in him the god of the modern world, the holy-noble god of 'five per cent,' the ruler and the master of ceremonies of our modern art."[19] However, the more Wagner rants, the more he talks himself into a position of radical opposition not just to Christian hypocrisy but to Christianity itself. If Christianity were the problem, then no mere change in political structures could bring about the solution. And the more Wagner rants, the more it becomes clear that Wagner the revolutionary *manqué* finds that Christianity in its most radical essence is the problem. "The art of Christian Europe," he maintains,

> could never proclaim itself, like that of ancient Greece, as the expression of a world attuned to harmony; for the reason that its inmost being was incurably and irreconcilably split up between the force of conscience and the instinct of life, between the ideal and reality.[20]

Wagner's choice of the word "harmony" in this context is both predictable and revolutionary at the same time. Wagner was of course writing as a musician at the time. But his use of the word "harmony" bespoke more than a simple professional interest. Harmony, even in Wagner's time, was still a concept that transcended the merely musical. Harmony was another word for order, the *tranquillitas ordinis* mentioned by Augustine that was manifest in creation, in society, and in the individual's soul in terms that were synonymous with terms musical. In addition to that, he was also drawing on a whole history of music in the West as associated with both external and internal order through the concept of harmony. "Each creature," wrote Goethe in a letter dated November 17, 1789, "is nothing more than a sound, a shading of a great harmony, which one must study in its magnitude and entirety. Otherwise each individual is nothing more than a dead letter."[21]

According to both the ancients and their Christian followers, the order of creation was love, bound together in a unity both mathematical and musical. Indeed, love, divine order, music, and mathematics are simply four different ways of saying the same thing. Harmony, as a result, had come to possess a cosmic meaning, that is, as a manifestation of the music of the spheres, a political manifestation, as seen in the well-ordered state, and a psychological manifestation, as seen in the well-ordered soul. In each instance, the most accurate description of that state of order is taken from the realm of music. So *sumphonia*, according to Leo Spitzer, "is the order introduced into the soul by music, an order which re-establishes the order of the cosmos."[22] Similarly, the Church Fathers were forced to employ a musical vocabulary when attempting to talk about love and the world order based on that love, not because they lacked a "scientific" way of talking about these things, but because the underlying unity they perceived in the universe was essentially musical. Saint John Chrysostom, in his praise of friendship, "explains the cithara as love, the sounds produced by it as the words of friends, the musician who brings about the harmonia and sumphonia as the power of love."[23] The Pythagoreans had taken the notion even farther, attributing to music the ability to cure disease. Theophrastus, according to Spitzer, "states that gouty pains in the hip, as well as snakebites, are cured by playing the flute."[24] The notion sounds slightly or more than slightly absurd to modern ears. However, perhaps not as absurd as it might have twenty years ago. The Surgeon General announced recently that—of the top ten causes of death—most were behavior related and, therefore, avoidable. In an age when AIDS is one of the chief causes of death in New York City, the correspondence between the moral and the medical, and moral disorder in the former leading to physical sickness, does not seem as far-fetched as it might have not very long ago.

Cicero drew on a tradition long established in his day when he claimed that *Pythagoras . . . per musicam refraenavit luxuriosum*" (Pythagoras. . . put a stop to the things of lust through the use of music).[25] In describing how Cicero could claim that Pythagoras could heal lust through music, Burbach claims that the ancients attributed to music

> a purifying and clarifying [*klärende*] power, as a result of which the soul is taken out of its state of confusion and returned to its normal condition. In his commentary on the Psalms, Thomas Aquinas cites another anecdote about Pythagoras, which is cited by Boethius in the foreword to his "Music." According to this anecdote, a young man who had been driven to frenzy by listening to melodies in the Phrygian mode was brought back to health by a changing of musical modes. In his commentary on the music theories in Aristotle's *Politics*, Peter of Alvern termed the Dorian mode as "*maxime moralis*" because it disposes the hearer to the Good and to constancy in action. Thomas Aquinas, in similar fashion, describes the "*cantus phrygius*," named after the region from whence the devotees of Dionysus came, as possessing the power to excite the emotions, a power that can lead the hearer to madness if the music is listened to immoderately.[26]

The common denominator, then, for the medical, the moral, the musical, the political, the theological, and the astronomical, is reason and measure. All things created by God participate in the being of their creator through the reasonableness that lies at the heart of their being. Proper order is synonymous with the divine mind, which makes it synonymous with Love and with the Good and, therefore, with the Beautiful. The antithesis of this order in creation is manifested according to the modality under which it appears. So disorder in terms of the body would be sickness, which transposed into the musical realm would be discord, which transformed into the political would be insurrection, which in the celestial spheres would correspond to comets and other bodies not held to the order implicit in the harmonious music of the spheres. "But when the planets," Ulysses tells the assembled Greeks in Shakespeare's *Troilus and Cressida*,

> In evil mixture to disorder wander,
> What plagues and what portents, what mutiny,
> What raging of the sea, shaking of earth. . . .

Feeling impelled to stress the importance of rank and degree in society, Ulysses falls hack on analogies from music:

> Take but degree away, untune that string
> And, hark! what discord follows!

The danger Ulysses perceives is that the obliteration of degree will lead to the obliteration of the distinction between right and wrong, whereupon the will to power or force becomes the moral measure:

> Force should be right, or rather, right and wrong,
> Between whose endless jar justice resides,
> Should lose their names, and so should justice too.
> Then everything includes itself' in power,
> Power into will, will into appetite,

> And appetite, a universal wolf,
> So doubly seconded with will and power,
> Must make perforce a universal prey,
> And last eat up himself.

Music is thus the antithesis to anarchy. Music bespeaks a receptivity to the order of nature apprehended through reason, rather than a false order imposed on nature by man's desires. Commenting on Psalm 32, Thomas Aquinas claims that the person who lacks the proper disposition cannot praise God properly because he does not want to conform his own will to the divine will but rather desires that the divine will be conformed to his own (*"Illi ergo qui non habent rectum affectum, non possunt bene collaudare Deum, quia nolunt voluntatem suam conformare voluntati divinae, sed divinam volunt potius conformari suae"*).[27] In the strictest sense of the word, the willful man is not musical. Inordinate desires are constantly interfering with the harmonious ordering of parts essential to music. When reason does not recognize and respect degree, there is no harmony in nature. Reason is replaced by will as the guide to human action, and chaos on the personal, political, and cosmic levels follows as a result. Inordinate desires held and nurtured by the individual will spread to the body politic and bring ruin. In each instance, the times will be "out of tune."

Order lacking in one area will make itself felt in another. Because political harmony will begin in the well-ordered soul and radiate out to encompass the body politic, music has an especially important part to play in society. Music acts directly on the soul. Disordered music leads to disordered lives, which lead to disorder in the state. Plato, sensing the importance of order in the soul, banned the playing of certain modes in his ideal republic in the certainty that the disorder this music introduced into the soul would soon put the state in jeopardy of insurrection.

Related thoughts go through the minds of Jessica and Lorenzo at the end of *The Merchant of Venice*. Jessica, Shylock's daughter, has escaped from his house, having disregarded what he had to say about listening to music in his absence: "Lock up my doors," Shylock tells her,

> and when you hear the drum
> And the vile squealing of the wry-necked fife,
> Clamber not you up to the casements then,
> Nor thrust your head into the public street
> To gaze on Christian fools with varnished faces,
> But stop my house's ears, I mean my casements.
> Let not the sound of shallow foppery enter
> My sober house.

Shylock's advice has little effect. Jessica elopes with Lorenzo and takes some of the family wealth with her as dowry. Shylock espouses an unmusical order. "I stand here for law," he says at one point; "I crave the law," he says at another. In either case, the order he chooses to impose is at odds with the musical order of the universe, first of all, because he ignores mercy; second, because in refusing to accept a greater amount of money, he proves himself willfully unreasonable. In the end he loses everything, and his daughter and future son-in-law are left to meditate on his stubborn adherence to the law and his own will to revenge. The reasonableness and order of the universe are all-pervasive and available to all who do not close themselves off to it:

> Sit, Jessica, Look how the floor of heaven
> Is thick inlaid with patines of bright gold.
> There's not the smallest orb which thou behold'st
> But in his motion like an angel sings,
> Still quiring to the young-eyed cherubins.
> Such harmony is in immortal souls,
> But whilst this muddy vesture of decay
> Doth grossly close it in, we cannot hear it.

Even brute animals, lacking in reason,

> Fetching mad hounds, bellowing and neighing loud,
> Which is the hot condition of their blood

are susceptible to the power of music.

> You shall perceive them make a mutual stand,
> Their savage eyes turned to a modest gaze
> By the sweet power of music.

Orpheus could even get "trees, stones and floods" dancing,

> Since naught so stockish, hard and full of rage
> But music for the time doth change his nature.

Since even brute nature succumbs to the divine order made explicit in music, the only thing that can resist it successfully is the human will, which is free to resist the order for which it was created. Milton makes the point, again in musical terms, in his sonnet "At a Solemn Musick." Original Sin is the original discord. Adam's disobedience is the "disproportion'd sin," which

> Jarr'd against nature's chime, and with harsh din
> Broke the fair music that all creatures made
> To their great Lord, whose love their motion sway'd
> In perfect diapason, whilst they stood
> In first obedience and their state of good.

Inordinate desire, in other words, as can only be manifest through the human will, is the only real threat to the order established by God. It epitomizes the disorder whose antithesis is musical harmony. Those who resist music are possessed of a self-will that endangers not only the individual's soul but the existence of the body politic as well. This is the gist of Lorenzo's speech to Jessica, and through it Shakespeare summarizes and recapitulates the thinking of both the ancients and of the Christian West on the relationship between music and the soul, the state, and the universe:

> The man that hath no music in himself,
> Nor is not moved with concord of sweet sounds,
> Is fit for treasons, stratagems and spoils;
> The motions of his spirit are as dull as night,
> And his affections dark as Erebus:
> Let no such man be trusted. Mark the music.

G. Wilson Knight has written an entire book on the conflict between music as a principle of order and the storm as the principle of chaos us the works of Shakespeare. He sees this conflict—"Music and tempests of discord are ever to be contrasted," we are told in 2 Henry VI (II, i, 54)—as Shakespeare's central idea: "the final impression of the whole of Shakespeare's work; tempests dissolved in a sublime unity of music."

Shakespeare's contemporary Sir Thomas Browne shared the view because it was the common patrimony of the West at the time. The ultimate order of the universe is musical insofar as it is an order, not of the rigid sort associated with Shylock and the law, but one based on love. "There is music," Browne writes,

> even in the beauty and the silent note which Cupid strikes, far sweeter than the sound of an instrument. For there is a music wherever there is a harmony, order, or proportion: and thus far we may maintain the Music of the Spheres; for those well-ordered motions and regular paces, though they give no sound onto the ear, yet to its understanding they strike a note most full of harmony. Whosoever is harmonically composed delights in harmony; which makes me much distrust the symmetry of those heads which declaim against all Church-Music. For myself, not only from my obedience, but my particular Genius, I do embrace it: for even that vulgar and Tavern-Music, which makes one man merry, another mad, strikes in me a deep fit of devotion and a profound contemplation of the First Composer. There is something in it of Divinity more than the ear discovers, it is an Hieroglyphical and shadowed lesson of the whole world and creatures of God; such a melody to the ear as to the whole World, well understood, would afford the understanding. In brief it is a sensible fit of that harmony which intellectually sounds in the ears of God.[28]

This consensus, however, had broken down by the time of the Enlightenment and had been replaced by what came to be known as the "scientific" worldview. Mozart's opera *The Magic Flute* is a cultural artifact that contains elements of both worldviews. The plot of the story is heavily Masonic in its orientation, often descending perilously close to propaganda. Both Mozart and Emanuel Schikaneder, the author of the libretto, were members of the same Masonic lodge in Vienna. In 1866, M. A. Zille claimed that Schikaneder's characters were allegorical representations of real people involved in Viennese Freemasonry. Tamino was the Austrian

Emperor Josef II; Pamina, the Austrian people; Sarastro, lgnatz von Born, leader of the Viennese Lodge; Monastatos, a traitor within the lodge; and the Queen of the Night, Empress Maria Theresa, who organized a raid on her husband's lodge.

But this is really only half the story. It may well be that Schikaneder felt that the Austrian people needed to he rescued from the "superstitions" associated with the Empress or the Catholic Church and led to Enlightenment, but Mozart's music, even when it incorporates the three knocks on the door of the initiate seeking admission to the Masonic lodge, is hardly affected by the ideology it portrays. Indeed, at the heart of the story is the myth of Orpheus retold. Tamino escapes from the threat of fire and water by playing his magic flute, which is capable of taming, that is, ordering, the elements. Musically as well as mythically, *The Magic Flute* espouses the traditional virtues of music, and Masonic elements in the opera do little to challenge all the old beliefs about the magical connection between world order, music, and love.

That those beliefs were under challenge is evident from Novalis' treatise "Christianity or Europe," which appeared in 1789, the same year as the French Revolution. According to Novalis, the "*musica mundana,*" which he associated with both the Middle Ages and Christianity, had been destroyed and replaced by the *Zeitgeist* that began with the Reformation and culminated its the French Revolution as the final expression of Enlightenment. Like Plato, Aristotle, Aquinas, and Shakespeare, Novalis, as his imagery makes clear, saw the destruction of Europe, Christendom, and world harmony as one event:

> The initial personal hatred against the Catholic faith gradually transmuted itself into a hatred of the Bible, the Christian faith, and finally a hatred of all religion. Beyond that, this hatred of religion extended itself quite naturally and consequently to include all objects of enthusiasm, persecuted imagination and feeling, common decency and the love of art. All past and future were placed in the ranks of the merely nawral under Necessity and this made the infinitely creative music of the universe into a monotonous thumping of some terrible mill, which, driven by the flow of coincidence and floating along with it, became a genuine *Perpetuum Mobile* which ended by grinding itself to pieces.[29]

Novalis, known as a proto-romantic, saw only one alternative for Europe, a return to an Augustinian *tranquillitas ordinis* based on what was increasingly seen as an outmoded worldview embracing religion, polities, and music. "Blood will continue to flow over Europe," he wrote, "until the nations . . . , moved and softened by sacred music, walk together to their former altars and undertake together works of peace and celebrate with ardent tears a feast of love and peace."[30]

Blood, unfortunately, continued to flow, and the tradition of world harmony was increasingly forgotten in the ever-increasing din of the industrial revolution and that of the apologists for a more "scientific" view of society. By the time Wagner got around to writing down his musical theories while in exile in Zurich, it was no longer considered oxymoronic to refer to "revolutionary art." The revolution in question was a curious amalgam of contemporary prejudice, which has subsequently become known as Romanticism. At some points, the Romantics were the implacable antagonists of the industrial revolution; at other points, however, they fostered the social dissolution, which the spread of industrialism also fostered, by their blanket attacks of the social order as oppressive and unjust. Had they been more limited in their scope, their reforms might have been implemented within a political or economic framework, but the whole Romantic *Zeitgeist* seemed to spurn just these limits, and so its quarrel with Christianity and the human condition seemed to eventuate almost of necessity in a cultural revolution that would have far-reaching effects.

In the fall of 1848, Eduard Hanslick, the Viennese music critic and thereafter implacable foe of Wagner, visited Wagner and remembered him as being consumed with politics and what he felt was the coming revolution. "Wagner was all politics.... He expected the victory of the Revolution to bring about a complete birth of art, society, and religion—a new theater and a new kind of music."[31] By the time Wagner got around to writing his treatise on art and revolution, he seems to have changed his tune, perhaps because of his experience of Dresden and Bakunin. One year after his conversation with Hanslick, Wagner was espousing art and not politics as the true vehicle of revolution. It was Nature herself bursting through the bonds of a moribund culture, and the very aperture of that breakthrough was the Revolution. No longer would revolution pave the way for true art; true art would bring about the revolution. "True Art," Wagner wrote in the summer of 1849, "is *revolutionary*, because its very existence is opposed to the ruling spirit of the community."[32] The role of the artist is to raise his "manly strength... against the arrogance of a culture that employs the human mind as naught but steampower for its machinery":[33]

> In the man-destroying march of Culture, however, there looms before us this happy result: the heavy load with which she presses Nature down will one day grow so ponderous that it lends at last to down-trod, never-dying Nature the necessary impetus to hurl the whole cramping burden from her, with one sole thrust; and heaping up of Culture will thus have taught to Nature her own gigantic force. The releasing of this force is—Revolution.[34]

The more global the revolution, the more Wagner needed a cultural rather than a political vehicle to bring it off. This seems to be the gist of his post-Dresden disillusionment with Bakunin and the political groups surrounding him. The chief goal of the Revolution was the liberation of Nature from the chains of Culture. Culture, for Wagner, was synonymous with Christendom, which he saw as "a truly unattainable ideal." "Its dogmas are not realizable."[35] Christianity was, to echo the formulation of Nietzsche, who got the idea from Wagner, "the negation of life." "How could those dogmas become really living," Wagner asks in *Art and Revolution*, "and pass over into actual life: when they were directed against life itself, and denied and cursed the principle of living?"[36]

Then as now, the culture/nature antagonism finds its truest explication in the sexual tensions and aspirations of the people who propose it. The chief objection against Christianity among the bohemian classes has always centered on that religion's sexual prohibitions, and the case with Wagner is no exception to the rule. Wagner began his indictment by claiming that Christianity's dogmas "were directed against life itself." The fault with Christianity was that it was "purely spiritual." It made no allowance for life's "inbred robust qualities,"[37] qualities concerning which Wagner had considerable firsthand experience: "Yet how strong this nature is," he opined,

> how unquenchable its ever fresh, productive fullness—it has shown all the more plainly under the universal incubus of the ideal; which, if its logical consequences have been fulfilled, would have completely swept the human race from off the earth; since even abstinence from sexual love was included in it as the height of virtue.[38]

Wagner for his part felt that love could reach its highest fulfillment only in the physical relationship between two members of the opposite sex. "Love in its fullest and truest sense," Wagner wrote,

> is possible only within a sexual context: only as man and woman can human beings fully and truly love, while all other forms of love are merely variants, derivatives, adjuncts or counterfeit copies of that original. It is mistaken to regard this love [i.e., sexual love] as simply one manifestation of love in its totality as though there existed other, and indeed higher, manifestations, besides this one.[39]

Yet it would be too simple to say that Wagner's attitude toward Christianity and specifically Christian prohibition of all sexual activity outside the bonds of matrimony was one of rebellion and negation. It was much more ambivalent than that. The ambivalence remained with him for his entire life. It is expressed most clearly at this point in his life in his opera *Tannhäuser* which he originally entitled the *Venusberg*, whose translation in English would have been the unfortunate *mons veneris*. Tannhäuser, the Christian knight, awakes inside of the mountain, which is the realm of pagan Venus and sensual delight, with a desire to leave and return to the world, which appeals to his surfeited senses in a way particularly human.

"Do you regret being a god?" Venus wants to know. Truth to tell, Tannhäuser does regret it. Whether his conscience is bothering him or whether his senses are surfeited, he longs to leave his privileged position "deep in the earth's warm lap" and take his chances with a cooler, more differentiated, more mutable, but more humanly appropriate, environment. The womb-like Venusberg where all of his desires are met is evidently getting on his nerves.

> I cannot measure
> the time that I have tarried here.
> Days, months, exist no more for me,

> for no more do I see the sunlight,
> no more the friendly stars of heaven.

The sexual satisfaction he has achieved in the Venusberg has become enervating, and Tannhäuser longs for a less godlike existence:

> But I must hence to the earthly world,
> with you I can only be a slave.

The unlimited satisfaction of sexual desire, which the Venusberg symbolizes, is fraught with ambivalence. Venus calls Tannhäuser a god; Tannhäuser for his part feels like a slave. In either case, the particularly human element is missing, and Tannhäuser can take it no longer. He renounces Venus by claiming that his "salvation lies with Maria," that is, the Blessed Virgin (*"Mein Heil! Mein Heil ruht in Maria!"*), and with that the Venusberg disappears and Tannhäuser finds himself in a valley near the Wartburg, where Luther spent time throwing inkpots at the devil. Seeing a group of approaching pilgrims, Tannhäuser joins them on their journey to Rome.

Tannhäuser, then, is Wagner's attempt to mediate a number of antitheses surrounding Christianity and its relation to sexuality. The opera is a meditation on sacred and profane love and the attraction each holds. In opposition to Venus and her obvious attractions, Wagner presents Saint Elizabeth. The poles of attraction are clear enough. Tannhäuser is offered either sacred or profane love. However, he can never seem to make up his mind which he finds more attractive. His calling on the name of the Blessed Virgin dissolves the Venusberg; however, in the middle of the song contest in the Wartburg, he feels compelled to sing the praises of the sensual love he learned at the feet of the recently spurned Venus, much to the consternation of Wolfram von Eschenbach, Walther von der Vogelweide, and a whole court of medieval literary notables. Similarly, after his rejection by the pope in Rome, Tannhäuser returns to the Wartburg with every intention of going back to the Venusberg he rejected at the opera's beginning. Tannhäuser, like Wagner, cannot seem to make up his mind when it comes to choosing between pagan sensuality and Christian virtue:

> It drove me here, where I once so enjoyed
> bliss and pleasure on her warm breast!
> To you, fair Venus, I return,
> to the sweet darkness of your spell;
> I will come down to your court,
> where your charms now shall ever smile on me!

It is only the impassioned plea of Wolfram von Eschenbach that stops Tannhäuser from entering the Venusberg again. The reality of past pleasure is especially palpable when juxtaposed with present disappointment so palpable, in fact, that Tannhäuser can virtually' see the nymphs dancing in front of him, promising him *"Wonn und Lust."* Venus for her part is only too happy to welcome him back:

> Welcome, fickle man!
> Did earth reject and banish you?
> And do you nowhere find compassion
> and seek love in my arms?

Tannhäuser, convinced that his salvation has been lost, is ready to console himself with the "delights of hell." The only thing that saves him is Wolfram calling on the name of Elizabeth, who, now dead and presumably in heaven, intercedes on the knight's behalf and saves him at the last moment from the jaws of hell. Tannhäuser dies, but his staff sprouts green shoots as a sign that he has been saved at last. If there is ambivalence here on Wagner's part, and I think there is, the ambivalence is at least definable between two clearly framed alternatives. Tannhäuser is confronted with the choice of dark pleasures, which are ultimately unsatisfying, or a pure love, which entails more suffering than he is willing to bear. Behind this polarity, we see an inchoate recognition of the struggle implicit in the human sexual condition. Tannhäuser is faced with the task of taming or humanizing his desires by bringing them into line with the light of divine order, apprehended as the order of reason or morality. The sexual drive must submit to the light of reason. The darkness of the Venusberg symbolizes the drive for sensual gratification without regard to the individual who is the object of that desire. The drama of psychic individuation arising from the darkness of the merely sexual encounter is told in Apuleius' tale *Amor and Psyche,* and brilliantly explicated by Erich Neumann. Pysche's refusal to meet with Amor in the dark brings about most immediately the calamity of his leaving, but eventually a synthesis of both love and light are united in the mature sexual love of the person, and not just the instincting acting out of natural drives as symbolized by Venus and her realm. "The Psyche," Neumann writes,

> who approaches the bed on which Eros is lying is no longer the languorously ensnared being, bewitched by her senses, who lived in the dark paradise of sexuality and lust.[40]

Psyche's (or the Soul's) individuation is accomplished only when she shines the light of reason on the undifferentiated darkness of instinctual desire, which Amor has chosen for his realm. The instinctual satisfaction of desire is lost, but it is eventually replaced by conscious love as a result of the Soul's bringing the light of reason to bear on Eros. The light of reason organizes Eros into something neither instinctual nor god-like (the Greeks were clever enough to realize that both were pretty much the same thing) but fully human. Eros, according to Neumann, did not want a Psyche aware of its light-bringing, that is to say, rational powers. Eros:

threatened her, he fervently implored her to remain in the paradise-darkness, he warned her that she would lose him forever by her act. The unconscious tendency toward consciousness (here toward consciousness in the love relationship) was stronger in Psyche than everything else, even than her love for Eros—or so, at least, the masculine Eos would have said. But wrongly so, for though the Psyche of the paradisiacal state was subservient to Eros, though she had yielded to him in the darkness, she had not loved him.[41]

Love, unlike mere sexual gratification, implies the activity of conscious agents. As such it cannot take place in the instinctual darkness that Eros finds congenial. Darkness is the realm of the erotic, which by its nature involves the blind acting out of instinctual drives. It is the task of the soul to subdue these drives and conform them to the light of reason and create out of animal/divine drives the subordination of instinct to the person, which is the essence of human love. Eros does not want this, so Psyche, the soul, must force it on him willy-nilly:

> To him [Eros] the masculine god, she [Pysche, the soul] was desirable enough when he was in the dark and he possessed her in the dark, when she was the mere companion of his nights, secluded from the world, living only for him, without share in his diurnal existence, in his reality and his divinity. Her servitude was made still deeper by his insistence on his divine anonymity: she was still more "devoured" by him.[42]

Tannhäuser is another version of this myth of sexual differentiation, of reason's light bringing love out of the darkness of sexual/instinctual chaos. Unlike Apuleius' myth, however, Wagner has provided us with a character who seems unable to make up his mind about whether he is more attracted to sacred or profane love. Tannhäuser leaves the sensual darkness of the Venusberg but cannot help singing about its charms in the song contest at the Wartburg, scandalizing all present. His subsequent pilgrimage to Rome to seek forgiveness ends in failure, and it is only the intercession of Elizabeth and the protest of Wolfram von Eschenbach that prevents him from returning to Venus' arms at the end of the opera. Tannhäuser is saved in spite of himself, and in the end only death succeeds in snatching him away from temptation.

In this he is much like Wagner himself. Wagner got the idea from a story by Heinrich Heine that appeared in print in 1837. Heine's version of the story was, according to Martin Gregor-Dellin, "an unremitting hymn to the senses."[43] Wagner found himself intrigued by the implications of sexual liberation he found in the story and spent his artistic career oscillating between the poles he established for himself in *Tannhäuser*. He struggled with the idea of renunciation in various ways, trying the Buddhist version, which he appropriated from Schopenhauer, and eventually settling at the end of his life on a quasi-Catholic version as evidenced in *Parsifal*. The pull in the opposite direction, however, remained just as strong, and Wagner's lifelong attitude toward what would come to be known as sexual liberation can only be described as ambivalent. At various points in his life, he would espouse both free love and renunciation with equal ardor. As with Tannhäuser, it was only death that brought an end to his indecisiveness.

In 1830, while still a teenager, Wagner fell under the influence of Heinrich Laube, a man six years his senior and one of the leading champions of the liberalism of his day. Then as now, liberalism's espousal of things "new" and "young" and "progressive" had a distinctly sexual cast. Laube believed in free love and pronounced the old morality dead. While at a ball in Leipzig, he attempted to persuade one young lady that the marriage laws should be overturned. That young lady, it turned out, was Wagner's sister. Because Laube became a frequent visitor to the Wagner household, Wagner got to know his views quite well and, as Gregor-Dellin puts it, "was enthralled by the erotic side of this secular creed."[44]

Wagner, as is often the case with young people exposed to such creeds, soon began to act on what he had learned. During the summer of 1834, the twenty-one-year-old Wagner and the young poet Theodor Apel set off on a six-week trip through Bohemia (the Czech one, not the artistic version), during which he worked on the libretto of *Das Liebesverbot*, based on Shakespeare's *Measure for Measure*. This early and not entirely successful opera became a vehicle for the views on free love and the triumph of youthful sensuality over puritanical convention that were being advocated by the Young German movement under Laube at the time, not without coming to the attention of the authorities. Laube was having troubles with the authorities in Saxony over his social views and would eventually end up in prison in Berlin. In August of that summer, Wagner accepted the directorship of the Madgeburg theater company and spent the late summer and early fall touring the various spas that had theaters associated with them. During his tenure as music director, Wagner was romantically involved with a young woman by the name of Toni, but his real attention was drawn to an actress with the troupe, almost four years his senior, named Christine Wilhelmine Planer, who went by the name Minna, which in medieval parlance meant love.

In his autobiography, Wagner claims that he tried out the Young German free-love line on Minna, but without effect:

> At any rate, I soon recognized upon closer examination that Young Europe, Ardinghello and my version of *Measure for Measure* wouldn't play with this lady. I also soon recognized that there was a very definite difference between the lively theatrical mood of my amorous fey and that of the honest bourgeois child who wanted a steady income.[45]

Minna, it seems, was still bourgeois enough to hope to land a husband who would be able to allow her to retire from acting to a comfortable middle-class domestic situation. At the time Wagner met her, Minna was generally considered engaged to a minor aristocrat by the name of von Otterstedt. The engagement was broken off when Herr von Otterstedt chose a wife in better economic circumstances. In reality it seems that the perplexity Wagner expressed in his autobiography stemmed from the fact that Minna acceded to his sexual advances but then still seemed indifferent to his proposals of marriage, causing a great deal of jealousy and consternation in the twenty-one-year-old composer, who found himself charmed by the mixture of sexual willingness and reserve he found in her.

Minna Planer had enough sexual history behind her to create an ambivalence that any young man would have found daunting. Seduced at the age of fifteen by a captain in the king of Saxony's guards, she had given birth to a daughter, Natalie, who was being raised by Minna's parents but who soon took to traveling with Minna as her sister. It is clear that Wagner saw in Minna much of what he separated into the two representatives of sacred and profane love in *Tannhäuser*. Minna was both Venus and Elizabeth wrapped up in one inscrutable, but deeply desired, love object. She was like Venus insofar as she acquiesced to his sexual desires, but she was distant, vaguely maternal, and in search of a respectable middle-class alliance that would guarantee some financial security as well. Gregor-Dellin describes the beginning stages of their love affair as "a sexual liaison of the kind extolled by Laube." As a result, it took on a character of instability, according to Wagner's testimony to Apel, that never really abated even after their marriage.

> Writing from Rudolfstadt on September 15, 1834, Wagner urged his friend to visit him soon, and added: You can have the Planer girl too—she has transfigured me quite sensually a couple of times—it made me feel splendid." So Minna was a trophy that belonged to his earthly paradise, and he was destined to atone like Tannhäuser—not until redeemed by an Elizabeth, but until the earthly and the celestial became one.[46]

At one of the spas, Wagner and Minna quarreled over Wagner's affair with Toni. Then later, in Berlin, Wagner learned that Minna had had an affair with a Jewish businessman by the name of Schwabe. And so it went before, during, and up to the end of their marriage. During the summer of 1835 Wagner considered himself engaged to Minna, a fact that did not deter her from leaving him for an acting position in Königsberg. During those early years, when Minna was still attractive and still unattached, Wagner's misgivings seemed to have been anesthetized by the numbing effects of his sexual addiction to her, but the effects of this drug were bound to wear off once he possessed the object of his desire. Wagner put up with one humiliation after another, and sharing his future wife's favors with a Jew probably contributed to his later anti-Semitism, but once the marriage was legally established, the balance of power began to change. There was, of course, a biological component to this as well. Since Minna was four years older than Wagner, and described as having the sort at beauty that fades quickly, her physical attractiveness and availability were bound to diminish even as Wagner's were on the rise. The difference has to do with the difference between men and women, between social arrangements and what has come to be known as the inequality of the sexes (against which Laube railed in his *Liebesbriefe*), over which Wagner effused: "Is it not a grand idea to give the world as many inhabitants again by emancipating women? You should associate with Negro slaves and Jews." [47]

Wagner married Minna on November 24, 1836, but the domestic acrimony that bad begun before the marriage not only continued but increased in intensity, according to the testimony of Minna's sister/daughter Natalie, who lived with the Wagners at the time. On April 1, 1837, Wagner took a position as musical director of the Königsberg Theater. Returning home after a rehearsal on May 31, Wagner found that his wife had taken Natalie and run off with a Königsberg businessman by the name of Dietrich. Herr Dietrich eventually tired of Minna, who returned to her parents, followed shortly by Wagner himself, who professed sorrow for the way he had treated her. Wagner contemplated divorce but eventually reconciled with his wife. The wound, however, would continue to rankle, and it left Wagner disposed to a number of other adulterous relationships in the future. In fact, Wagner's mature career revolved around a constellation of three major adulterous affairs. It was as if a sexual consummation so easily achieved in his youth never really took, never blossomed into a relationship that stimulated him sexually and, at the same time, provided the security he needed.

His relationship with Minna came to be viewed as disappointing on both accounts. By the time he had to flee Saxony for exile in Zurich, Minna's physical charms were beginning to fade, a decline accelerated by heart disease. During the early period of his exile, Wagner had the opportunity to meditate on her past infidelities and, as the aggrieved husband, contemplate future infidelities of his own. It was a situation that was bound to seek release in some way. In addition to that, this same period saw the apogee of Wagner's revolutionary thinking. *Art and Revolution* was written during the summer of 1849 in the first few months after his escape from an almost certain jail term in Saxony. In the spring of 1851, Wagner was invited, through the finagling of Liszt, to the estate of a prosperous Bordeaux wine merchant by the name of Eugene Laussot. His wife, it had been intimated, might be willing to make a substantial contribution toward helping him complete his operas.

Jessie Laussot, the daughter of an Englishwoman of independent means by the name of Ann Taylor, had heard *Tannhäuser* a few years earlier, in 1846, when she was only sixteen, and the music had created the beginning of an infatuation with things Wagnerian that reached its height when Wagner himself arrived on the Laussot doorstep. Mrs. Taylor offered to support Wagner to the tune of three thousand francs a year. Wagner was clearly overwhelmed by his good fortune, but the wine of this good fortune clearly went to his head and caused an intoxication that made him reckless. Instead of just taking the money, Wagner decided to take Laussot's wife as well. Since Mrs. Taylor had already engaged in an affair with her son-in-law before marrying off their daughter to him, this audacity might have succeeded if Wagner had observed the "proprieties" necessary for a clandestine affair. Wagner's plans were, perhaps in keeping with his operas, much more grandiose. He proposed that he take half of his allowance and give it to his wife, while taking the other half to "seek oblivion" in Greece or Asia Minor.[48] Wagner hinted that Jessie should join him, and Jessie hinted that she was ready to acquiesce in such a plan.

The impossible plot blew up in Wagner's face with recriminations on all sides. Wagner complained to Julie Ritter that Jessie Laussot lacked the strength to emancipate herself from the bourgeois attachment to marriage. Minna, for her part, wrote Wagner a long letter, especially instructive for our purposes, that saw a connection between his reckless behavior and his involvement in revolutionary politics during the past few years, culminating in the uprising in Dresden.

> I beseech you, what is going on inside you again this year? Nothing is sacred to you, nothing more remains for you to destroy but our conjugal happiness. That is why you guard yourself against reproach by fabricating the meanest, most unjust and contemptible accusations; why you persuade yourself of things that have never existed between us; and why you ultimately deceive yourself in order to excuse the abominable treatment to which you are once more subjecting me.[49]

Minna saw the crisis in their marriage as coinciding with Wagner's involvement in revolutionary politics, "which have already destroyed so many happy relationships."[50] Minna was convinced that "no good would come of your revolutionary activities."[51] Minna was hardly a disinterested observer, but the fact of the matter is that no one close to Wagner as she was could be. She was hardly an innocent herself in the affairs of the heart that troubled their marriage. However, the crucial difference between the two seems to be in their attitude toward revolution. Neither Minna nor Wagner was a model of connubial chastity; however, Minna remained, in spite of her failings, still committed to matrimony as an institution and to their own marriage in particular. Beyond that, she was not moved to project her own personal failures onto the institution, whereas Wagner was. Wagner "guards himself against reproach by fabricating. . . contemptible accusations." This was the essence of projection. It was a sign that the burdens on Wagner's conscience, perhaps as a result of the Laussot affair, had reached critical mass. In situations like this, something has to give. The guilty party conforms either his behavior to his beliefs or his beliefs to his behavior. Minna's letter is a strong indication that Wagner was headed in the latter direction. It is an especially strong temptation for those who are intellectually inclined, and Wagner was not only that; he had absorbed as well the most corrosive of revolutionary thinking at the time. In addition, he was in the throes of bringing together an entire pre-Christian mythology based on German legend, which would espouse all that Christianity had repressed. At a certain point, it must have become clear to Wagner that the revolution he needed would not be brought about by political concessions from the king of Saxony. Wagner's intellectual contact with Feuerbach, as well as his personal contact with the free-love ideology of Laube, Herwegh's redaction of Marx, and the jovial anarchism of Bakunin as the two inspected the barricades in Dresden convinced him that something much more thoroughgoing was needed. By the same token, the failure of the revolution in Dresden and his subsequent flight convinced Wagner that politics was not the vehicle for that longed-for transformation of the social order. In the parallelogram of forces that these intellectual and historical events construct, the median line that resolves them is art, specifically opera, which Wagner saw as the art work of the future.

The Laussot affair was the first of a triad of adulteries that provide the matrix not only for Wagner's revolutionary art, but also for the musical innovation that would sound the anthem for cultural revolution for the next fifty years. *Tristan und Isolde* was from the moment of its inception musical adultery, and adultery was simply the manifestation of sexual liberation that appealed most passionately to Wagner at the time. He seemed always to be drawn to someone already spoken for by someone else.

> Wagner was attracted only by "attached" women. If the psychologists are to be believed, he suffered from the traumatic notion that he was depriving someone else of a wife (mother). He was even tactless enough to make this clear to Cosima. He had never had an untouched woman in his life, he told her; none of them had ever been "new." . . . It would appear that their fixation creates a block that renders it hard to find release in other loving relationships, so the unconscious manufactures an obstacle to their fulfillment: The love object is already taken.[52]

Adultery is essentially an impossible situation. Someone always gets hurt. As Wagner proceeded from one reckless affair to another, inflicting more and more psychic damage on his already ailing wife, the notion of impossibility began to find expression in his music. Its culmination came in the musical innovations at the heart of *Tristan und Isolde*. This important work of musical modernism grew out of the climate of adultery established by the Laussot affair, which found its continuation in the Wesendonck affair (whether it was consummated or not), and which found its culmination in the affair with and subsequent marriage to Cosima von Bülow. By the time Wagner went into exile at the midpoint of the nineteenth century, a number of forces were coalescing in his life. Wagner had become a revolutionary, but the revolution, as epitomized by Bakunin, had failed. He had become desperately unhappy in his marriage with a woman who was both older than himself and fast losing her good looks to heart disease. In this context, it became clear to Wagner that a change in political structure would not really scratch where he itched. As a result, he broadened the scope of his revolutionary thinking to the point where it transcended the merely political and began to take on a more cosmic or cultural scope, one that would deal with his unhappy marriage, his economic woes, the baleful effect of Christianity, and a host of other ills, not through political insurrection but through works of art, which would make his impossible longings if not morally justifiable then at least aesthetically plausible to an increasingly large number of disaffected bohemians (of the artistic, not the Czech, kind) who desired nothing more ardently than the overthrow of Christian morality and the repressive social order based on it. By the time he arrived in Zurich, Wagner had reflected on Bakunin's failures enough to see a different road. Revolutionary art was to become the vehicle for social and cultural revolution. Before this new paradigm of cultural revolution could succeed, a number of elements needed to fall into place. Wagner needed a new woman, a new philosophy, and a new vocabulary of musical expression. Schopenhauer's *Die Welt als Wille und Vorstellung* supplied the second requirement; the first came in the form of another well-to-do married woman in her twenties by the name of Mathilde Wesendonck. The new musical vocabulary was to come last, because it had to come from Wagner himself. It was something that, up until that time, no one had thought of, perhaps because no one's need was as urgent as Wagner's, perhaps also because Wagner could sense that he was not alone in his need.

Up to this point, Wagner was fairly clear in talking about revolutionary works of art. However, the idea of "revolutionary music" was still (and in a sense always would remain) an oxymoron. But the idea of expressing his revolutionary feelings in "revolutionary" music was on his mind as early as late 1850, when Wagner was fresh from his disappointments in Dresden and hard at work on a theoretical work that would come to be published under the title *Oper und Drama* one year later. In the discussion of music in *Oper und Drama*, Wagner makes the same connections between music and the state that Plato and Aristotle did, but he inverts their values and looks at the idea from a revolutionary point of view. Just as orderly music led to an orderly state, Wagner's music would lead to revolution. The vehicle of the rebellion is the overthrow of the "Absolute Melody" that Wagner found in the music of Rossini:

> As Metternich, with perfect logic on his side, could not conceive the *State* under any form but that of *Absolute Monarchy*: so Rossini, with no less force of argument, could conceive the *Opera* under no other form than that of *Absolute Melody*. Both men said: "Do you ask for Opera and State? Here you have them;— there are no others!" [53]

The connection between Metternich and music is not immediately clear, but before long, the ramifications begin to make themselves apparent. "It should not be forgotten," Wagner reminds us," that Metternich, only two years before the writing of this sentence, had played an important part in suppressing the Austro-Germany revolutionary movement." [54] Monarchy was the rule of one man in the political sphere; melody in music was the domination of a row of notes by a tonal center. By the mid-nineteenth century, monarchy had come to be seen as *the* form of government sanctioned by Christian culture. Melody, as the coherent organization of notes around a tonal center that dominated and organized its emotion, had become the prime expression of music. Melody was the soul of music; it was to music what plot was to tragedy, according to Aristotle. By now, it should be obvious that Wagner and his bohemian contemporaries had become radically dissatisfied with both forms of order. The alternative to monarchy was easy enough to figure out. Both Wagner and Bakunin had agitated for it behind the barricades of Dresden. But what was the alternative to melody? Was "revolutionary" music possible? Or was it to prove as chimerical as its political counterpart?

It was not as if Wagner were proposing the abolition of melody. Rather he thought of melody as antithetical to drama, or emotion, and, as if proposing a constitutional monarchy in the realm of music, he proposed limiting melody's powers as a way of heightening drama or emotion. The problem with Rossini was that melody had taken over the dominant role in music to the exclusion of emotion. Wagner makes oblique reference to Novalis in one more denigrating reference to the established order in both its political and musical sense, a conjunction in which Wagner saw intimate and far-reaching relations:

> What with our romanticizing *poets* betrayed itself as an ogling with the one eye at Roman-Catholic mysticism and with the other at feudal-chivalric amours expressed itself in Music as homelike, deep and broad-breathed Tune, instinct with noble grace,—Tune as listened from the last vanishing sigh of the naive spirit of the Folk.[55]

The modern orchestra, that is, the one bequeathed by Beethoven to Wagner, had made enormous strides in its ability to articulate an increasingly wide range of emotion, but melody remained the measure of musical structure. Emotional intensity "was always subordinated to that melody; and where it even reached so far as to take a direct share or interest in its delivery, still it really only served to render mistress Melody more dazzling and more proud, by sumptuously adorning, as it were, her court."[56] Music without melody as its essence—"this essence was enunciated in that hard-and-fast [*scharf gezeichneten*] rhythmic and melismatic Form, whose surface the composer might haply vary, but never wash away"—ran the danger of turning into pure arbitrary sonic chaos. The composer who spurned melody ran the danger of "completely drowning himself in a chaos of the most hopelessly indefinite expression."[57] On the other hand, "self-sufficing melody" ruled out "unflinchingly true dramatic expression," leaving the composer with the choice of "either Melody or Drama. Rossini sacrificed the Drama; the noble Weber wished to reinstate it by force of his more judicious [*sinnigeren*] melody."[58]

Wagner's solution to this dilemma is to import into music a whole new architectonic principle, namely, the text. With the text taking over the direction of where the music is going, the music is free to devote itself to the luxurious cultivation of emotion, unrestrained by the intramusical organization of melody. In order to explain himself Wagner once again falls back on sexual metaphors. "Music," he tells us, "is a woman.... Music is the bearing woman, the Poet the begetter."[59] Music, in other words, becomes the handmaid of a message imposed upon her from without. She has no need for an organizational principle of her own, because the man, that is, the text, provides one for her. "Woman," Wagner tells us,

> first gains her full individuality in the moment of surrender. She is the Undine who glides soulless through the waves of her native clement, till she receives her

soul through the love of a man. The look of innocence in a woman's eye is the endlessly pellucid mirror in which the man can only see the general faculty for love, till he is able to see in it the likeness of himself. When he has recognized himself therein, then also is the woman's all-faculty condensed into one strenuous necessity to love him with the all-dominant fervor of full surrender.[60]

Since Wagner's concept of liberation entails the removal of the rational organizing principle or soul from both women and music, it is not difficult to conjure up what sort of music he would write to accompany his "masculine" texts, nor what he would do when left alone with an attractive woman. He would attempt to dominate both. He would attempt to subjugate both to his overweening desire. Wagner's creed could be called Romanticism, it could also be called the first musical ideology, one that sees, *à la* Schopenhauer, the musical realm as no longer possessing its own laws and rights, but rather nothing more than pure "feminine" potentiality, which can be fecundated or organized according to his puissant and world-creating masculine will. "No truth," writes Schopenhauer, "is more certain and from all others more independent and less in need of proof than this, that everything that is capable of being known, in other words the entire world, is nothing more than an object that exists in relation to a subject. The view of a viewer, in one word a product of the imagination." "The world," Schopenhauer says at another point, "is my Will." [61] Since the world is the product of my imagination (*Die Welt ist meine Vorstellung*), it is also a function of my will. Schopenhauer's ability to carry German idealism to its logical conclusion (or *reductio ad absurdam*) allowed Wagner to break with the revolutionary materialisms of Feuerbach and Marx and provided the perfect philosophical vehicle for the revolutionary *manqué* who was now going to bring about his subversion of the social order through art instead of armed insurrection. It is hardly a coincidence that Nietzsche, the man who so apotheosized the Will to Power, would be immediately attracted to Wagner and his music. His music is incipient revolution, sexual liberation, and totalitarianism all rolled up into one overly emotional, overly long "endless melody," which the liberation wanna-bes of his day found irresistible.

Thomas Mann sums up the attraction of Wagner to his generation in a passage from *Buddenbrooks*:

> And what now began was a feast, a triumph, a boundless orgy of this single phrase.... There was something brutal and stupid and at the same time religious and ascetic... in the fanatical worship of this trifle, this scrap of melody..., something impious in the excessiveness and insatiability with which he relished and exploited it, something cynically desperate like the will to perish in an ecstasy in the avidity with which he drew from it all the sweetness it could yield.[62]

The attraction was essentially erotic. This music bespoke emotion liberated from reason. In the musical realm, the assault on tonality corresponded to an assault on sexual restraint in the moral realm and an attack on the social order in the political realm. Wagner could achieve all three, which would correspond to the deepest needs he felt as a failed revolutionary, simply by playing the half-diminished seventh chord that introduced the prelude to *Tristan und Isolde*. He had become a negative Orpheus, calling forth disorder out of order with his deranged and hypersensual music.

Revolutionary music was a caricature of both femininity and emotion all at once. Just as Wagner's music was liberated from the domination of melody, so his emotion was liberated from the "domination" of reason, which liberation, interestingly enough, has always been the classic definition of sin. Wagner kept returning to the classical notions of world harmony even in proposing his most revolutionary changes. Indeed, he could only propose revolution of the moral and musical order by positing the ordered universe of the ancients in the first place. By attacking the hegemony of the dominant note over the line of notes that follows, Wagner attacked the heart of what music is: "Melody the first real Shape of music." [63] In doing this he proved himself, in the words that Lorenzo used to describe Shylock, to be "fit for treasons, stratagems, and spoils." Men like this should not be trusted, certainly not alone with other people's wives. This is a lesson that his conductor Hans von Bülow found out too late.

Wagner never really invented a musical vehicle for this erotic antinomianism. He simply took something that had existed in the history of music for some time and developed it. That musical idea was known as chromaticism. It was based on an octave of twelve semitones instead of the seven-note diatonic scale. "In the baroque era," according to the *New Grove Dictionary of Music*, "the use of chromaticism was closely linked with the doctrine of affections." It had always been used as a way of expressing emotion, by adding "color" to the melodic line. Diatonicism became the norm for Western music in the late Middle Ages, and with the rise of the architectonic potentiality of the diatonic scale, emotion was subordinated to the organizational principle. Chromaticism reached its highest expression in *Tristan und Isolde*, but the tradition was continued in Schönberg (more on him later) and the development of chromaticism into atonality and then beyond that to the twelve-tone system. The latter, for all its modernity, always retained a Wagnerian flavor because Wagner's music made use of the twelve-tone chromatic scale.

In Wagner's works, this musical fact quickly takes on dramatic significance. In *Tannhäuser*, for example, the already-mentioned dichotomy between sacred and profane love takes on a specific musical coloring. Tannhäuser finds himself at the middle of a musical and sexual tug-of-war between melody and emotion, between musical lust, portrayed in chromatic tones, and diatonic Christianity. Venus' aria beginning "*Geliebter, komm! Sieh dort die Grotte*," in which she attempts to lure Tannhäuser back to the Venusberg, is heavily chromatic and a clear hearkening forward to *Tristan und Isolde*. On the other hand, one of the strongest diatonic melodies in all of Wagner, the pilgrims' chorus, pulls Tannhäuser away from the Venusberg into a pilgrimage to Rome, where he repents and, as in a moral analogue to melody itself, tries to conform his sexual life to the dominant note of reason, as expressed in the Christian moral code.

Although he never mentions Wagner directly, John A. Oesterle, writing a neoscholastic critique of music,[64] sees more than coincidence in the difference between the two tonal systems. Because of the two irregular half-step progressions in the diatonic scale, Oesterle sees in it, not a uniformity, but a progression with a beginning, middle, and end, and one that is naturally attuned to the "movement of emotions as reflected in the movement of the human voice," which is the object of imitation in music.[65] Neither the whole-tone progression of six whole notes nor the chromatic scale of twelve half-tones possesses the diversity of the natural scale and so cannot convey the same emotional satisfaction, the same catharsis, the same sense of emotion aroused and resolved that is so satisfying in the best music of the West. Music, according to Oesterle, can fail by either excess or defect.

> Music suffers by defect if regularity is pursued to the point of monotony. Music suffers by excess if irregularity is pursued to the point of inducing a state of disordered agitation in the movement of the emotions. Either extreme, pursued directly, attacks the end of music: the tonal representation of the movement of the emotions in conformity with reason. The intermediate in rhythm is the judicious combination of the two which fully realizes the end of music.
>
> Melody, so far as it can he analyzed, is based upon a unity proportion and order of tones recognizable as such by the mind through the ear and representing the arousal and release of the emotions. Music suffers by defect if melody has little or no relation to the movement of the emotions (sometimes to the extent that melody is not even a recognizable element in a composition), or if the unity and order of tones rend to be determined by purely intellectualistic or arbitrary principles of tonal progression as, for example, in the twelve-tone progression (so far as it aims at atonalism), which is more a technical manipulation than an artistic principle. Music suffers by excess if melody sacrifices an intelligible unity or order of tones to sheer emotional intensity, making the emotions as such the principle tonal progression instead of the reasoned order of the emotions. This latter extreme was pursued by the romanticists to the point of emotional exhaustion by the end of the last century. The true mean in melody acknowledges the emotional content present, but balances it by informing the tonal representation of the movement of the emotions with an orderly progression induced by reason.[66]

Wagner was attracted to the twelve half-tones of the chromatic scale precisely because their indeterminacy bespoke a freedom from order (musical, sexual, and political) that the diatonic melody would not allow. Wagner felt tyrannized by Melody, Minna, and Metternich because his own emotions were not conformant to the canons of reasonable behavior. His rebellion was the rebellion against the moral order; his musical innovation was simply the discovery of a musical analogue to the rebellion against reason that his troubled conscience and increasingly impetuous desires craved. His description of the new music he aspired to create was full of a curious blend of sexual and political metaphors applied to the music he aspired to write. The importance of love in the Christian view of things had to be liberated from the Christianity that gave it its meaning in the first place and then allowed to develop in a purely sensual direction. Free tonality would then come to equal free love, and the notes that had been held in bondage to patriarchal "keys" would be set free, like emancipated women, to follow their inclination to whichever tones they find sexually/musically attractive. Musical key, Wagner wrote, referring to the German term *Tonart*,

> is the most united, most closely kindred family of the whole tone-genus; it shows itself as truly of one kin with the whole tone-genus, however, where it advances to an alliance with other keys, through the instinctive inclination of its individual members. We here may suitably compare the tone-key with the ancient patriarchal families of the various human stems: by an instinctive error the kinsmen of these families considered themselves as a peculiar people and not as members of the entire human race; yet the individual's sexual love was not enkindled by a wonted, but solely by an un-wonted object, and thus it climbed the barriers of the patriarchal family, to knit alliances with other families. In a prophetic transport Christianity proclaimed the oneness of the human race: the art that owes its most characteristic development to Christianity, the art of Music, has taken up that evangel into itself, and has transformed it, as our modern tone-speech, into a sybaritic message to the sensuous feeling. If we take those *ur*-patriarchal national melodies, the genuine heirlooms of particular stems, and compare them with the Melody that the advance of music through Christian evolution has made possible to us today; we shall find as their characteristic token, that they almost never move away from one definite key, appearing positively engrown therewith: whereas the Melody possible to us has acquired the most unheard variety of power of placing its initial chief-key in alliance with the remotest tone-families, by means of harmonic Modulation; so that in a larger composition the *ur*-kinship of all keys is presented to us, as it were, in the light of one particular chief-key.[67]

It all sounds vaguely Hegelian and sexual at the same time; Christianity, with its universalization of love, has enabled an evolution to take place, which now with the advent of Hegel and/or Wagner has the golden opportunity of becoming conscious of itself and moving beyond the confines that restrained it in the past. All the tone families can now be related to one another directly beyond the narrow confines of the patriarchal family/melody. Harmonic modulation in combination with the fecundating power of the poetic text snakes virtually any and all combinations, either sexual or musical, now possible. The doctrine of Christian love, initially so promising, is freed from its narrow confinement inside the Christian moral law and can now expand to embrace all mankind in an "orgiastic, enravishing announcement of sensual emotions."[68] Without the text, which is to say, without the will of the poet, which imbues the music with both direction and meaning, the Absolute-musician, for example, the composer of symphonies,

> swam aimlessly and restless to and fro, until at last he lost his nerve: before him he saw nothing but an endless surge of possibilities, albeit he was conscious in

himself of no definite purpose to which to put those possibilities—just as the Christian all-humanitarianism (*Allmenschlichkeit*) was merely a floating sentiment, without any holdfast to vindicate it as a definite feeling; and this holdfast is the actual Man. Thus the musician was found to well nigh bewail his immoderate power of swimming: he yearned to go back to his primal homeland's quiet creeks, where the water flowed restfully between its narrow shores and always in one definite tide. What moved him to this return, was nothing but the experienced aimlessness of his rovings on the high seas; to put it strictly; the admission that he possessed a faculty he was unable to use,—the Yearning for the Poet.[69]

Wagner was thus faced with a choice that would have terrible consequences for the music of the West. He could have either melody or emotion. He could either subordinate his desires to the logic of the music or the music to the logic of his desires. That he saw the two terms, emotion and reason, as antinomies bespoke a personal tragedy that was gradually to become a pan-cultural tragedy as well. The diatonic scale with its ability both to arouse the emotions and to subdue them to the demands of reason had unleashed a burst of musical creativity without precedent in the history of the human race, a creativity that found one of its more significant expressions in the German-speaking lands of the eighteenth century. The price of admission, however, was the rigor of the tonal, diatonic system, which conformed so admirably to the movement of human emotion. Because it possessed a beginning, middle, and end, the diatonic scale could evoke a catharsis of emotion unprecedented in other musical systems. But there was a price to pay here, and the price was adherence to the canons of reason. The emotions that were aroused could be resolved only by returning to the key note from which they originated. To modulate the notes unceasingly from one key to another, as Wagner's chromaticism did, was tantamount to blunting their emotional focus; to lead them away never to return to the dominant note gave the feeling of tumultuous and unsatisfied passion, a passion that never got resolved. From a human perspective, there was generally only one emotion that demanded this sort of extension *ad infinitum*, and that was the sexual. The music that was the fullest expression of this modulation of emotion from key to key for hours on end with no resolution in sight had a lot in common with pornography. It was musical pornography and was having a sort of enervating, deranging, and debilitating effect on the audiences that heard it. It was a classic example of what Oesterle would call missing the mark by excess in music. The emotions were strained in one direction, and, before they could be resolved into the initial key, they headed off in the direction of another key to be strained again. The chromatic modulation that found its most forceful expression in *Tristan und Isolde* could now allow the musical movement to drift from one key to another in a seemingly endless orgy of sensual emotion, unchecked by either the principles of the moral law or the exigencies of the diatonic scale, both of which, according to Wagner's view, found their perfection in the life-denying and hypocritical beliefs of Christianity. In 1850, when Wagner was still struggling to come up with a musical principle that would fit his revolutionary frame of mind, he kept coming back to something that was inevitably seen as a violation of the "patriarchal" family. The chromatic modulation that would find its fullest expression in *Tristan und Isolde*, which is after all a play about adultery, found its theoretical explication in a description of maidens "stepping beyond the family."

> The Key of a melody is that which presents to Feeling its various included tones in their earliest bond of kinship. The incitement to widen this narrower bond to a richer, more extended one, is derived from the Poetic Aim, insofar as that has already condensed itself in the speaking-verse to a moment-of-feeling; while this extension is governed by the particular expressional character of single chief-tones, which have themselves, in turn, been prompted by the verse. These chief-tones are, in a sense, the adolescent members of the family, who yearn to leave its wonted surrounding for an unhindered independence: this independence, however, they do not gain as egoists, but through encounter with another being, a being that lies outside the family. The maiden attains her independence, her stepping beyond the family, only through love of the youth who, himself the scion of another family, attracts her over to him. Thus the tone that quits the circle of the Key is a tone already prompted and attracted by that other key, and into the latter must it therefore pour itself according to the necessary law of Love. The leading-tone [*Leitton*] that urges from one key into another, and by this very urgency discloses its kinship with that other key, can only be taken as prompted by the motive of Love. The motive of Love is that which drives the "subject" [*Subjekt*] out beyond itself, and compels it to an alliance with another.[70]

Given then the collapse of "patriarchal" melody, the only organizing principle left is the will of the poet, "the Yearning of the Poet," which spurned all rational restraint, both musical and moral. Will, after all, created the world. The world is nothing more than my will and my imaginative construct (*Vorstellung*). It was the titanic will of the Poet, knowing no other law than itself and at last become conscious of itself as a result of the lucubrations of German idealism, which was to protect the music from drifting into aimlessness. Wagner, perhaps still imbued with the feelings evoked during his revolutionary days in Dresden, saw the last movement of Beethoven's Ninth Symphony as the watershed separating the older "patriarchal" music from the more revolutionary, text-informed art work of the future.

> If, now, we compare the broad melodic structure of the whole musical setting of the verse "*Seid umschlungen*" with the melody that the master, in his absolute-musical capacity so to say merely spread above the verse "*Freude Schöner Götterfunken*," we shall gain an exact understanding of the distinction between that patriarchal melody—as I have called it—and the melody that grows forth upon the word-verse through the working of the Poetic Aim. As the former made itself intelligible only in the most straitened of tone-family ties, so the latter—not only without becoming un-understandable, but to first become rightly understandable by the Feeling—can stretch the narrower kinship of the Key to the broad *ur*-kinship of all Tones, through alliance with other keys akin; and thus it widens the surely-guided feeling, into the endlessly Purely-human Feeling.[71]

Richard Wagner

When the melody, maligned as "patriarchal," is banned from music, or at the very least subordinated to something extramusical like the poet's text, expressive of his "yearning," the musical consequences are catastrophic. In Wagner's opera, the consequences can be seen by comparing *Tannhäuser* and *Tristan und Isolde*. In *Tannhäuser*, the tension between the chromatic and the diatonic, mirroring of course the conflict between reason and desire, carries the opera along to a successful musical conclusion. In *Tristan*, on the other hand, the struggle between reason and desire is, for all practical purposes, over. Venus' chromatic seductiveness in *Tannhäuser* is opposed by the pilgrims' Christian, "patriarchal" melody, and Tannhäuser is forced to choose between the two. *Tristan*, on the other hand, is like a musical vertebrate without bones. It rolls out of the orchestra pit and onto the audience like a huge, tepid water balloon. It sloshes, but it cannot dance; in fact, it can hardly move at all except in its amoebic fashion. It emotes endlessly but can find no resolution to the emotions it evokes, and so, instead of ending in catharsis, it promotes exhaustion. *Tannhäuser* deals with sexual conflict; *Tristan* is an exercise in *coitus reservatus*. Tristan succumbs to sexual desire during the first act, and the rest of the opera is filled with gaseous chromatic drifting.

Act Two provides the culmination of the already-expressed desire to be liberated from patriarchal constraint. Set at night, it provides an interesting cultural antipode to Mozart's *The Magic Flute*. Mozart, perhaps unduly influenced by Masonic propaganda, saw his opera demonstrating the triumph of the light of reason over the darkness of superstition. *Tristan*, written sixty-five years later, celebrates the triumph of sensual darkness over the light of reason. In literary historical terms, the change could be described as the move from Enlightenment to Romanticism, from *Aufklärung* to *Verklärung*, to give two expressive German terms. This description, however, gives little insight into the catastrophic cultural consequences of this decision. Once again Wagner makes use of the counters of his culture to turn the project of his culture on its head. Sitting in the comfort of the drawing room of the Wesendonck villa on the shores of Lake Zurich, a small group of Wagner's devoted admirers, including the three current women in his life, listened in rapturous silence as Wagner read his Tristan poem aloud. Minna was there, along with Mathilde Wesendonck, the immediate inspiration for the poem and the woman Wagner construed as the Isolde to his Tristan. Cosima von Bülow, the wife of the man who would be the first to conduct *Tristan*, and Wagner's future wife, was there, too. Cosima, Wagner's second wife, would name one of their children Isolde. On that evening Cosima listened to the recital with downcast eyes, saying nothing, Wagner would testify in his autobiography. When he asked her what she thought, Cosima burst into tears. When Mathilde was presented with a copy of the libretto dedicated to her, she embraced him and said that all her wishes were fulfilled and, according to one account, added that it was time for her to die.

And what did this cultured group of passionate ladies find so overpowering? Not just adultery, but rather the creation of a huge enabling symphonic/poetic context for adultery, the scene of the second act of Tristan, in which Isolde spurns Brangäne's warning not to extinguish the torch, which symbolizes the light of reason. Isolde's response is interesting in its vehemence,

> Even if this lamp were the light of my life
> I wouldn't hesitate to extinguish it.

Wagner got to pose the question first, but since he proposed it in such an aesthetically convincing way, ever-widening circles in the countries that had received the patrimony of Christianity could ask the question themselves over and over again: Just how much are we willing to pay for sexual liberation? Is it worth death, either individually or collectively? Sitting at the peak of a musical achievement unprecedented in human history, Wagner took a peek into the abyss and thought it not all that deep. Tristan in the throes of passion chooses darkness over the light. Once again Wagner appropriated cultural symbols in an almost uncanny way and turned the tradition they represented on its head. But in so doing he only substantiated the tradition he had set out to overturn. Act Two is a replay of the Venusberg, but this time without the moral scruples evinced by Tannhäuser. As a result, the music suffers: morals suffer: culture suffers, but Tristan/Wagner, comfortably ensconced in the Wesendonck's drawing room, seems willing to chuck it all for the "*Wunderreich der Nacht.*" Taking the notes of the famous Tristan chord and spinning them into a melody of sorts, he comes up with the famous duet, "*O sink hernieder*":

> *O Night of Love,*
> *Descend*
> *and grant forgetfulness*
> that I live;
> Place me in your lap.
> Dissolve me from this world.
> Extinguish now the last lamp;
> What we thought
> All thought,
> All remembering,
> Holy Twilight,
> Sublime Foreboding,
> Extinguish the horror of our imaginings
> In one world-dissolving stroke.

Just how much are we willing to risk to gratify sexual compulsion? Enough to dissolve the world? Are we willing to foster sexual license to the point of social breakdown? The question seems much more pertinent to our age than to Wagner's. How much darkness we willing to call down on ourselves to obliterate the recognition of our deeds? How much reason are we willing to banish from our lives in order to justify this sensual gratification? How much of our cultural patrimony are we willing to pawn for liberation from the norms of reason applied to the sexual drive? In Act Two of *Tristan* we find the culmination of Wagner's activity as a cultural revolutionary. Emboldened by Schopenhauer's philosophy, which proposed that the self not only created the world but *was* the world, "*selbst—dann bin ich die Welt*," both Tristan and Isolde sing their hymn to unreason, the "O sink hernieder" duet, and press on toward sexual gratification under the illusion that the cultural revolution can be prosecuted according to its own laws. But day dawns and both are drawn back into the harsh daylight of the truth, whether they wish to be or not.

The moral import of the light/darkness imagery was not new with Mozart and *The Magic Flute*. It is part of the universal patrimony of mankind, found among the world's religions and given its Christian redaction in the Gospel according to Saint John (3:19-21):

> Though the light has come into the world
> men have shown they prefer
> darkness to the light
> because their deeds were evil.
> And indeed, everybody who does wrong
> hates the light and avoids it,
> for fear his actions should he exposed....

The passage could hardly have been far from the consciousness of the audience listening in rapture to Wagner's panegyric to the extinction of the light of reason. Nor could it have been far from Wagner's mind itself, given what he had had to say previously about the baleful influence of Christianity. This direct contradiction of Christianity and the light of reason was, however, the main attraction it held for precisely that audience. The West would meditate with increasing intensity over the next century and a half on the price it was willing to pay for sexual liberation, liberation from the light of reason, liberation from the cultural achievements that were based on society's subjugation of individual passion to the order of reason. Was it worth it after all? The audiences that found themselves awash in the tepid chromatic modulations of *Tristan* could ask themselves this question over and over again. Was it really worth it? Would it not be better to perish in one exquisitely consummated burst of passionate *Liebestod*?

> Lovely death
> longed for, sought after
> Love Death!
> Freed from the need to awake
> This bliss
> Far from the sun.

All the metaphysical questions revolved around the sexual issues that were coming more and more to dominate the thought of the cultured classes as Christianity's attraction began to dwindle throughout the nineteenth century. If the world is nothing but an externalization or projection of the will, meditation on the exigencies of the will shows that, to a large extent, the will is focused by the sexual appetite. If that is the case, then perhaps anything that hinders the will is ultimately self-destructive. One can almost feel this strangely compelling thought being turned over again and again in the minds of Wagner's cultured followers. Thomas Mann tells us that he "never missed a single performance of *Tristan* at the Munich Hoftheater." Mann, like Wagner inspired by Schopenhauer, tried to work out the dynamics of the relationship between sexual liberation and cultural achievement. Like Wagner, he found in himself a deeply ambivalent frame of mind. Mann's Gustav Aschenbach is faced with a similar dilemma in *Death in Venice*. Is Achenbach's impossible love for a Polish teenage boy worth dying for? The cultured Aschenbach, trapped in the disease-ridden cultural monument that is Venice, seems to think so. It is a sentiment that has captured space even on condom ads in the age of AIDS. Is sexual liberation something we are willing to risk death to attain? The jury is still out. Thomas Mann saw the culmination of Schopenhauer's world-as-will philosophy taken to its logical conclusion in Wagner's hypersexual music:

> The part of Schopenhauer's teachings that influenced Wagner, and in which he recognized himself, was the explanation of the world in terms of the "will" or instinctive drive, the erotic conception of the world (sexuality as the "focus of the will"), by which the music of *Tristan* and its cosmogony of longing are shaped. Some have denied that *Tristan* is influenced by Schopenhauerian philosophy— and rightly so, in so far as the denial of the will is concerned. For this, after all, is a love poem; and nowhere does the will affirm itself more powerfully than in love and sexuality But it is precisely as a mystery of love that the work is steeped to the very core in Schopenhauerian ideas. Here the erotic sweetness, the intoxicating essence of Schopenhauer's philosophy has been sucked out, so to speak, leaving the wisdom untouched.[72]

Wagner's achievement in *Tristan* resided in his ability to put the sexual question to his audience in a compelling way. The flight from reason in morals is in effect not different from the flight from reason in music. Music provides the argument with a plausibility the argument lacks on its own, a fact that both Plato and Aristotle recognized and the reason why Plato banned certain musical modes from his republic. Wagner returned to this tradition of world harmony, but with the intention to plot its overthrow. In accomplishing his intention, however, he subverted his own message. The republic was endangered by certain modes much more radically than it was by anarchists like Bakunin. Wagner's *Tristan* was the perfect mirror of his disordered desires, and, more than that, it also mirrored the disordered desires of the cultured classes that came to hear him and found encouragement in his music:

> *Tistan's* chromatic conflict, its soulful, painful descent from one key to another, is a "literary" device that transcends the bounds of music and expresses disen-

chantment with a real world whose fixed points of reference are steadily disappearing. As a resort to artistic means, it characterized the decadent aspect of romanticism, which attained its last and most mature consummation in *Tristan*. Bourgeois ideals had withered in the outside world and resistance could be offered only in art itself, by revolutionizing its means. Flaubert and Wagner were confronted by the same problem. *Tristan* and *Madame Bovary* both presuppose a real world in the throes of instability: King Mark is not alone in his weariness. The conventions are mocked with a candor that would have been unthinkable only a decade earlier. The outrage felt by both men's contemporaries, or those of them who upheld the conventions, was not surprising. That *Tristan* did not cause a far greater stir requires some explanation. Given the nature of the second act, Wagner was just as open as Flaubert to a charge of "offending against public morals, good manners, and religion." Minna, who found the libretto "disgusting" and "almost indecently passionate," loathed the whole opera because she was aware of its "instigation." But it was the music that brought its lasciviousness and "immoral" tendencies to life. If this point did not sink in at once, it was because Wagner overtaxed the ears of his audience, and because the urge for release and resolution was confined to a deeper level by a self-imposed framework and carefully calculated intervallic tension: in short, by the dialectic of subtlety.[73]

For the next one hundred fifty years, the West would pose the *Liebestod* question again and again in various ways, from Nazism to Woodstock, and never be able to come up with an answer. In the process, enormous amounts of cultural patrimony were thrown overboard. Classical music, freed from patriarchal melody by Wagner's chromatic modulations, would go into a state of terminal decline. Sexual morals would follow suit. It was an expensive way to find out that Shakespeare had been right all along and that this sort of man should not be trusted.

Notes

1. Martin Gregor-Dellin, *Richard Wagner: His life, His Work, His Century*, trans. J. Maxwell Brownjohn (San Diego and New York: Harcourt Brace Jovanovich, 1980), p. 167.
2. Gregor-Dellin, p. 165.
3. Richard Wagner, *Mein Leben* (Munich: Paul List Verlag, 1963), p. 451.
4. Wagner, *Mein*, p. 467.
5. Wagner, *Mein*, p. 469.
6. Wagner, *Mein*, p. 469.
7. Wagner, *Mein*, p. 452.
8. Wagner, *Mein*, p. 453.
9. Wagner, *Mein*, p. 454
10. Gregor-Dellin, p. 164.
11. Wagner, *Mein*, p. 468.
12. Wagner, *Mein*, p.473.

13. Wagner, *Mein*, p. 475.
14. Gregor-Dellin, p. 179.
15. Gregor-Dellin, p. 179.
16. Richard Wagner, *Prose Works*, trans. William Ashton Ellis, vol. 1, *The Artwork of the Future* (New York: Broude Brothers, 1966), p. 24.
17. Wagner, *Prose*, p.37.
18. Gregor-Dellin, P. 188.
19. Wagner, *Prose*, vol. 1. p. 42.
29. Wagner, *Prose*, p. 39.
21. Leo Spitzer, *Classical and Christian Ideas of World Harmony: Prolegomena to an Interpretation of the Word "Stimmung"* (Baltimore: The Johns Hopkins Press, 1963), p. 1.
22. Spitzer, p. 13.
23. Spitzer, p. 16.
24. Spitzer, p. 15.
25. Hermann-Josef Burback, *Studien zur Musikanschauung des Thomas von Aquin* (Regensburg: Gustav Bosse Verlag, 1966), p. 52, n.6.
26 Burback, p. 54, (my translation).
27 Burback, p. 69.
28 Sir Thomas Browne, *Religio Medici*, cited in Spitzer. p. 288.
29 Novalis, *Christenheit oder Europa*, cited in Spitzer, p. 76, (my translation).
30. Novalis, p. 77, (my translation).
31 Gregor-Dellin, p. 153.
32 Wagner, *Prose*, vol. 1, p. 52.
33. Wagner, *Prose*, p. 54.
34. Wagner, *Prose*, p. 55.
35. Wagner, *Prose*, p. 59.
36 Wagner, *Prose*, 59.
37. Wagner, *Prose*, p. 60.
38. Wagner, *Prose*, p. 60.
39. Mann. *Pro and Contra Wagner*, trans. Allan Blunden (Chicago: University of Chicago Press, 1985). p. 98.
40. Erich Neumann, *Amor and Psyche: The Psychic Development of the Feminine, A Commentary on the Tale by Apuleius* (Princeton, NJ: Princeton University Press, 1956). p. 78.
41. Neumann, pp. 80-81.
42. Neumann, p. 81.
43. Gregor-Dellin, p. 110.
44. Gregor-Dellin, p. 57.
45. Wagner, *Mein*, p. 113.
46. Gregor-Dellin, p. 68.
47. Gregor-Dellin, p. 71.

48. Gregor-Dellin, p. 197.
49. Gregor-Dellin, p. 200.
50. Gregor-Dellin, p. 200.
51. Gregor-Dellin.
52. Gregor-Dellin, p. 23.
53. Richard Wagner, *Prose Works*, trans. William Ashton Ellis, vol. 2., *Opera and Drama* (New York: Broude Brothers, 1966), p.45.
54. Wagner, *Prose*, p. 54.
55. Wagner, *Prose*, 51.
56. Wagner, *Prose*, p. 77.
57. Wagner, *Prose*, p. 78.
58. Wagner, *Prose*, p. 87.
59. Wagner, *Prose*, p. 111.
60. Wagner, *Prose*, p. 111.
61. Arthur Schopenhauer, *Die Welt als Wille und Vorstellung* (Zurich: Haffmans Verlag, 1888), pp. 32, 33, (my translation).
62. Mann, p. 14.
63 Wagner, *Prose*, vol. 2, p. 104.
64. John A. Oesterle, "Toward an Evaluation of Music," *Thomist* 14 (1951), pp.325-34.
65 Oesterle, p. 326.
66. Oesterle, p 330.
67. Wagner, *Prose*, vol. 2, p. 288.
68. My translation of the original "*zu schwelgerisch enzückender Kundgebung an das sinnliche Gefühl*," rendered in the above passage "a sybaritic message to the sensuous feeling.
69. Wagner, *Prose*, vol. 2, p. 289.
70. Wagner, *Prose*, p. 291.
71. Wagner, *Prose*, p. 290.
72. Mann, p. 194.
73. Gregor-Dellin, p. 276.

Chapter 2

Friedrich Nietzsche
Transvaluation of All Values as the Prosecution of the Cultural War

> Does one finally understand—does one want to understand?—what the Renaissance was? The transvaluation of Christian values, the attempt undertaken with every possible means, with every instinct, with every genius, to bring about the victory of counter-values Up 'til this time there was only this major war, there was no more decisive posing of the question than the formulation presented by the Renaissance. My question is their question.
>
> —Friedrich Nietzsche
> *The Anti-Christ: A Curse on Christianity*

On Saturday, May 15, 1869, Friedrich Nietzsche, a young philology professor at the nearby university of Basel, walked up the gently sloping carriage road that approached Tribschen, the imposing house on a grassy knoll situated between Mount Pilatus and Lake Lucerne, now the home of Richard Wagner and his domestic ménage. Wagner's first wife, Minna, had died in 1866, but since 1863 he had taken as his mistress Cosima von Bülow, wife of the conductor of his operas and one of the three illegitimate daughters born to Franz Liszt and the Countess Marie d'Agoult. Wagner's life had oscillated between economic extremes. When prospects seemed good, Wagner would recklessly furnish whatever house he had chosen in the most expensive style money could buy, either using up whatever windfall he had just happened to come upon or placing himself impossibly in debt, or a combination of both. More than once, the only way he could come up with a plausible solution to his financial problems was by simply leaving town with his debts unpaid. He and Minna had left Riga in this manner as newlyweds; his disastrous affair with Mathilde Wesendonck around ten years earlier had ended in pretty much the same manner, when his distraught wife had put an announcement in the paper causing a run on his property and assets by local creditors.

Within a few years of going into exile, Wagner had gone through two wealthy patrons and reached the end of his financial rope. As in the Jessie Laussot affair, his impetuous sexual inclinations had ruined his relationship with the Wesendoncks. Wagner had proposed that Mathilde Wesendonck, the wife of the man who was bankrolling him in Zurich, run off with him. The composer at the time was in full-blown creative heat composing the music to *Tristan und Isolde*, his paean to impossible adulterous love. As in the case with Jessie Laussot, Mathilde Wesendonck was either too tied to her children or too wary of breaking bourgeois conventions or too comfortable living with her wealthy husband, or sensible enough to see that living with Wagner would be no bed of roses. Whatever the reason, Wagner left for Venice on his own, there to brood and continue scoring the composition of *Tristan und Isolde* in a rented palazzo, while nursing himself though bouts of abdominal pains and wondering how he was going to make it financially.

By late April 1864, Wagner was staying at the Hotel Marquardt in Stuttgart, making plans to complete the *Meistersingers of Nuremberg* somewhere or other and still wondering how he was going to pay his bills. He had separated from Minna, who, suffering from heart disease, would be dead within two years, but who was at the time still very much alive and refusing to grant him a divorce. One year before, he had embarked upon his affair with Cosima von Bülow. Less than one year later, their first child, Isolde, would be born in Munich on April 10, 1865. In spite of this, he was at the time thinking of improving his financial situation by marrying into wealth. He had even gone so far as to ask his sister, Luise Brockhaus, wife of the orientalist and encyclopedist, to pressure Minna into granting him a divorce. Luise flatly refused and suggested he get a job as *Kapellmeister* in Darmstadt.

Then, on the evening of Monday, May 2, Wagner was handed a card informing him in French that the court secretary of his majesty the king of Bavaria would like to speak with him. Wagner at first thought it was a ploy on the part of his creditors so he sent word that he was not available and packed his bags for a morning's journey of, up until then, no specific destination. The visitor, however, persisted, and Wagner suddenly found himself the beneficiary of a *deus ex machina* that he would probably have considered too implausible to use in one of his music dramas. Ludwig II, the young Bavarian king and a passionate devotee of Wagner's music, had heard of his plight and was now earnestly requesting a personal audience with him with the indication that he wanted to keep him "forever at his side in friendship."[1] Wagner could hardly believe his good fortune and sat down immediately to write a letter to the king expressing his gratitude, not omitting to mention "these tears of the most heavenly emotion."[2]

Ludwig II, when still a fifteen-year-old crown prince, had been no stranger to tears of emotion either. He had shed tears of joy upon hearing Wagner's *Lohengrin* for the first time. The king, who was not especially musical, was likewise so overcome by the passage in *Tannhäuser* where Tannhäuser entered the Venusberg that "his body," according to Embassy Secretary von Leinfeder, "would go into positive convulsions each time. They were so severe on one occasion that I feared he would have an epileptic fit." [3]

By the time Nietzsche arrived at Wagner's doorstep in May of 1869, Ludwig's financial bailout of the Wagnerian enterprise was having its full effect. The king of Bavaria had not only paid off Wagner's debts, he had set him up handsomely at Tribschen. The three-story house bad been redecorated in the rococo style, including much pink satin and many *putti*, and in the drawing room there were matching busts of both Ludwig and Wagner himself. This sensual extravagance was not confined to the decor in Wagner's house; it extended to his taste in clothing as well. According to Robert W. Gutman, Wagner's "need for silks, satins, furs and perfumes had reached the fetishistic.... That his skin was extremely sensitive may explain his silk chokers and underwear but hardly those quilted, shirred, bowed, laced, flowered, fringed, and furred gowns he dragged through his private rooms." [4]

Nietzsche did not get to see the master that day. "I stood for a long time in front of the house," he recounted later, "and heard a painful chord repeated constantly." [5] Wagner was hard at work on the third act of *Siegfried* and had left word with the servants that he was not to be disturbed. While walking away from the house, Nietzsche was accosted by a servant who wanted to know if he was the Herr Nietzsche whom Wagner had met in Leipzig. Replying that he was, Nietzsche was asked to stay for lunch, but because of previous commitments their meeting had to be postponed until the coming Monday. Nietzsche, like Ludwig II, was a young man with a troubled sexual history who saw in the older Wagner a combination of father figure and minor deity. Like Ludwig II, Nietzsche had been exposed to the Wagnerian *oeuvre* as a teenager and had been swept away by the emotions he found portrayed there. (Nietzsche was an extraordinarily sensitive musician all his life and might have studied music if the training had been available and he had not opted for the theological studies his father had pursued.) In the fall of 1861, the seventeen-year-old Nietzsche was exposed to a piano score of *Tristan und Isolde* by his friend Gustav Krug. The two, according to Nietzsche's sister Elizabeth, spent that fall playing the score on the piano and singing its arias well into the night. It was a fascination that never left Nietzsche. In *Ecce Homo*, one of his last books and one written after he had publicly repudiated Wagner, Nietzsche described how "beginning from the moment when there was a piano version of *Tristan*, I was a Wagnerian." [6] Even as a committed anti-Wagnerian, Nietzsche could still write about the fascination that *Tristan*, "Wagner's *ne plus ultra*," exerted over him:

> Nonetheless I'm still looking to this day for a work that possesses the same dangerous fascination, the same sweet and horrifying infinitude as *Tristan*, and I continue to search in vain. All of the strangeness of Leonardo da Vinci is made mundane by the sounding of the first note of *Tristan*. This work is without a doubt Wagner's *ne plus ultra*; he recovered from it by writing the *Meistersinger* and the *Ring*. But getting better was a step backward for a nature like Wagner's. . . I take it as a good fortune of the first order having lived at the right time and

particularly to have lived as a German, so that I was mature enough for this work, so great is the curiosity of the psychologist in me. The world is a poorer place for those who have never been sick enough to appreciate this "lust of hell." It is permissible, in fact, it is practically obligatory to come up with some sort of mystical formula. I suspect that I knew better than anyone the monstrosities of which Wagner is capable, the fifty worlds of alien delight, which no one but he had the wings to reach, and since I'm strong enough to turn even the most dangerous and questionable aspects to my advantage, I name Wagner as the greatest benefactor of my life.[7]

As this passage makes clear, *Tristan* was the quintessential Wagner as far as Nietzsche was concerned. Nietzsche's deranged sensibilities, so sensitively attuned to the slightest nuance in music, found something deeply satisfying in the musical invention Wagner brought forth in *Tristan*. Judging from the vocabulary Nietzsche used, he was also not unaware of the sexual underpinnings of this derangement. In a musical vocabulary that could have been taken (and for all we know was taken) straight from the classical sources on music (Nietzsche was after all a classics professor and most certainly read Aristotle and Plato in the original), Nietzsche states that "getting better" (Gesünder werden), that is, writing more conventional and accessible operas like the *Meistersinger*, was a step backward for Wagner. Nietzsche preferred musical sickness of the sort expressed in *Tristan*, that "simultaneously horrible and sweet infinity." The world is impoverished because it has never been sick enough to appreciate the "lust of hell" of which *Tristan* is the closest musical approximation. Thomas Mann, a student of both Wagner and Nietzsche, cites the "lust of hell" passage in *Ecce Home* in support of his claim that "Wagner's *Tristan* is a thoroughly obscene work."[8] Likewise Mann, a contemporary of Schönberg, with whom he would share exile in Hollywood in the forties while he was at work on his Nietzsche/Schönberg music novel *Doktor Faustus*, gave some indication of the influence *Tristan* had had on the proto-modern generation. "There was a time," he wrote, "when I never missed a performance of *Tristan* at the Munich *Hoftheater*—that most sublime and dangerous of Wagner's works, which in its sensuous-suprasensuous passion, its lascivious desire for bed, is really' something for young people, at the age when the erotic is all important."[9]

Adolescence is precisely the time of life when Nietzsche was exposed to *Tristan's* lascivious musical charms. Adolescence is always a difficult and formative age. Aristotle warned against allowing certain sensual modes to be played among the young for fear of damaging their character. If the notion was ever heeded, it was not during the 1860s in Germany. Mann wondered that a work like *Tristan* could get played at all in the German theaters of that day, so subversive did he consider it. But the fact is that it was being played regularly, perhaps because its scope and pace exerted a counterbalancing, calming effect on the passions. The notion that music can be obscene is not widespread anyway, even though Mann used precisely that expression. It comes across as a vaguely poetic concept, unlike, say, obscene drawing or literature, which is something readily understandable.

Tristan's effect on Nietzsche, however, seems real enough. Nietzsche, the sexually confused adolescent and aspiring theologian, was quite simply swept away, and nothing, not even Wagner's later prostration before the cross in *Parsifal*, could bring him back.

There were other currents at work as well. The revolutionary spirit had died down since 1849, but the writings of those who had inspired it were still in circulation and having the same effect on Nietzsche as they had had on Wagner. Nietzsche would eventually come to Schopenhauer as the apotheosis of German idealism and its transmutation of those currents into the doctrine of the world-creating will. But at the time there were other documents that affected the theology student more intimately. There was the effect of the newly emerging historical critical method on the beliefs of young Lutherans like Nietzsche, whose faith rested on the foundation of *sola Scriptura*. In 1864, David Strauss brought out a popular version of his life of Jesus, *Das Leben Jesu für das Deutsche Volk bearbeitet*, and both Nietzsche and his friend Paul Deussen bought copies and found the undermining of the biblical faith Strauss propounded there "irresistible." "There is a serious consequence," wrote Nietzsche, evidently thinking down the road a bit, "—if you give up Christ, you will have to give up God too."[10]

In addition to the intellectual ferment, which in the form of Strauss' book was weakening his faith and in the case of Wagner's music, heating up his passions, Nietzsche was subjected to the moral dangers associated with growing up just about anywhere. In February of 1865 the then twenty-year-old Nietzsche, while sightseeing in Cologne, asked a street porter to take him to a restaurant. The man instead took him to a brothel. "I found myself," he told his friend Deussen in a letter afterward, "suddenly surrounded by half a dozen apparitions in tinsel and gauze, looking at me expectantly...."[11] If they expected a paying customer, they were disappointed. Instead of going to one of the girls, Nietzsche went to the whorehouse piano, played a few chords (diminished sevenths out of *Tristan und Isolde* perhaps?), and then left.

The real question in Nietzsche scholarship is whether he went back, either to the brothel in Cologne or to another one in Leipzig. Thomas Mann, for one, thought he did, and not only that, but that he went back and deliberately infected himself with syphilis. The idea, based on material from Deussen's book on Nietzsche, forms the basis for Mann's Nietzsche novel, *Doktor Faustus*. In that novel, Mann describes the meeting between the Nietzsche character, Adrian Leverkühn, and a prostitute, who

> learned from his own lips that he had made the journey thither on her account. She thanked him, even while she warned him against her body. I know it from Adrian: she warned him—is not this something like a beneficent distinction between the higher humanity of the creature and her physical part, fallen to the gutter, sunk to a wretched object of use? The unhappy one warned him who asked of her, warned him away from "herself"; that meant an act of free elevation of soul above her pitiable physical existence, an act of

human association from it, an act of sympathy, an act if the word be permitted me—of love. And, gracious heaven, was it nor also love or what was it, what madness, what deliberate, reckless tempting of God, what compulsion to compromise the punishment in the sin, finally what deep, deeply mysterious longing for daemonic conception, for deathly unchaining of chemical change in his nature was at work, that having been warned he despised the warning and insisted upon possession of her flesh.[12]

According to Mann's telling of the story, Nietzsche deliberately infected himself with syphilis in some sort of demonic initiation and pact with the devil. The payoff for Adrian Leverkühn was the invention of the twelve-tone scale, a piece of poetic license that annoyed Schönberg, who claimed at the time to be the sole inventor of that musical system. (More about Schönberg's hypersensitivity on the matter later.) The artistic conflation of Nietzsche and Schönberg in Mann's *Faustus* novel posits the rise of modem German philosophy out of German music and the further development of that music coming as the result of a pact with the devil. The sensual music of *Tristan* led Nietzsche/Leverkühn to the brothel, where he dedicates himself to the devil to produce a truly deranged music in response. Virtually all of German cultural life in the twentieth century, but most especially its music, philosophy, and politics, arose out of this syphilitic sexual consecration. The Nietzschean transvaluation of all values, atonal music, and Nazism were all cultural manifestations of an age that was conceived in a pact with the devil.

Pia Daniela Volz in a recent book gives an exhaustive account of Nietzsche's illnesses. In spite of the disparities from one source to another, and in spite of the handicaps inherent in trying to diagnose an illness in a body that no longer exists, the evidence seems fairly clear that Nietzsche did have syphilis. He was, at any rate, a man whose life spun itself out almost entirely in the shadow of illness. The most productive years of his life, before the time of his collapse in paralysis and madness, were spent in a fruitless search after the one doctor, spa, medicine, or cure that would relieve him of the almost constant pain he experienced. In an entry in the medical records dated January 10, 1889, the attending physician wrote that Nietzsche "admits that he specifically infected himself twice."[13]

The interesting point for our purposes is not the medical details of his physical and mental collapse in early 1889 but rather the fact that Nietzsche's life, from his seventeenth year on, seems to have been lived out under the influence of Wagner's music in general and of *Tristan und Isolde* in particular. *Tristan*, at least the piano version, preceded syphilis by a number of years. On the occasion of hearing the *Tristan* Prelude performed by an orchestra for the first time, on the evening of October 27, 1868, around six months before he showed up at the door at Tribschen, Nietzsche had difficulty giving adequate expression to the enormous influence the music had had on him:

> I cannot bring myself to take a critically cool view of this music. It sends a thrill through every fibre, every nerve, and for a long time I have not had such a sustained feeling of being swept away [*Entrücktheit*] as the Overture gave.[14]

Friedrich Nietzsche

Being swept away (*entrückt*) and crazy (*verrückt*) are etymologically related in German and, not surprisingly, related in the life of Nietzsche the German philologist as well. His desire to be swept away by Wagner's music culminated in a madness that was either the result of syphilis or self-induced. Nietzsche's friend, the composer Peter Gast, was convinced when he visited Nietzsche in an insane asylum toward the end of his life that that madness vas self-willed. Even in the throes of madness, Nietzsche would still play music influenced by *Tristan*, and if one remembers the extinguishing of the light of reason that takes place in the second act of *Tristan*, it is not hard to see why Nietzsche would still find it attractive. "*O sink hernieder Nacht der Liebe*" was a swan song that could apply to Nietzsche's mental powers equally as well as it did to the consummation of Tristan and Isolde's illicit love.

As early as his first book, *The Birth of Tragedy*, the one written almost totally under Wagner's influence, Nietzsche portrayed Socrates as the villain in the cultural history of the West. Socrates banished the spirit of music from tragedy because of his desire to subordinate life to reason. Socrates, "in whom the brave madness of artistic enthusiasm never glowed," "turned his cyclopic eye on tragedy and was incapable of peering into the Dionysian abyss."[15] Socrates' "deep-seated madness" consisted in this: his unshakeable belief that thinking could follow the thread of causality into the deepest abyss of being and that thought could not only recognize being but could correct it as well. If reason mastering will can drive music out of tragedy and bring about the Christian/Classical age in the West, then Nietzsche as Dionysos/Antichrist could bring about the reversal of that process by subordinating reason to will according to the spirit of music he had imbibed in Wagner's *Tristan*. Socrates was guilty of the "optimistic dialectic," which used "the whip of its syllogisms to drive music out of tragedy."[16] But Nietzsche, taking his cue from Schopenhauer, saw in music "the immediate replica of the will itself" and, as a result, the metaphysical substratum of all reality.[17] Music, and here again one must remember that Nietzsche had Wagner's music in mind, specifically *Tristan und Isolde*, would bring about the overthrow of the age of Christ/Socrates and usher in the age of Dionysian excess that Nietzsche had discovered in texts such as Euripides' *Bacchae*. In Nietzsche, Wagner found an heir and explicator of his theory of cultural revolution.

When Nietzsche finally got into the drawing room at Tribschen, he noticed, in addition to the busts of Wagner and Ludwig II and the various *objets d'art*, Gemelli's painting of *Dionysus among the Muses*. Like Nietzsche, Wagner saw the drama of the ancient Greeks as superior to the Christian art that succeeded it. In his essay on "Art and Revolution," Wagner made invidious comparisons between the pagan Greeks and the hypocritical, life-denying Christians:

> Christianity adjusts the ills of an honourless, useless, and sorrowful existence of mankind on earth, by the miraculous love of God: who had not—as the noble Greek supposed—created man for a happy and self-conscious life upon this

earth, but had here imprisoned him in a loathsome dungeon: so as, in reward for the self-contempt that pointed him therein, to prepare him for a posthumous state of endless comfort and inactive ecstasy. Therefore the poor wretch who, in the enjoyment of his natural powers, made this life his own possession must suffer after death the eternal torments of hell! Naught was required of mankind but *Faith*—that is to say, the confession of its miserable plight, and the giving up of all spontaneous attempt to escape from out this misery: for the undeserved Grace of God was alone to set it free.[18]

Wagner's redaction of Christianity, like Nietzsche's, was distinctly Lutheran, and their program for cultural revolution was a function of this worldview in crisis, Wagner remained in a state of ambivalence about not only Christianity but also the Protestant/Catholic split for his entire life. Tannhäuser, it should be remembered, not only oscillates between Venus and Elizabeth, he also vacillates between the Wartburg and the Vatican. "Love me," the then sixty-four-year-old Wagner wrote to a considerably younger Judith Gautier, "and let us not wait for the Protestant kingdom of heaven: it will be terribly tedious. Love!"[19] Nietzsche's meditation on Protestant Christianity was at once more profound and more corrosive. In this, Nietzsche and Wagner were like their American contemporaries Ralph Waldo Emerson and Walt Whitman. Emerson's repudiation of not only the fatally attenuated redaction of Christianity that was Unitarianism, but the whole claim of the past on the present was avidly adopted by the much younger Whitman, who went on to dedicate *Leaves of Grass* to Emerson. When Emerson objected to some of the explicitly homoerotic poems, Whitman responded by quoting "Self-Reliance" back at Emerson: "No law can be sacred to me but that of my nature. Good and bad are but names very readily transferable to that or this; the only right is what is after my constitution; the only wrong what is against it."

Both Nietzsche and Wagner came from the birthplace of Lutheranism; both repudiated their background. "Both men," according to Gregor-Dellin, "felt deeply rooted in the Central German cultural area bounded by the Harz, the Thuringer Pforte, and Elster—the home of Martin Luther, Heinrich Schutz, and Novalis—without ever quite mastering their aversion to its endearing but provincial atmosphere."[20]

Wagner's Catholic proclivities kept popping up in his operas, from *Tannhäuser* through *Parsifal*. In the end, nothing got resolved. Wagner wrote a myth that was as much a part of the Cathar tradition as it was Catholic. Because of his repudiation of reason, there is a sense in which Nietzsche is a Lutheran "saint." Because of his inability to pursue that rejection of reason to its logical conclusion, there is a sense in which Wagner is a Lutheran apostate. In both instances, both reason and will are viewed in a sexual context. Wagner said that music was a woman, by which he meant some formless matrix upon which the poet could impose his meanings. Nietzsche called truth a woman, by which he meant pretty much the same thing. In both instances, the will simply imposed its own desires on the ever-compliant and, therefore, female reality. In Nietzsche, Wagner, and

Friedrich Nietzsche

Schopenhauer, desire takes precedence over truth. In all three, desire is in some sense the ultimate truth. Schopenhauer formulated the relationship by saying that the world was my will and my imaginative construct. In each man the energy flow of the intellectual life has been reversed. Making reason a servant of will is a German invention. Luther hated reason every bit as much as Nietzsche and, in trying to think up the worst insult imaginable, came up with the formula "Reason is a whore." Nietzsche, raised by his Protestant pastor father in the sanitized Lutheranism of the nineteenth century, took the Lutheran anti-rationalism to unheard-of peaks of fanatical piety. He absolutized the hatred of reason; he provided a cultural program for banning the entire tradition of the Christian/Classical West, which was based on a reverence for reason, whose cause he traced back to Socrates. In *The Birth of Tragedy*, Nietzsche's first book and the one he wrote when under the maximal influence of Wagner, Nietzsche proposed a "new dichotomy?": "the Dionysian and the Socratic principles." [21] The advent of Reason among the Greeks signified the death of music and tragedy, the banning of the worship of Dionysos. With the advent of Socrates and the demise of tragedy, music was henceforth to conform itself to reason. This is, indeed, the gist of both Plato's commentary on music in the *Republic* and Aristotle's in the *Politics*. It is also the source of the tradition of world harmony in the West, which held its sway with diminishing power and comprehensibility even over people as close to Wagner in time and culture as Novalis and Beethoven. It was the latter who wrote to Bettina Brentano, explaining that:

> Like all the arts, music is founded upon the exalted symbols of the moral sense: all true invention is a moral progress. To submit to these inscrutable laws, and by means of these laws to tame and guide one's own mind so that the manifestations of art may pour out: this is the isolating principle of art. To be dissolved in its manifestations, this is our dedication to the divine, which calmly exercises its power over the raging of the untamed elements and so lends to the imagination its highest effectiveness. So always art represents the divine, and the relationship of men towards art is religion: what we obtain from art comes from God, is divine inspiration, which appoints an aim for human faculties that we cannot attain.[22]

Nietzsche's attitude toward morality is well known. His program for man's liberation is the "*Umwertung aller Werte*," the transvaluation of all values. Like Beethoven, who is merely restating something well within the Christian/Classical tradition, Nietzsche also sees a connection between music and morality, as well as a relationship between music and reason. For Nietzsche, however, the poles have been reversed. With the advent of Socrates, music was subjected to reason. In order to end the Christian/Socratic age, reason would now be subject to music, which is, according to Schopenhauer, the immediate expression of the will. The reason Nietzsche could feel so sanguine about the coming advent of the new post-Christian age lay chiefly in the fact that he felt that the vehicle of this transvaluation of all values was now at hand in the music drama of Richard Wagner in general, but most particularly the deranged chromaticism of *Tristan und Isolde*, which bespoke for Nietzsche "the lust of hell."

During the entire period surrounding the creation of *The Birth of Tragedy*, Nietzsche steeped himself in Wagner's thought, music, and life. After reading Wagner's essay on Beethoven, Nietzsche wrote to tell him that as far as he was concerned Wagner's philosophy of music was "*the* philosophy of music." Wagner's strictures against Christian culture, his praise of the Greeks, his growth away from the Lutheranism of his childhood, all struck deep chords of affinity with the musically sensitive Nietzsche, whose adolescent mind had been formed by the piano score of *Tristan*. *Tristan* had in fact become the key to understanding Wagner:

> Through this preliminary study I have arrived at the point of understanding—completely and with profound pleasure—the necessity of your line of argument. ... I feel that to contemporary aestheticians you will seem like a somnambulist. ... I should think that to follow you, as thinker, in this case is possible only for those to whom *Tristan* has yielded up its secrets.[23]

Wagner, the revolutionary *manqué*, had come upon a musical invention in *Tristan* so powerful that it would provide the vehicle for overturning the hegemony of Christian culture in the West. The twenty-four-year-old Nietzsche would write the operator's manual for this soon-to-be-born cultural revolution that would herald an age of sexual excess and unfettered will. That manual would bring back to the West the ceremonies of lust and cruelty that had been lost since the ascendency of Socrates. At the center of this new age would be a rebirth of irresistible sexual license, which would overwhelm the order of every family and unleash the wildest bestiality of nature in a mixture of lust and cruelty, Nietzsche described what he had in mind in *The Birth of Tragedy*:

> In just about every instance the center of these festivals could be found in an overpowering sexual licentiousness, whose waves broke over each and every family and their honorable laws. In particular the wildest beasts of nature were unleashed here, even to the point of the hideous mixing of lust and cruelty, which always seemed to me to be the real witches' brew.[24]

The writing of *The Birth of Tragedy* corresponds not only with Nietzsche's reading of Wagner's revolutionary writings. The meeting of the minds was much more intimate than that. The gestation period of this work corresponded to Nietzsche's entrance into Wagner's family circle. Less than a month after his initial arrival at Wagner's door in mid-May, Nietzsche was invited to spend his first weekend at Tribschen, on June 5, 1869. The timing was either fortuitous or regrettable, depending on your point of view. Cosima was pregnant with her third child by Wagner and almost ready to give birth. As luck would have it, she went into labor the night of Nietzsche's first stay at Tribschen. Wagner noted in his journal that he spent a "tolerable evening" with Nietzsche. He said good night to Nietzsche at around eleven, and then Cosima's labor pains began. The midwife arrived at three A.M., and at four Cosima gave birth to Wagner's first son, whom they named Siegfried. Wagner considered the presence of Nietzsche a good omen. Nietzsche for his part seems to have felt the same. He was completely under Wagner's influence, claiming that Wagner "fulfills every wish which we could possibly have."[25] It was a time of new beginnings. The birth of Siegfried, *The Birth of Tragedy*—Nietzsche, in a reversal of historical metaphors, was to preside over the birth of Socrates' demise.

In this, Wagner's domestic arrangement was just as important to Nietzsche as his writings, and it should be clear that Nietzsche saw in the Wagner ménage the antithesis of bourgeois marriage. It was clear to Nietzsche that Wagner was living in adultery, certainly at the time of Siegfried's birth and during the time in which *The Birth of Tragedy* was in its gestative period. Even the Wagners' marriage after Cosima's divorce seems not to have affected Nietzsche's understanding of their relationship. Toward the end of his sanity, around the time of the composition of *Ecce Homo,* Nietzsche wrote that "Frau Cosima Wagner is by far the most elegant nature that there ever was, and in relationship to me I have always interpreted her marriage to Wagner as adultery. . . . the case of Tristan."[26] Wagner, it should be remembered, was living in sin and profiting handsomely from it. Protected by Ludwig II, who had settled his debts, and was taking a personal hand in seeing that his operas were performed, Wagner was the prime example of the Promethean figure who took morality and fate into his own hands and wrestled it into conformity with his will.

Music, according to Schopenhauer, was the immediate language of the will, which was the constitutive element in the world. The world was will, which was music. Nietzsche, contemplating Wagner and his music, began to visualize a sort of anti-Orpheus, whose disordered melodies might bring about the demise of the world as they knew it. Civilization had arisen with the subjugation of music to reason; now the Dionysiac culture could be brought about by the subjection of reason to music, the sort of music which Wagner had invented in *Tristan*:

> Perhaps we can gain some point of departure for our meditation if I propose the following example, that the Satyr, the imaginary natural being, relates to the man of culture in the same way that Dionysian music relates to civilization. Of the latter, Richard Wagner says that civilization is superseded by music in the same way that candle glow is superseded by daylight. In the same way, I think, the Grecian man of culture felt himself superseded when confronted by the Satyr chorus, and this is the most immediate influence of Dionysian tragedy, that state and society as well as the separation of one man from another all disappear in the light of an overpowering feeling of unity, which leads directly back to the heart of nature. The metaphysical consolation. . . that life at its most basic, in spite of all variability of appearance, is irreducibly powerful and joyous. This consolation appears in its most corporeal clarity embodied as the Satyr chorus, as the chorus of natural beings, which lives ineradicably behind all civilization and in spite of the changes of generations and the history of various peoples always remains the same.[27]

Just as under the old dispensation, salvation depended on subordinating the individual will to the will of God—as manifested primarily in the order of the universe, specifically the moral order and the order of the family and the state—the new civilization was to be an inversion of that ideal. Now everything was a function of will, and salvation was achieved by pursuing that will as single-mindedly as possible. In the place of the myth of the fall, Nietzsche proposed a return to the myth of Prometheus, who stole fire from the gods. Nature as the representative of God's order was, like music, like truth, and like reason, an essentially feminine entity that waited to be coerced by a superior will. The greater the coercion, the more abundant would be the reward. Wagner seemed in many ways living proof of this. Always on the brink of ruin, he seemed to have a knack for dancing away from the pit of disaster and ending up better off than before. He had forced the issue with Cosima and had ended up with Ludwig II as his protector in clear defiance of bourgeois morality. Wagner had not only created *Tristan*; he seemed destined to live it as well. And the sickly Nietzsche, whose success with women was hardly Wagnerian, could only admire the man who brought all these things off so well. Not only could he admire him; he would philosophize a principle out of what he perceived in Wagner. Wagner was the new Oedipus, who forced the Sphinx to divulge its secrets:

> with regard to the mother-wooing, riddle-solving Oedipus, an immediate interpretation comes to mind, that where, through oracular and magic powers, the force of both present and future, the rigid law of individaution as well as the magic of nature are broken, the preconditioning cause is the fact that beforehand a monstrous act against nature—something on the order of incest must have taken place; then how is one to force nature to reveal her secrets other than by victoriously going against her, that is, through an act contrary to nature. I see this recognition sketched out in that hideous trinity of Oedipus' fate: the same man who solves the riddle of nature—that double-edged Sphinx—must also violate the most holy order of nature as both parricide and spouse of his mother. Indeed, the meaning of the myth seems inescapable, that wisdom, and especially Dionysian wisdom, is an unnatural horror, and that the man who through his knowledge plunges nature into the abyss of annihilation experiences in his own being the disintegration of nature. "The point of wisdom turns against the wise; wisdom is a crime against nature." [28]

The passage is seminal to the modern age. In it we see, down to the minutest details, where Freud got the Oedipus Complex. "Wisdom is a crime against nature." A crime like incest fit nicely into Freud's compulsions at the time. His sexual desire for his sister-in-law dovetailed with his desire to force nature to reveal her secrets and get his stalled career moving again. Only the man who is willing to commit some "terrible act against nature—something like incest" can force nature to reveal her secrets. He who wants to know nature's secrets must be willing, through the murder of the father and the taking of his mother as wife, to smash the holiest order of nature.

Just as reason, as epitomized by Socrates, "the specific non-mystic," as Nietzsche described him, gave birth to the culture of order, so music of the sort banned from Greece when Socrates won out over Dionysos will bring the new order magically back into existence; "With this explicit historical example we have attempted to explain that, just as tragedy is destroyed by the disappearance of the spirit of music, it can alone be reborn out of this same spirit." [29]

Unlike reason, which Nietzsche saw as its antithesis, music is not *about* being; it *is* being in its full sexual manifestation. It is the will willing itself, and when it attains its full force, the individual and his illusory individuality are absorbed into it like spit into a raging river. In this, Nietzsche was just forging a union of his two heroes, Schopenhauer and Wagner, both of whom saw music as an "immediate representation of the will." "As a result of this," Nietzsche quotes Schopenhauer as saying, "we can speak of the world of appearances or nature and music as two different expressions of the same nature and music as two different manifestations of the same thing":

> All possible strivings, excitements, and expressions of the will, as well as all possible psychic events in the interior of man, which Reason refers to derogatorily as feelings, achieve their expression through the infinitely possible melodies, but always in their most general form without content, always according to the thing itself and not according to appearances, resembling in this the innermost soul without a body. Out of this intimate relationship that music has to the true being of all things, it is easy to explain that when fitting music is played alongside any scene, action, or event, this music seems to reveal the deepest meaning of the event and provides it with its most appropriate and clearest commentary. This is so because music is, as I have said, different from all of the other arts in that it is not a representation of the event or more exactly the adequate objectivity of the will, but rather the immediate replica of the will itself and the metaphysical principle to the physical world. It is the thing itself in relation to all appearance.[30]

We have here a doctrine remarkably close to the one the ancients ascribed to Pythagoras. Just as Pythagoras could subdue lust by his flute playing, so Wagner could incite it through *Tristan*. Nietzsche's *Birth of Tragedy* is a program for cultural revolution based on his reading of *Tristan und Isolde*. It presages a new age of sensate culture based on a neo-Lutheran rejection of reason in all its modalities, but specifically the moral and the musical, and the substitution of a culture of ecstasy, sexual license, and intoxication in its place. Not only does sensual, Dionysian music dull human reason and unleash revolutionary forces in society; it also tends to become an object of worship, as in places like Bayreuth or Woodstock.

In April 1870, Nietzsche sent the manuscript of *The Birth of Tragedy*, then known as *Musik und Tragödie*, to his publisher with the explanation that "the real function [of the book] is to illuminate Richard Wagner, that extraordinary enigma of our age, in his relation to Greek tragedy." [31] To his friend Rohde, Nietzsche wrote from Bayreuth, where Wagner was busy with rehearsals, "if only a few hundred people get from this music what I get from it, then we will have a completely new culture."³²

It took Nietzsche to philosophize out of Wagner's music a program for cultural revolution that would shake the coming age to its foundation. The twentieth century was to become the proving ground for Nietzschean philosophy in its various permutations. There were the Nazis, and then there was the global cultural revolution of 1968-1969, and then there are the people who have taken over the universities of the West and have held them until this day. All are descendants of Nietzsche in one way or another. In his explanation of "Why I Am a Fate" in *Ecce Homo*, Nietzsche gives a sketch of the future that is uncanny in its accuracy. "I know my lot," he writes.

> At some point, the remembrance of something monstrous will be attached to my name—a crisis unlike any that has existed on earth before me, the most profound collision of conscience, a decision, conjured against everything that to that time had been believed, promoted, or called holy.³³

Given the prescience in the statement, it is not surprising that Thomas Mann would link Nietzsche with a pact with the devil in his Faustus novel. The whole notion of the will pursued to the point of violating nature as a way of becoming privy to her secrets is a profoundly demonic idea. And it was that idea that lay at the heart of the new civilization Nietzsche was proposing in *The Birth of Tragedy*. However, there is more specific evidence as well. Around the same time that he was becoming more intimate with the Wagner family at Tribschen, he wrote the following peculiar entry in his diaries:

> What I am afraid of is not the frightful shape behind my chair, but its voice; also not the words, but the terrifyingly unarticulated and inhuman tone of that shape. Yes, if only it would speak as human beings do.³⁴

Writing to his friends von Gersdorff and Rohde after celebrating his twenty-seventh birthday with them, Nietzsche proposed that at exactly ten o'clock the three of them should drink half a glass of red wine and pour the other half out into the night in greeting the demons who had made the evening possible. Nietzsche repeated the same ceremony a few nights later as, with Burkhardt, they poured two glasses of Rhine wine down on the street below. "In earlier centuries," he wrote describing the incident, "we might have been suspected of witchcraft. As I then came home, somewhat demonically, at 11:30, I was astonished to find Deussen there."³⁵ Nietzsche goes on to give the impression that it might have been only a spectral simulacrum of Deussen. "I have an almost ghostly memory of him because I saw him only by pale lamplight and moonlight." ³⁶ At another point, Nietzsche, fearing that he might not meet his friends at a Wagner concert, suggested, "Let us quickly make a sacrifice to demons, so that they do not frustrate me over this wish." ³⁷

Without Wagner's music there would have been no *Birth of Tragedy*; however, once in existence, the philosophy that Nietzsche formulated based on Wagner's music was quite capable of going on without him. Indeed, it had to, because Wagner in *Parsifal*, his final work, returned more to the ambivalence he had expressed in *Tannhäuser* than to the paean to free love and adultery that had inspired Nietzsche so much in *Tristan*. The Wagner-Nietzsche collaboration reached its apogee during the summer of 1870, when *The Birth of Tragedy* was completed and sent off to the publishers. During that spring, Nietzsche had watched the rise of the Paris Commune from afar. In May there were savage reprisals on both the part of the revolutionaries, who shot hostages, including the Archbishop of Paris, and the national army, which was equally brutal in putting down the revolutionaries. Nietzsche, who considered himself both a good Prussian soldier and a German nationalist but, at the same time, someone deeply committed to overturning the social order, began to think of the two spheres of culture and revolution under a common guise. It was his genius to come up with a plan for cultural revolution that would antedate and ultimately succeed all the programs for political revolution spawned in the nineteenth and found wanting by the end of the twentieth century. Faced with the example of politicians like Bismarck and events like the Commune of 1870, interpreting those events under the influence of thinkers like Feuerbach and Marx, Nietzsche began to think of the intellectual life, as manifested by his own life as a professor of philology in Basel, as impotent and irrelevant to the issues of the day. That someone who glorified the will at the expense of the intellect should feel this way is to be expected. In fact, it may be that the whole glorification of the will to power was simply his transmutation of *Realpolitik* into the cultural realm. With Bismarck as his model, it is not surprising that Nietzsche would come up with his own notion of *Kulturkampf*. However, given his rage against the social order and his sickly constitution, it seems inevitable that his notion of the intellectual life would simply be war transposed onto the intellectual sphere. Not for him the professor who sat in docility before the truth, hoping to achieve wisdom. Nietzsche, having learned from the experiences of Wagner in 1849, was now proposing an intellectual assault against the foundations of the Christian/Classical ideas of world harmony and order. It was, besides, an order he saw collapsing all around him. "What use is an intellectual," Nietzsche wondered,

> faced with such a cultural earthquake? One feels like an atom One uses one's whole life and the greatest part of one's strength to come to a better understanding of one's cultural period, and to expound it. How is this profession to be regarded when in a single wretched day the most precious documents of such periods are burned to ashes? [38]

Nietzsche was both bellicose and an intellectual, and *Kulturkampf* was the logical outcome of these two tendencies. He had a revolutionary's hatred of the established order but neither the physical strength nor the inclination to pursue that hatred in the political realm. In a letter to his friend von Gersdorff, he urged him to pursue a "vigorous cultural life as if you were still fundamentally a soldier, and striving to transpose your military attitude into the realm of philosophy and art. And that is correct: only as fighters can we, in our time, have a right to exist, as fighters in the vanguard for a new spirit." [39]

As in any relationship where there is a difference of thirty-one years in age, Wagner and Nietzsche found themselves moving in opposite directions as the 1870s progressed. There was also an ideological component to the growing rift. It was as if their common religious and geographical background proved less and less binding the more each man moved along the trajectory his thought provided. The Lutheran background they shared was proving to be an untenable middle position between the stark antinomies of sensual Dionysiac nihilism and Catholicism, which is to say, a more sacramental and "mythic" reading of Christianity. Their meeting of the minds over *Tristan* began to fade. On July 18, 1870, Cosima von Büllow received her divorce from her husband Hans. On August 25, Cosima and Wagner were married in Lucerne. Wagner had not only written *Tristan*; he was also willing to live the sexual sacrilege that opera endorsed as a way of forcing nature to reveal her secrets. From Nietzsche's point of view, Wagner the sexual Prometheus was now safely back within the bounds of bourgeois respectability. Considering his wholesale repudiation of Christianity, Nietzsche was oddly Catholic in his inability to recognize the marriage, as well as in his inability to countenance divorce. As we have seen, he could never see anything in the Cosima/Wagner relationship but adultery, even after the divorce and remarriage.

Wagner, for his part, seems to have had his revolutionary sensibilities softened by family life in a way that would never happen with Nietzsche. Wagner's revolutionary period corresponded to his childless marriage with Minna. Now he was, in addition to a success throughout Europe and the protégé of the king of Bavaria, the father of a growing family. His children gave him a stake in the future, which Nietzsche did not have. As Wagner's family grew, so did Nietzsche's sickness and isolation. Throughout the 1870s and 1880s, Nietzsche's life was one never-ending pilgrimage looking for the right doctor, the right cure, or the right medicine. After a while, Nietzsche became his own pharmacist, dosing himself with everything from tannic enemas to opium to knockout drops. As Wagner's life increased in domestic harmony, Nietzsche's increased in sickness, isolation, and a demonic obsession to turn his illness into a philosophical weapon that would bring the world down around his head. At the end of his sanity, Nietzsche claimed that Wagner was "the greatest benefactor of my life." "The thing that binds us," he continued, "is that we have suffered more deeply than people of this century were capable of suffering...." [40]

All things, they say, look yellow to the jaundiced eye. In Nietzsche's case, the lack of psychic and physical harmony began to manifest itself as a predilection for dissonance. It appears in *The Birth of Tragedy* as the characteristic of the Dionysian personality. The world can he justified only as an aesthetic phenomenon, but the Dionysian is the "womb" out of which both music and tragic myth are born:

that even the ugly and disharmonious is an artistic game that the will, in the eternal fullness of its desire, plays with itself. This most basic and primeval phenomenon of Dionysian art, so difficult to understand, becomes immediately grasped and easily understood in the wonderful meaning of musical dissonance. Just as music alone, when juxtaposed with the world, can give some conception that the justification of the world is at its basis only understandable as an aesthetic phenomenon. The desire that is the creator of the tragic myth has the same home as the lustful sensitivity to dissonance in music. The Dionysian, with its lust perceived as pain, is the common womb of both music and the tragic myth.[41]

Only musical dissonance can make the Dionysian world comprehensible. The spread of dissonance will make the new age of unbridled sexual lust and cruel abandonment to primal forces plausible to the "German genius," which too long has lived in bondage to "malicious dwarves," that is, Christianity.

Music and tragic myth are in the same way an expression of the Dionysian capacity of the people and inseparable from each other. Both derive from an artistic region, which lies beyond the Apollonian: both illuminate a region, in which lustful chords make both dissonance as well as this terrible view of the world sound attractive; both play with the goad of revulsion, relying on their mighty magical arts; both justify through this play the existence of even the "worst world."[42]

The Dionysian is "the eternal and original artistic violence" that brings the world of appearances into existence. Everything, in other words, springs from the womb of dissonance, which remains for Nietzsche the ultimate musical and, therefore, metaphysical phenomenon. "Is it possible to imagine a human manifestation of dissonance," Nietzsche wonders, and then as if to correct himself, adds the question, "and what is man other than that?"[43] The true or Dionysian man is a manifestation of dissonance. The ugly and the disharmonic are simply games the will plays with itself.

Once again, as in the "Why I Am a Fate" passage of *Ecce Homo*, Nietzsche waxes prophetic, in the light of the history of music, a history that at the time of his writing had yet to come into existence, a history that he in many ways called into existence himself. *The Birth of Tragedy* was written under the influence of *Tristan*, but it clearly looks beyond *Tristan*, which does resolve the dissonance in Isolde's Verklärung. The resolution, it must be admitted, was a long time coming, but it is there in a way that avoids the conclusions that Nietzsche seems to want to draw in *The Birth of Tragedy*. In the universe of musical meaning, there are basically two emotional/tonal elements, consonance and dissonance, corresponding to tension and resolution. In *Tristan*, the resolution is delayed but still there. In the music Nietzsche seems to be proposing, the dissonance is unrelieved, because that is the best expression of the psychic state of Dionysian man. According to the musically sensitive Nietzsche, universal dissonance is the best vehicle for bringing about the cultural revolution he so ardently desired, the ascendancy of Dionysian man and the defeat of the Classical/ Christian culture of world harmony. Nietzsche's prescription is both Promethean and Epimethean. It looks both forward and back. It looks forward to the music of Schönberg and the twentieth century and to the calamities that music will accompany as if in a film score. And it looks back at the tradition of world harmony and pronounces its curse on it. Nietzsche's doctrine is also the exact fulfillment of what the classic tradition had warned against. Musical discord and social disharmony go hand in hand. Ulysses' speech in *Troilus and Cressida*, when taken in the light of what Nietzsche had to say about the Paris Commune and dissonance in *The Birth of Tragedy*, becomes a roadmap for the cultural catastrophes—from the Third Reich to Woodstock—of the twentieth century. If we untune the string, discord follows, in both the musical and political realms. Reason is the criterion of measure. The triumph of Dionysian music over Socratic reason brings about a society in which "each thing meets in mere oppugnancy." Might becomes right:

> Strength should be lord of imbecility,
> And the rude son should strike his father dead.
> Force should be right, or rather, right and wrong,
> Between whose endless jar justice resides,
> Should lose their names, and so should justice too.
> Then everything includes itself in power,
> Power into will, will into appetite,
> And appetite, a universal wolf,
> so doubly seconded with will and power,
> Must make perforce a universal prey,
> And last eat up himself.[44]

To jump ahead roughly one hundred years: Jim Morrison described his band The Doors as "erotic politicians." "We're interested in everything about revolt, disorder, and all activity that appears to have no meaning."[45] It is difficult to imagine what Nietzsche would have thought of the music, but it is hard to imagine him withholding his approval from statements like that. But in a sense, even The Doors did not believe in dissonance. In order to make their anarchic message palatable to an audience beyond, say, the salons of *fin de siècle* Vienna, they had to return to the tonality their musical fathers despised. As the sophistication of the listener declined, dissonance became less and less suitable as the vehicle to emancipate the West from reason, morality, and social order. Tonality returned in simplified form as the maidservant to the relentless and barbaric rhythm of rock music. Rock music bespoke in many ways the return of the repressed, that is, tonality, but in a way completely compatible with the Dionysian aspirations Nietzsche expressed in *The Birth of Tragedy*. It was the fate of the tradition of subversion. Like the deconstructor who complained about being misunderstood, it could only convey its message by being false to its philosophy.

In this regard even Wagner the revolutionary was probably never willing to go as far as Nietzsche would have wanted him to. Wagner the pamphleteer and ideologue was always subject in a way to Wagner the musician and dramatist. Musical ideology was an invention that would have to wait for the twentieth century. In this, Nietzsche was more prophetic than he knew. The ideology of dissonance would come to pass, but he would never hear it. One year before Nietzsche's death, Schönberg wrote *Verklärt Nacht*, but that piece was simply warmed-over *Tristan*. The real move into dissonance, which Schönberg would bring about, would not occur for another eight years. Wagner, whose *Tristan* provided the musical vocabulary for *Verklärte Nacht*, turned away from the dissonance it would ultimately spawn when he wrote *Parsifal*. At the same time that Nietzsche was becoming more anarchic, more dissonant, and heading step by step toward madness, Wagner was turning back to the struggle he had left unresolved with the completion of *Tannhäuser*. The clash between the two men was inevitable.

In January of 1878, Wagner sent Nietzsche the text of his newly completed opera *Parsifal*, and Nietzsche was appalled at what he read. In the instinctive reaction of one lapsed Lutheran to another, Nietzsche came up with an insult he thought both could understand. *Parsifal*, he claimed, bespoke the "spirit of the Counter-Reformation." It smacked of Liszt; it was "all too Christian, timebound, limited; purely fantastic psychology; no flesh, and far too much book especially at the Holy Communion." Nietzsche felt that the libretto sounded "like a translation from a foreign language." [45]

And in a sense it was, foreign to Nietzsche at least. When Nietzsche's friend Heinrich Romundt not only converted to Catholicism but decided to become a priest as well, Nietzsche took the decision as a personal rebuke of himself and all that he stood for. "I sometimes feel," Nietzsche wrote, "it is the most evil thing anyone could do to me. . . . Our good, clean, Protestant atmosphere! . . . Does the wretch want to turn his back on all these liberating influences? Is he still in his right mind or should he be treated with cold baths?" [47] If Nietzsche felt this way about Romundt, then his reaction against the man whom he idolized must have been that much stronger. Nietzsche saw *Parsifal* as tantamount to Wagner's conversion to Catholicism and, beyond that, the wreck of his hope that Wagner would write the music drama that would bring about the advent of the Dionysian age.

Wagner, for his part, was more ambivalent on the matter than Nietzsche gave him credit for. Wagner did seek advice from a Catholic priest in Munich for details on the Holy Eucharist, which would be central to the opera. But his own psychic state was still akin to what it was when he was writing *Tannhäuser*. In a sense, this bespoke a turn away from what he had written in *Tristan*, but the conflict was far from resolved. Wagner was, in a sense, the old man Amfortas, who had been wounded by lust and weakened to the point where he doubted he could achieve the holiness that was his destiny. Amfortas is what Wagner was, Parsifal what he would have liked to be. By the time *Parsifal* was brought to the stage, Wagner was almost seventy years old, a success in almost every sense of the word, the father of three children, and yet still subject to the same sexual infatuations that had dominated him since his teenage years. At the time, Wagner was hard at work on the sublimely spiritual *Parsifal* but still infatuated with a number of different women. On September 4, 1877, he wrote to Judith Gautier, wondering: "Was it for the last time that I put my arms around you this morning? No, I shall see you again. I want to because I love you." [48] On October 1, he wrote to her again, urging her, "Love me, and let us not wait for the Protestant kingdom of heaven: it will be terribly tedious. Love!" [49] Perhaps nothing symbolizes the ambivalence more than Wagner's sending her a sheet of his Communion music, "*Nehmet hin mein Leib*," and asking her to send him in return various perfumes that evoked her presence. If *Parsifal* is any evidence of his psychic state, Wagner seemed both aware of the debilitating effect of lust and yet quite unable to do anything about it. His wound was incurable: someone else would have to procure the spear that would heal him.

For Nietzsche, however, the fact that Wagner would prostrate himself even symbolically before the cross was an indication that the time of his apprenticeship with the master was over. It was clear now that the Dionysiac music that Europe needed was not going to come from Wagner. Depending on one's point of view, either Nietzsche had moved beyond Wagner or Wagner had moved beyond Nietzsche. Either way, a break was inevitable. The stories describing the break vary. Nietzsche's sister claims that Nietzsche and Wagner discussed *Parsifal* while walking along the cliffs at Sorrento. Wagner spoke of the religious experience that provided the inspiration for *Parsifal*, whereupon Nietzsche, disillusioned by Wagner's conversion, walked away never to return. The biographical consensus today is that the incident never happened. More to the point according to contemporary students of Nietzsche and Wagner is the exchange of letters between Wagner and Nietzsche's physician, Dr. Eiser, over the state of Nietzsche's health. Wagner let it be known that he felt that Nietzsche's illness was the result of excessive masturbation. Dr. Eiser imprudently concurred. When Nietzsche got wind of the exchange, he broke with Wagner for good. In a letter written in February 1883, shortly after Wagner's death, Nietzsche confided to his friend Franz Overbeck, "There is something between us like a mortal insult, and it could have become terrible had he lived any longer." [50] He is more specific in a later letter to the musician Peter Gast. "Wagner is rich in malicious ideas," Nietzsche wrote on April 21, 1883, "but what do you say to his having exchanged letters on the subject (even with my doctors) to voice his *belief* that my altered way of thinking was a consequence of unnatural excesses, with hints at pederasty?" [51] Gregor-Dellin thinks that any disagreement over *Parsifal* was minor in comparison with the insult Nietzsche sustained at Wagner's hand over masturbation. Hayman, on the other hand, feels that nothing was more disappointing to Nietzsche than the dashing of his hopes for the rebirth of tragedy out of Wagner's music drama:

> Of all the reasons for his breach with Wagner none was more important than the realization that tragedy was not going to be reborn through music-drama. To call *Parsifal* "the spirit of the Counter-Reformation" was to anathematize it. Accord-

ing to *Menschliches, Allzumenschliches*, the Counter-Reformation had blocked all the progressive forces launched by the Renaissance, permanently frustrating all hope of interpenetration between antiquity and the modern spirit. Having arrived at this equation of Wagner with baroque medievalism, Nietzsche felt that he was himself "a hundred paces closer to the Greeks than ever before."[52]

Either way, the break was there, and in describing it Nietzsche gives every indication of disillusionment not only with Wagner but with Germany and the whole of European culture as well. In his two polemics against Wagner, Nietzsche refers to Wotan as the god of bad weather and sees rain and bad weather as determinative of the German spirit. All of this, however, is a subterfuge for reacting against Wagner's "apostasy" in writing *Parsifal*, "that poor devil and nature boy, who with such insidious means gets made into a Catholic."[53] The more one reads Nietzsche's anti-Wagner tracts, the more one realizes what a blow to Nietzsche's hopes *Parsifal* was. Nietzsche begins by wondering whether Wagner was being serious when he wrote *Parsifal* and follows with a series of rhetorical questions that get more serious and pointed as he proceeds. Was it, he wonders,

> an apostasy and a conversion to Christian/pathological and obscurantist ideals? And ultimately a negation of himself, a self-negation on the part of an artist who up until that time had dedicated himself with all the power of his will to the exact opposite, to the highest sort of spiritualization and sensualization of his art? And not only of his art but also of his life as well? One recalls how enthusiastically Wagner in his day trod in the footsteps of the philosopher Feuerbach. Feuerbach's motto concerning "healthy sensuality" resonated with Wagner as much as it did with so many other Germans during the thirties and forties— one called them "young Germans"—like the word that brought salvation. Did he suddenly forget everything he had learned? . . . Has hatred of life become his lord and master as it has with Flaubert? . . . .I mention this because *Parsifal* is a malicious work, a work of vindictiveness, a secret poisoning of the wellsprings of life, and a bad work as well. His sermon on chastity remains an incitement to acts against nature. I hold anyone in contempt who does not see *Parsifal* as an outrage against decency.[54]

Wagner's "apostasy" has to do most of all with his conversion to chastity," which entailed turning his back on the "healthy sensuality" of Feuerbach. The "sermon on chastity" that is *Parsifal* is an incitement to acts repugnant to nature, that is, prostration before the cross. It is difficult not to hear in Nietzsche's increasingly hysterical indictment of Wagner's apostasy from the faith of libertinism some sense of betrayal. And perhaps this was in a way that even Nietzsche himself could not admit. "No serious biographer of Nietzsche," writes Gregor-Dellin, "dares to dispute that his subject was stricken with the aftereffects of youthful experiments in sex."[55] Nietzsche's commitment to sexual liberation was total. In an age in which there was no cure for syphilis, he p his life on the line by going to a brothel. What is more, he went to the brothel in 1866, two years after his first hearing of the piano score of *Tristan*. To have dedicated oneself to sexual liberation to the point of contracting an incurable disease for that cause was one thing, to have the man whose work incited him to that dedication turn on him and then "sink suddenly, helpless and broken. before the Christian cross"⁵⁶ was enough to drive a more balanced man crazy. It was a betrayal of the deepest sort, and Nietzsche felt it as such. Wagner's inquiries into how frequently Nietzsche masturbated were nothing compared to this sort of betrayal. Nietzsche had sacrificed his health and his soul on the promise of Dionysiac sexual liberation held out in the second act of *Tristan und Isolde*, and now Wagner was reneging on that promise.

The shock drove Nietzsche not only away from Wagner, it drove him away from Germany as well. In *The Case of Wagner*, Nietzsche bids farewell to the "moist north, as well as to the mistiness of Wagnerian ideals *[von allem Wasserdampf des Wagnerschen Ideals]*." ⁵⁷ In place of Wagner, Nietzsche then proposed Bizet's *Carmen* as the new ideal in Dionysian music drama. Nietzsche admired Bizet, not because it was French as opposed to German, but because its liveliness (*Heiterkeit*) was not European at all. It was rather "African."

> This music is lively, but its liveliness is neither French nor German. Its liveliness is African. It has this destiny; its happiness is short, sudden, and without pardon. I envy Bizet, therefore, because he has the courage to give expression to this sensibility, a sensibility that up 'til this time had no expression in European music, a more southern, browner, more burned sensibility. . . . How the yellow afternoons of this happiness give us pleasure! We look out and believe that we have never seen the sea calmer. And how this Moorish dance speaks to us so tranquilly! How even our insatiability learns satiety from its lewd melancholy! Finally we have a love that has been transposed back to nature. Not the love of some "higher virgin!" No sentimentality! Rather love as fate, as fatality, cynical, without guilt, cruel—and as a result just like nature. That love which is war in its means, and at its basis the deadly hatred of the sexes.⁵⁸

Embittered by Wagner's betrayal of the "healthy sensuality of Feuerbach," Nietzsche turned his gaze beyond Europe, across the Mediterranean, to the "Moorish dance," which speaks to us so reassuringly. In the lascivious melancholy of the Negro, the insatiable European learned satiety. Here in the dark continent, the diseased European, who seemed unable to throw off the yoke of Christianity without being betrayed by his fellow cultural revolutionaries, would learn what the true love that has returned to nature is. This natural love is not the love of a "celestial Virgin," but rather fate, fatality—cynical, guiltless, and cruel. It is a love that is totally within nature, which is to say, partaking of war and a deadly hatred of the sexes.

It is not difficult to see why Nietzsche would be attracted to *Carmen*. The attraction, however, lay more with the plot line than with the music, which is hardly the dissonant sort he praised in *The Birth of Tragedy*. Since Nietzsche was someone who ruined himself through "love," that is, an intemperately pursued liaison, he would feel more comfortable with a character like Don José, who did something similar in *Carmen*, than he would with *Parsifal*, whose renunciation of a sexual liaison with the Bacchic Kundry allows him to redeem the Grail brotherhood and cure Amfortas' hitherto incurable wound. What is equally clear is that he would not feel particularly happy with Wagner proposing Christian chastity as the means whereby Amfortas' incurable wound was healed. Remember, Nietzsche suffered from the incurable wound of syphilis, probably contracted at the incitement he got from listening to *Tristan und Isolde*. Since the wound was incurable, Nietzsche's commitment to sexual license and immorality in general was irrevocable. Wagner, who had never made the commitment Nietzsche had under Wagner's instigations, was trying to welsh on the deal, and Nietzsche was furious enough with Wagner to want to make him repudiate not only Christianity—he had already repudiated that—but all of Europe and its high culture as well.

A close reading of *The Case of Wagner* shows Nietzsche in the role of the spurned woman. He gave his life for Wagner in the bordello in Leipzig only to have Wagner turn on him and fall down in front of the cross. It is difficult to imagine a greater betrayal from Nietzsche's point of view. "Being a disciple of Wagner is an expensive proposition. . . ." Nietzsche tells us revealingly, "Wagner is a seducer of the grand style. . . . Wagner is bad for young people":

> Ah, this old sorcerer! This Klingsor of all Klingsors. How he makes war on free spirits like us. . . . One would have to be a cynic not to be seduced by him; one would have to be able to bite, in order not to pray here.[59]

Nietzsche knew just how bad Wagner was for young people from personal experience. Nietzsche could have contented himself with a sort of sexual tit for tat, infecting unsuspecting girls up and down the continent. But he seems to have taken a lesson from the syphilitic spirochetes circulating in his system, germs that, according to Mann, have a propensity to rise to the head. Instead of infecting people literally, Nietzsche decided to sublimate his disease into an intellectual attack on the culture of the West. Instead of choosing France over Germany, because of the promise he found in Bizet's *Carmen*, Nietzsche chose the "Moorish dance" of Africa and the "lascivious melancholy" of the Negro. "I for my part," he writes at the end of *Nietzsche contra Wagner*, "am seeking the black continent, where I can free 'the slaves.'"[60] Nietzsche turns his back on Wagner by seeking in Africa the Dionysian liberation he promised but failed to deliver. Bizet's music, at least in Nietzsche's almost deranged mind (we are talking about 1888 here, six months before his mental collapse), holds the promise of Africa, a sensibility that is "more southern, browner, more burnt."

Once again, the objective observer is struck by the uncanniness of Nietzsche's prescience. In 1888, Nietzsche repudiated Wagner's music and predicted the rise of an African sensibility that would replace it. Eleven years later, Arnold Schönberg would compose *Verklärte Nacht*, his homage to Wagnerian free love, and begin a trajectory that would eventually bring about the destruction of the music of the West, and that of Germany in particular, more effectively than the Allied bombs would destroy German cities. In the same year *Verklärte Nacht* was composed, another musical event took place thousands of miles away on another continent, which was not Africa but which had a great number of transplanted Africans who were beginning to forge a musical heritage all their own. In 1899, Scott Joplin composed the "Maple Leaf Rag." The two pieces of music are significant because they both correspond to the program of cultural revolution that Nietzsche was proposing for music. His program was, of course, mutually contradictory. It proposed dissonance and sensuality, sonic ugliness and Dionysiac frenzy. But actually, Nietzsche got exactly what he wanted in a way he could not have understood at the time. The twentieth century got both the "lascivious melancholy of the Negro, as Nietzsche put it in *The Case of Wagner*, and the wonderful meaning of musical dissonance," as he put it in *The Birth of Tragedy*. No one could do both. (Frank Zappa at one point said that he found nothing reprehensible in atonal music played over a Boogaloo rhythm, but he never really succeeded in doing it or making the idea culturally viable on a wide scale.) But between the two, between the destruction of classical music that Schönberg and his followers accomplished and the rise of the Negro Dionysiac in the vacuum that this destruction created, the stage was cleared for cultural revolution of the sort envisioned by both Nietzsche and Wagner on a worldwide scale. If the cultural elite were willing to certify Schönberg's "Three Pieces for Piano," op. 11, as music or, beyond that, the "performances" of John Cage, then it could hardly object to the songs of Elvis Presley, which were much more recognizable as music than either of the others. By mid-twentieth century, the notion of contemporary music in the classical Western tradition had become an oxymoron. Either it was music or it was contemporary, but it could not be both at the same time. Nietzsche, to give him credit, even if it is for something he did not completely understand, was able to predict the two predominant strains of music in the twentieth century: the African and the dissonant. He was also correct in predicting music as the vehicle of cultural revolution.

In this he was far more accurate than many who knew better, a fact that makes his prescience doubly remarkable. At the same time the mortal insult that was Wagner's betrayal was festering in Nietzsche, the freed Negroes of the southern United States were picking up the discarded band instruments of the two armies that had clashed on their soil and were experimenting with them in a musically illiterate but creative way, bringing about an unprecedented amalgam of the African and the European in the American South. Jazz was the result, and it was being born right around the time that Nietzsche turned his eyes to the "black continent," looking for an African lasciviousness that Wagner could no longer provide. No one, so far as I know, has said that Nietzsche was at all familiar with African music, much less with the music that would come to be known as jazz. Mahler was, but Mahler was unimpressed. Beyond that, Mahler lacked Nietzsche's urge for cultural warfare. In his capacity as director of the New York Philharmonic, Mahler spent time in America and was exposed to Negro music, probably ragtime, the manifestation of Negro music that was most popular at that time. Mahler, however, because he lacked a cultural axe to grind, had difficulty seeing its merit: "It seems to me," he wrote,

> that the popular music of America is not America at all, rather that kind of music which the African Negro transplanted to American soil has chosen to adopt. . . . I cannot subscribe myself to the doctrine that all men are born equal, as it is inconceivable to me. It is not reasonable to expect that a race could arise from a savage condition to a high ethnological state in a century or two. It took Northern Europe nearly one thousand years to fight its way from barbarianism to civilization. That the Negroes in America have accomplished so much is truly amazing. In their music they doubtless copied and varied the models of the white people to whose households they were attached. They are great imitators, I am told, but that is no reason why the American composer should imitate their distorted copies of European folk-songs. The syncopations introduced in Negro songs under the name of "ragtime" are not original, but may be found in the folk-songs of Hungary and other European nations. Syncopation as a part of national folk-songs existed in Europe before the first Negroes were transported from Africa. . . . Just why the American composer should feel that he is doing something peculiarly American when he employs Negro folk-songs is difficult to tell.[61]

Mahler's difficulty lies not with his knowledge of music but with his knowledge of race relations in the United States. Accepting an appointment as director of the New York Philharmonic, he arrived in the United States during the first decade of the twentieth century, a time when the revolution against Christian values that was modernity was happening among the cultural elite of his wife's generation. That this revolution was sexual in nature was something that Mahler would have to discover the hard way. His wife, Alma, had an affair with Walter Gropius, the creator of Bauhaus architecture. In 1907, Gropius had designed the Fagus Werk, a shoe factory in Allfeld an der Leine that is now generally conceded to be the first modern building. Around the same time, a young Spaniard living in Paris by the name of Pablo Ruiz (he would later take his mother's name, Picasso) was venting his fury at being betrayed by his mistress onto a large canvas that would come to be known as "Les Demoiselles d'Avignon." The title referred to the red-light district in Barcelona; the faces of the whores looked a lot like African masks. The movement born out of this sexual disgust was known as cubism. It was in this same year Schönberg went atonal and Thomas Mann wrote *Death in Venice*, that quintessentially modern meditation on whether Western culture was worth the price it exacted in sexual sublimation. *Death in Venice* is completely suffused with homoerotic fascination, to the point where Gustav Aschenbach, Mann's archetypal German and, therefore, European intellectual, is willing to chuck a whole life of the most rigorous, nay, heroic effort on the off chance of some sexual contact with a Polish teenager. "His armpits," sighs Aschenbach in a moment of pederastic ecstasy, "were as smooth as a statue's." Is the chance to gratify a lust like that worth risking not only your own life but the cultural achievements of the West? Ask a homosexual what he thinks. Gustav Aschenbach thought so. He could not bring himself to leave Venice even though he knew that a cholera epidemic had already broken out and that the information was being suppressed by the city authorities in order to preserve that year's tourist trade. Is any social order worth the price of suppressing our sexual desires? Gustav Aschenbach, as the stand-in for the secularized Western intellectual, meditates on the question over and over again; he is a study in ambivalence. He is filled with indignation at the cover-up of the cholera epidemic and yet, at the same time, "filled with satisfaction" at the opportunities this abrogation of the social order offers to his perverted sexual appetite, an appetite that could be satisfied only if the social order were held in abeyance:

> For passion, like crime, is not suited to the secure daily rounds of order and well-being; and every slackening in the bourgeois structure, every disorder and affliction of the world must be held welcome, since they bring with them a vague promise of advantage. So Aschenbach felt a dark contentment with what was taking place, under cover of the authorities, in the dirty alleys of Venice. This wicked secret of the city was welded with his own secret, and he too was involved in keeping it hidden. For in his infatuation he cared about nothing but the possibility of Tadzio's leaving, and he realized with something like terror that he would not know how to go in living if this occurred.[62]

In the end, Achenbach's ambivalence is resolved us favor of decadence. Yes, it would be worth it after all, to paraphrase Prufrock, to sacrifice a life of the most rigorous intellectual effort to gratify an impossible passion. Aschenbach is the ultimate modern intellectual and a true disciple of Wagner's *Tristan*. Just as Wagner is willing to annihilate melody, the principle of musical order, in *Tristan* for the sake of greater sensual effect, so Aschenbach is willing to subvert the entire social order along with the cultural achievement that goes with it on the oft chance of gratifying his sexual infatuation with the Polish teenager. If satisfying sexual passion means extinguishing the light of reason, then Aschenbach is willing to pay the price.

> [For] you must know that we poets cannot take the road of beauty without having Eros join us and set himself up as our leader. Indeed, we may even be heroes after our fashion, and hardened warriors, though we be like women, for passion is our exaltation, and our desire must remain love that is our pleasure and our disgrace. You now see, do you not, that we poets cannot be wise and dignified? That we necessarily go astray, necessarily remain lascivious, and adventurers in emotion? The mastery of our style is all lies and foolishness, our renown and honor are a farce, the confidence of the masses in us is highly ridiculous, and the training of the public and of youth through art is a precarious undertaking which should be forbidden. For how, indeed, could he be a fit instructor who is born with a natural leaning toward the precipice: We might well disavow it and reach after dignity, but wherever we turn it attracts us. Let us. say, renounce the dissolvent or knowledge.... This then we abandon with firmness, and from now on our efforts matter only by their yield of beauty, of, in other words, simplicity, greatness, and new rigor, form, and a second type of openness.[63]

Friedrich Nietzsche

In this passage we detect a struggle between Mann the artist and Mann the homosexual, a struggle resolved, as is often the case with homosexuals, by identifying self with homosexuality. But in spite of the whining to which the passage descends at the end, it does give a burly coherent explication of the aesthetic of modernity. Modernity is rationalized sexual misbehavior. Reason is extinguished; passion is exalted in its place. But with reason go light and clarity: passion can exist only in the dark. And so correspondingly, modern art opts for an openness that reveals in increasingly otiose detail nothing more than the opacity of the human mind obscured by passion. The techniques of modernity—cubism, atonality, stream of consciousness—so promising to Aschenbach and Mann in 1907—had all exhausted themselves by the time of the 1929 stock-market crash. The promises of the soon-to-be explored *terra incognita* of the human psyche found their culmination in the Dexedrine-fueled monologues of beatniks like Jack Kerouac or William Burroughs. When inspiration failed, there was always Dexedrine or sex. Sartre used drugs to fuel his philosophical writing. Schönberg used them to write music. The drug epidemic that is a worldwide phenomenon now is only the logical outcome of modernity and the educational system that has been commandeered to propagate its values. Nietzsche was admittedly a sick man, but he was also a walking medicine cabinet drugging himself with a variety of substances. Freud, his disciple, not only was a cocaine addict but also got a number of his patients addicted as well, with tragic consequences. By focusing the mind on consciousness divorced from reason, by situating the whole of human intellectual endeavor in the arid vacuum of quasi-scientific materialism, modernity had nowhere to turn but to drugs. Drugs became its god, the *deus ex machina* in a materialistic universe in which consciousness refused to disappear. If thought was simply an electro-chemical epiphenomenon secreted by the brain, then why try to influence it by reading poetry? Why not go to the chemicals directly? The apotheosis of sexual passion that Gustav Aschenbach registers in *Death in Venice* is simply the middle term in the equation. Nietzsche, Mann's mentor in this, had called for intoxication after all. Intoxication was the typically Dionysian emotion. Sex was simply the first step, the most important step albeit, in the achievement of a Dionysian culture. Aschenbach thought it worth the risk, even if it eventually killed him. In this he was a typical modern.

In the United States, which would become the world's premier cultural power within the next half century (it would have to defeat Germany twice to do this), the whole notion of cultural revolution was refracted through the peculiar lens of race. The antinomies current in American bohemia were essentially Nietzschean; however, in America their matrix was racial. The American *Kulturkampf* would be fought along racial lines. I have discussed this elsewhere (see *Modernity and the Negro as a Paradigm of Liberation*), but the cultural transaction was quite simple. The moderns, the cultural revolutionaries, simply took the worldview of the Ku Klux Klan and reversed the values, in a typically Nietzschean fashion. So according to that world view, the white man stood for family, sexual morality, Christianity, and the social order; the black man, on the other hand, stood for what Dean Moriarity, in Jack Kerouac's novel *On the Road*, called "spade kicks," that is, sexual license, drugs and alcohol, and, above all, the music that made it all plausible, jazz. By identifying with the Negro, the cultural revolutionaries simply accomplished the transvaluation of all values. "Whites were the mind," writes Michael Ventura in a recent study linking jazz and rock to voodoo, "blacks were the body." [64] Is Ventura claiming that blacks are mindless? Well, in a sense he is, but isn't that a racist notion? Not to the indefatigably sensual modern intellectual. Ventura's advocacy of Ku Klux Klan anthropology is redeemed, in his eyes at least, by putting it at the service of anti-Christian cultural revolution. "Blacks," he continues,

> were supposed to be incredibly potent, incredibly sexy, incredibly tough, and they had the infamous "natural sense of rhythm"—everything whites at least whites like Ventura wanted and missed in their bodies was projected onto blacks. Christianism [sic] had always despised the body, and so most of its people despised blacks.[65]

Ventura is right about one thing. The whole field of race relations m America was suffused with projection of the most rabid sort. Ventura and a whole host of white cultural revolutionaries (Norman Mailer's White Negro essay comes immediately to mind) projected onto the Negro race their own fantasies of sexual liberation. *Pace* Mr. Ventura and the Ku Klux Klan, there is no set of moral codes associated with any race. The Negro, like the Caucasian, puts his moral pants on one leg at a time, which is to say, by effort, not by inheritance. The happy-go-lucky, jazzin', guilt-free, sexually liberated darky is a cultural construct created by white moderns who wanted to implement the transvaluation of Christian sexual mores. Jazz was the cultural vehicle that made this artificially constructed paradigm not only plausible but compelling. Jazz, and eventually rock 'n' roll, persuaded millions of whites that they could throw off Christian or Jewish morality in the name of racial solidarity. Eventually the two streams, the Nietzschean and the Negroid, would coalesce. Allan Bloom saw them as epitomized by one figure, Mick Jagger, "a teen-aged satyr up until he was forty," who possessed "this strong stimulant, which Nietzsche called Nihiline."

> This gutter phenomenon is apparently the fulfillment of the promise made by so much psychology and literature that our weak and exhausted Western civilization would find refreshment in the true source, the unconscious, which appeared to the late romantic imagination to be identical to Africa, the dark and unexplored continent. Now all has been explored: light has been cast everywhere; the unconscious has been made conscious, the repressed expressed. And what have we found? Not creative devils, but show-business glitz. Mick Jagger tarting it up on the stage is all that we brought back from the voyage to the underworld.[66]

It is no coincidence that the civil rights movement in the United States preceded the largest push for sexual liberation this country had seen since its inception.

This is not surprising because the two movements were inextricably combined through their advocacy of freedom and the fact that both rose out of proto-modern events like the Harlem Renaissance.[67] The 1960s were an erotic Great Awakening. As Nietzsche had predicted, the Negro was the catalyst for the overturning of European values, which is to say, the most effective enculturation of Christianity. The civil rights movement was nothing more than the culmination of an attempt to transform the Negro into a paradigm of sexual liberation that had been the pet project of the cultural revolutionaries since the twenties.

The social dislocation caused by World War I in the United States brought large numbers of Negroes up from the South, where they had lived essentially rural lives, to places like New York City, where they were exposed to the ferment of modernity firsthand. Harlem (or Chicago) was in a sense the meeting place between modernity and the southern Negro. Once places like Harlem became established as Negro cultural centers in the United States, a number of cultural transformations could take place. The Negro got to see the values of the moderns first hand, and those who wanted to get ahead adopted them. A complex symbiotic relationship developed between the upwardly mobile blacks and the whites who needed them for their own purposes. In exchange for literary advancement, blacks became involved in an unspoken agreement whereby they would portray the values of the primitive that the whites wanted to project on them. The whites with literary connections, people like Carl Van Vechten, promoted blacks who would be willing to act like paradigms of sexual liberation. In his book on the Harlem Renaissance, Nathan Irvin Huggins traces white desire to "Freud and the new psychology," which "caused sophisticated people to deny the artifices of civility and manner and to seek the true self through spontaneity and the indulgence of impulse."[68] Freud's was an essentially Nietzschean project, but in America it was acted out according to the racial scheme of things familiar to white Americans. "The creation of Harlem as a place of exotic culture," according to Huggins,

> was as much a service to white need as it was to black. So essential has been the negro personality to the white American psyche that black theatrical masks had become, by the twentieth century a standard way for whites to explore dimensions of themselves that seemed impossible through their own personae.[69]

Harlem was simply an elaborate extension of the "darktowns" that were part of most American cities, places where "the respectable white citizenry sought pleasure in their brothels and cabarets. And their patronage shielded the extralegal life of Negroes from legal harassment."[70] Harlem was a pan-cultural version of this suspension of the moral law, its exaltation into an antinomian decadence of the sort proposed by Gustav Aschenbach shortly before he died. Before World War I, white Americans were willing to tolerate these enclaves as sexual safety valves. After the war they were to become paradigms for the liberation of the entire culture from white, "Puritan" values. "Looking at Harlem," Huggins writes, "it was easy to believe that Negroes had more fun."

> Post-war America was prepared to view the Negro from a different angle. Afro-Americans and Harlem could serve a new kind of white psychological need.... White Americans had identities of their own to find, and black men were too essential to them to be ignored. Men who sensed that they were slaves to moral codes, that they were cramped and confined by guilt producing norms which threatened to make them emotional cripples, found Harlem a tonic and a release. Harlem Negroes' lives appeared immediate and honest. Everything they did—their music, their art, their dance—uncoiled deep inner tensions. Harlem seemed a cultural enclave that had magically survived the psychic fetters of Puritanism.
>
> How convenient! It was merely a taxi trip to the exotic for most white New Yorkers. In cabarets decorated with tropical and jungle motifs... they heard jazz, that almost forbidden music. It was not merely that jazz was exotic, but that it was instinctive and abandoned.... melody skipping atop inexorable driving rhythm. The downtown spectator tried to encompass the looseness and freedom of dance. ... In the darkness and closeness, the music, infectious and unrelenting, drove on. Into its vortex white ladies and gentlemen were pulled to dance the jungle dance.[71]

Jazz was the musical initiation rite for those who were interested, if not in the transvaluation of all values, then at least in a sexual life that had been released from what they perceived as the increasingly nonsensical burden of "Puritan," that is, Christian sexual morality. If the Negro could get away with it without a guilt-burdened conscience, why couldn't whites who aspired to "Negro" values get away with it as well?

> Harlem was also therapy for deeper white needs. The most forbidden was most available: whiskey of course, but also cocaine and sex. The fantasy of Negro sexuality is fed by deep springs in the white psyche. Brown and black bodies—the color seemed lustier than white—full lips that quickened flesh to move, whole selves enlivened to blood-heat, seemed closer to the jungle source. Negroes were that essential self, one somehow lost on the way to civility, ghosts of one's primal nature whose very nearness could spark electric race-memory of pure sensation untouched by self- consciousness and doubt.[72]

Harlem bespoke, as I said, symbiosis. Whites got to project their aspiration for sexual liberation onto the Negro race, and aspiring young Negro writers got to foster their careers by telling the whites just what they wanted to hear. The young Negroes who came there to make their way in the publishing world—Langston Hughes, Claude McKay, Zora Neale Hurston, to name just a few—did so under the patronage of white people who were interested in promoting the primitive. Mrs. Charlotte Mason set up Langston Hughes in his own apartment and had her chauffeur pick him up in her limousine. Hughes, who must have felt at some point as if he had died and gone to heaven, tried his best to conform to her notions of how a "primitive" African might behave, but since he had grown up in Cleveland, Ohio, the project was doomed to failure. "She wanted me to be primitive," Hughes wrote after the fact in his autobiography, *The Big Sea*,

> and know and feel the intuitions of the primitive. But, unfortunately, I did not feel the rhythms of the primitive surging through me, and so I could not live and write as though I did. I was only an American Negro—who had loved the surface of Africa and the rhythms of Africa but I was not Africa. I was Chicago and Kansas City and Broadway and Harlem.[73]

Hughes' collaboration with Carl Van Vechten was more productive and lasted longer than the ill-fated arrangement with Mrs. Mason, perhaps because Van Vechten was more single-minded than the rich patroness of primitive man from Park Avenue. Van Vechten was a homosexual who was interested in decadence. He got Hughes' first book of poetry published at Knopf and introduced him to the pages of *Vanity Fair*. Van Vechten was a white Midwesterner from Cedar Rapids, Iowa, who came to New York as a music critic and quickly became acquainted with the newly circulating currents of modernity. He was an initial promoter of both Stravinsky and Schönberg and a writer of light but decadent fiction, which entailed, in Huggins' words, "a deliberate dislocation of conventional moral sensibilities."[74] At some time in the early twenties, Van Vechten became enamored of things Negro. "It was in 1922," he recounted later, that he became "violently interested in Negroes." "I would say violently," he emphasized, "because it was almost an addiction."[75]

If it was an addiction, Van Vechten had lots of codependents. In fact, at some point after World War I, the cultural revolutionaries as a class turned away from the classical tradition as the prime vehicle of cultural revolution and focused their attention on jazz. It is difficult to find one cause for this change. The mantle of the German classical tradition had passed from Wagner to Mahler to the thin shoulders of Arnold Schönberg, who carried it into the hothouse environment surrounding his school in Vienna never to reemerge. After listening to the thin gruel the Vienna group was putting out in the period before, during, and immediately after World War I, it must have become evident to people like Van Vechten that another Wagner was not in the making. Besides, as Nietzsche had prophesied, and was saying posthumously to increasingly large numbers of people as his books became more popular, Wagner had never really lived up to the promise he had shown in writing *Tristan und Isolde*, at least not as far as sexual liberation was concerned. As the writings of Thomas Mann and any number of cultural revolutionaries had shown, *Tristan* dominated the consciousness of the avant-garde for at least fifty years after its first performance. But one work cannot a revolution sustain, and the revolutionaries were becoming impatient with the increasingly inaccessible material the musical avant-garde was producing. As a result, they began looking elsewhere for the musical accompaniment to their dramas of liberation. They began to look to the Negro. In this, Van Vechten was symbolic of his class. And Van Vechten had the precedent of Nietzsche to follow as well. After all, Nietzsche had pointed them toward Africa after Wagner had failed him. It was only a matter of time before the avant-garde caught on, especially in the light of the thin fare Wagner's successors were producing.

In giving his version of what happened to classical music and its connection to the avant-garde in the period surrounding World War I, the composer George Antheil seems to indicate exhaustion both on the part of the people who were expected to carry the tradition forward and on the part of the public that was supposed to keep up with the sonic arcana that progress in music had become. Everyone was tired after the war, especially the Germans. In this atmosphere, nothing spiritually demanding could survive in music, especially not the sort of hyper-intellectual atonal and (later) twelve-tone stuff that the Germans were producing at the time. When the Negroes arrived in Paris after World War I, everyone heaved a sigh of relief. It was okay to tap your feet again. Tonality was exacting its revenge after all. It was the return of the repressed, although Antheil did not use that term:

> Since Wagner, music has had two gigantic blood infusions: First the Slavic, and in recent times the Negroid. The Russian Five, leading gradually into young Debussy, and eventually into young Stravinsky, seemed to pass naturally into the present Negroidian epoch, especially after the great and world-shaking events of the *Sacre du Printemps* and *Noces*. It is not difficult to understand the transition when one examines and realizes how completely they exhausted Slavic music, and how the Negroidian music, already used to existence under the heat when all other life and music must perish, was the predestined influence to carry music through the difficult after-war period until the present time. . . . It was the only thinkable influence after *Sacre* and *Noces* had exhausted once and for all every last drop of blood that the primitive Slavic music had in it. The first Negro jazz band arriving in Paris during the last year of the great war was as prophetic of the after-war period immediately to come as the *Sacre* was prophetic of this selfsame war, declared only a year after the stormy scenes in the Champs Elysées Theatre in 1913. And this was the war which exhausted the world and left it without a grain of its former "spirituality. . . ." Nothing could survive underneath this dense heat and smoke except Negro music. It absorbed this period so naturally that in 1919 we find the greatest Slavic composer living [that is, Stravinsky] writing Piano-rag-music" and "Ragtime" almost without knowing it, and a whole school of young composers springing up in Paris deeply influenced by American Negro music.[76]

American Negro music was, in other words, sexier in a more immediately apprehensible way than *Tristan und Isolde* had been. And in spite of the mammoth expansion of the post-Wagnerian megaorchestra, there had been really no follow-up to what Wagner had been proposing in *Tristan*. There was only the repentance of *Parsifal*. And no one wanted to hear about that. "The Message of Negro Music" is nothing if not accessible and not burdened by an extensive emotional vocabulary. It is to Wagner what *O sink hernieder* is to "Shake That Thing!" According to Antheil, it

> is strongly marked and recognizable never to be mistaken, even by the musical illiterate. Rhythmically it comes from the groins, the hips and the sexual organs and not from the belly, the interior organs, the arms and legs as in the Hindu, Japanese, and Chinese musics, or from the breast, the brain, the ears, and eyes of the white races.[77]

With the arrival of the first Negro jazz band after the war, Paris finally "had turned her back on Wotan."

> In the circles where ideas and tastes count, a gradual tension was being felt; a grim, inevitable drifting towards a great catastrophe was evidenced in the tremendous artistic revolutions of that time: the *Sacre du Printemps* alone was enough to herald it if nothing else. Then came the war, one single terrible flattening blast; indeed what could survive after this whirlpool of ideas and events? The American Negroes advanced upon musical Paris, took command, reigned for a time, and then disappeared, leaving everywhere gigantic mulatto patches; musicians particularly seemed to have turned at least to octoroons. Like wildfire, the Negro patch spread everywhere in Europe.... Waking up one morning somewhere around 1925, the musical world of Europe became alarmed at its racial problem.[78]

The transition is captured in what has become the most famous English-language poem of the twentieth century. *The Waste Land* begins by citing *Tristan und Isolde*, "Frisch Weht der Wind der Heimat zu," and then moves on to a music-hall version of the Shakespearian Rag: "It's so elegant, so intelligent." In the meantime Eliot follows the trajectory of a halfhearted proletarian seduction: the young man carbuncular is by implication the modern Tristan, and the demise of the land's fertility results from the incurable wound of the fisher king, of which Parsifal is the prime type. The connection between Wagner and jazz is made all the more striking by the fact that, according to the normal canons of influence, there is no connection. The only real link between Wagner and jazz is the sexual liberation both espoused. But this one link was the central concern of the avant-garde at the time. The link is fortuitous, but then again, so is most of history. Nancy Cunard, the model for Eliot's Fresca in the fire sermon section of *The Waste Land*, was early exposed to Wagnerian free love though her mother, Maud or Emerald (she shed names like chrysalides), who carried on an affair with the conductor Sir Thomas Beecham throughout Nancy's formative years. "Maud recalled," writes Cunard's biographer describing the atmosphere at Holt, the Cunard country estate, around the turn of the century,

> one of the guests had thrown open his bedroom window and had given the Valkyries' cry, and from window after window other voices had answered until the whole place resounded with Wagnerian melodies. "When my husband came

back," Lady Cunard once told Cecil Beaton, "he noticed an atmosphere of love. 'I don't understand what is going on in this house,' he said, 'but I don't like it.'"[79]

Nancy did not like it either. She did, however, become a passionate devotee of free love in the decade following the war. And just about the time all the other sexual drugs were wearing off, she picked up an American Negro piano player by the name of Henry Crowder in a bar in Venice, and her career as a crusader against racial segregation was launched. Nancy had been raised a modern, exposed to all its currents. Describing the autumn of 1912 spent at a boarding school in Munich, Nancy Cunard's novelistic alter ego in *The Green Hat* claimed that "transition and danger were in the air."[80] Eliot claimed that Fresca had been ruined by what she read:

> Women grown intellectual grow dull,
> And lose the mother wit of natural trull,
> Fresca was baptized in a soapy sea
> Of Symonds—Walter Pater—Vernon Lee.
> The Scandinavians bemused her wits,
> The Russians thrilled her to hysteric fits.

"We responded," Cunard relates in her own words,

> like chameleons to every changing colour, turning from Meredith to Proust to Dostoevsky, slightly tinged by the Yellow Book, an occasional absinthe left by Baudelaire and Wilde, flushed by Liberalism, sombered by nihilistic pessimism, challenged by Shaw, inspired by young Rupert Brooke, T. S. Eliot, Yeats, D. H. Lawrence; jolted by Wyndham Lewis's *Blast* into cubism and the Modern French Masters, "Significant Form," Epstein's sculptures; Stravinsky's music (booed and cheered); the first Russian ballets and American jazz. . . .[81]

Jazz followed Wagner in much the same way that Nancy's compulsive promiscuity followed Lady Cunard's more discreet affair with Sir Thomas Beecham. Both were in a way a reflection of their age. They reflected the transition from the Victorian to the Modern Age in England as well as a decline in morals as well as a decline in musical sophistication. In this regard, jazz was a punishment for *Tristan*: "My mother's having an affair with Thomas Beecham," Nancy said, "I can do as I like."[82] It was also a way of punishing her American mother, who was now subjected to statements of the following sort from Margot Asquith: "Hello, Maud, what is it now—drink, drugs or niggers?"[83] Jazz was Nancy's revenge on the Wagnerian free love practiced by her mother. Jazz was simultaneously the *Aufhebung* of the classical tradition and revenge against it. Jazz was quite simply a more accessible musical form of the same thing Wagner had proposed so long ago, an idea no one seemed capable of developing in any significant fashion beyond the language in which Wagner presented it. Schönberg was to try in *Verklärte Nacht*, but it was clear that that piece lacked the gravity to motivate a whole generation. And besides, Schönberg had quickly gotten into other things. Nothing on the cultural horizon in the years around World War I promoted sexual liberation as simply and as insistently as Negro jazz. Jazz succeeded Wagner in a way that defied any orderly progression of musical history, but no one was claiming that history at the time involved orderly progression—certainly not Nietzsche, who before his death at the turn of the century had predicted both the sensuality of jazz and the dissonance of atonality.

Wagner had bequeathed a musical bow no one could bend any more. That part of the avant-garde that was committed to music fled into the confines of a sterile hyperintellectuality; the musically non-committed avant-garde, those who were in it just for the decadence, people like Nancy Cunard and Carl Van Vechten, simply jumped ship and went with Negro music. By the 1920s, classical music was no longer in a position to represent the aspirations of the cultural revolutionaries. It would be another forty years before popular music would be in that position. In the interim, revolution was pursued primarily by other means, and the successors of Wagner were left to their own devices to bridge the gap. All that Antheil can say about Schönberg is that "his last opera [probably *Von Heute auf Morgen*] contains some of the very worst jazz that a white man has ever written."[84] The Viennese under Schönberg's direction simply were not providing what the culturally aware needed at the time. At a time of artistic exhaustion after World War I. Schönberg's forays into musical numerology simply did not speak to the audience that had been aroused by Wagner. Jazz became Wagner's heir, by default for the most part; jazz filled the vacuum created when Schönberg tried and failed to fill the space Wagner left vacant. "Negro music," according to Antheil,

> appeared suddenly (after a gigantic preparation) after the greatest war of all time. . . . It came upon a bankrupt spirituality; to have continued within Slavic mysticism would have induced us all, in 1918, to commit suicide; Negro music made us remember at least that we still had bodies which had not been exploded by shrapnel. . . . Without knowing it we were learning to live again in the bright torrid sunshine of reasonable animals without mystical northern lights [that is, Wagner], without any spiritual food except that which we lay in wait for or trapped ourselves. . . . The Negro taught us to throw away our useless folding baths, our hot-water bottles, our travelling frigidaires. . . to put our noses to the ground, to follow the scent, to come back to the most elementary principles of self-preservation. We found ourselves in the Parisian veldt; Chirico, Picasso, Stravinsky, Cocteau were hunters who roamed the wild jungles and trapped every day, every month, without fail, our existence. No longer could we arrive at the water-well with an automatic graph or synthetic compass. The Viennese meanwhile, full of "automatic-synthesis," invented a system whereby they could reproduce genius on purely mechanical principles; they thought their science would outdo itself in reproducing life, but so far it has produced nothing but a breath-taking and awesome system. The twelve-tone system is such that each and every melody to attain pure atonal balance must sound at some point within itself the whole chromatic scale. . . no more, no less. In consequence, the soul of music has passed out of the hands of the old Germans (Schönberg and followers) into the hands of the young Germans. And the young Germans embraced mulattoism after their fashion. It is true that they are often as much Negroid as a performance of *Green*

Pastures with native Berlinese in blackface might be, but at least they black their faces unabashedly; "Jonny Spielt Auf" [an opera by Ernst Krenek] did a considerable lot of good in opening up the operatic movement in Germany.... The hero of this last-named opera is a Negro called "Jonny" (!), albeit a beery and Viennese Negro who achieves his highest moment by breaking into "Swanee River." [85]

By this point it should be apparent that music of the period after World War I found itself in a bind. It was condemned to err either by defect of emotion, as in the twelve-tone school recently established by Schönberg, or by excess, as in the jazz that was filling the vacuum created by the hyperintellectualization of the classical tradition. The notion that music could give a sophisticated explication and/or replication of emotion according to tonal reason was gone by the mid-twenties, and as of the mid-nineties, it has yet to return. The fact that so few people were troubled by its passing is attributable to the general desire for sexual liberation that haunted the cultured classes. As Aristotle had said, "a man receives pleasure from what is natural to him." Music will correspond to the mind of those who produce it and the tastes of those who pay for its production. Perverted minds, Aristotle reminds us in chapter six of the *Politics*, lead to perverted musical modes. The tendency is accentuated in a democratic polity where culture tends to descend to the lowest common denominator anyway. According to Antheil, the cultured classes at the time were suffering from a sort of burnout. The war had made the sublime seem hypocritical. Hemingway captured the sense in his disquisition on place names as opposed to hollow terms like "glory" in *A Farewell to Arms*. Antheil explicates the same feeling from a musical perspective and in doing so explains why suddenly the Negro and his music had become so popular:

> The great war had come and gone, we had been robbed and ransacked of everything; and we were on the march again. Therefore we welcomed this sunburnt and primitive feeling, we laid our blankets in the sun and it killed all of our civilized microbes. The Negro came naturally into this blazing light, and has remained there. The black man (the exact opposite color of ourselves!) has appeared to us suddenly like a true phenomenon. Like a photograph of ourselves he is the sole negative from which a positive may be drawn! Holding this negative up to the sun we see in essence that which so many eyes and ears have been trying to demonstrate on canvas, paper, and stone... the other side of that which we cannot see, but which we can put our arms around; the hard indestructible object with or around it, a world transferred over into the opposite world, a new start, the black man. [86]

The Negro was the photographic negative not only of the white man, but of his Christian values as well. The fact that, on the average, the Negro was more consistently committed to Christianity than his white counterpart meant nothing to the arbiters of modernity and to the Negroes who were willing to go along with the white boys' *Kulturkampf* for whatever gain it would bring them. The actual Negro, whatever his spiritual inclinations, was really nothing in comparison with what the moderns could make him represent. He had become the vehicle for the transvaluation of all values, which Nietzsche had predicted, and, just as Nietzsche had predicted as well, it would be music that would provide the Dionysian breakthrough: not Wagner, though, who had betrayed the cause of sexual liberation and liberation from Christian morality by prostrating himself before the cross, but the happy-go-lucky Negro, whose sex life seemed so unencumbered by German-Christian guilt and other unpleasant heaviness.

The trend of portraying the Negro as a paradigm of sexual liberation continues up to this day. The primary vehicle for this transaction is, of course, Negro music, be it jazz or rock 'n' roll. Michael Ventura makes a convincing case that jazz rose out of the religion of voodoo, particularly as it was practiced in New Orleans in the mid- to late nineteenth century.[87] The voodoo ceremony was accompanied by fevered African drumming. Its purpose was ecstasy, which also entailed possession by one of the voodoo gods. Henry Edward Durell described the dances in Congo Square in New Orleans as of 1853:

> Upon entering the square the visitor finds the multitude packed in groups of close, narrow circles, of a central area of only a few feet; and there in the center of each circle sits the musician, astride a barrel, strong-headed, which he beats with two sticks to a strange measure incessantly, like mad, for hours altogether, while the perspiration literally rolls in streams and wets the ground; and there, too, labor the dancers male and female, under an inspiration of possession, which takes from their limbs all sense of weariness and gives to them a rapidity and a duration of motion that will hardly be found elsewhere outside of mere machinery. The head rests upon the breast, or is thrown back upon the shoulders, the eyes closed, or glaring, while the arms, amid cries, and shouts, and sharp ejaculations, float upon the air, or keep tune, with the hands patting upon the thighs to a music which is seemingly eternal.[88]

The ritual is, to use a term we have become familiar with, Dionysian. The Dionysiac ritual was not Nietzsche's invention. He got his idea from Euripides, whose tragedy *The Bacchae* was commenting on the practices of his day. Bacchic frenzy probably holds a universal attraction to all cultures. The author of the Book of Wisdom refers to "loathsome practices... deeds of sorcery and unholy rites, hated as ruthless murderers of children ... initiated while the bloody orgy goes on" (Wisdom 12:4-6). Just how many forms of sensual ecstasy are there, after all, and could any of them exist without sexual license or intoxication coming from either drugs or wine? Would the music played there be something along the lines of a Bach cantata? So we may be dealing with some sort of constant in human nature here. The desire for ecstasy bespeaks a desire to transcend the limits of human existence, the most onerous of which often seem to involve the moral law. Whenever this law is seen as something external and imposed from without, the attraction to Dionysiac orgy will grow. The modern era, beginning with Nietzsche and lasting up to the present, is just one such era. Relying on the very Christian social restraints he scorns, Nietzsche can see the dissolution into Dionysiac frenzy

Dionysos Rising

in a much more benign light than could the author of the Book of Wisdom (or than could Euripides for that matter):

> Tragedy is enthroned in the middle of this superfluity of life, sorrow, and desire in sublime rapture, listening to a distant, melancholy chorus, which recounts the mothers of being whose names are: madness, will, and woe. Yes, my friend, believe in me and Dionysian life and the rebirth of tragedy. The age of Socratic man is over. Crown yourselves with ivy, and take the Thyrsus wand in hand and be not surprised when tigers and panthers sink fawning at your knees. Dare now only to become tragic men, because this is your salvation. You shall accompany the Dionysian procession from India to Greece. Prepare yourselves for difficult struggles, but believe the more in the miracles of your god![89]

No dead babies here. Nietzsche's Bacchanal is a bit like a bunch of dancing philology professors. But as time went on, and the consequences of sexual liberation became more apparent, the images darkened accordingly. By the time Thomas Mann gave his version in *Death in Venice*, the stakes had gone up: blood was flowing again as once it had in the Book of Wisdom account:

> The obscene symbol, huge, wooden, was uncovered and raised up; then they howled the magic word with more abandon. Foaming at the mouth, they raged, teased one another with ruttish gestures and caressing hand; laughing and groaning they stuck the goads in one another's flesh and licked the blood from their limbs. But the dreamer now was with them, in them, and he belonged to the foreign god. Yes, they were he himself as they hurled themselves biting and tearing upon the animals, got entangled in steaming rags and fell in promiscuous unions on the torn moss, in sacrifice to their god. And his soul tasted the unchastity and fury of decay.[90]

As the passage indicates, Mann is describing a dream here. Gustav Achenbach's dream of pederastic Eros has turned into a Dionysiac nightmare. But he can still wake up from it. Sixty-two years later, the culture decided to try out Achenbach's dream as reality. In attempting to do a replay of that summer's mammoth rock festival at Woodstock, the Rolling Stones gave a free concert at an abandoned California race track on a bleak day in December of 1969. Just as Mann trumped Nietzsche with Gustav Achenbach's nightmare, reality trumped both in a Dionysiac festival that offered not promiscuous unions on the torn moss but rather Hell's Angels clubbing naked teenagers crawling over broken glass toward the stage where the Rolling Stones were singing about Sympathy for the Devil. "The more they were beaten and bloodied," wrote Tony Sanchez, *quondam* factotum and drug supplier to the Stones in his memoirs,

> the more they were impelled, as if by some supernatural force, to offer themselves as human sacrifices to these agents of Satan. The violence transcended all comprehension; it had become some primeval ritual; the victims were no longer merely tolerating pain and evil and bestiality but where actively collaborating in it. And now the pounding voodoo drumming and the primitive shrieks echoed out and the Stones were into their song of homage to the Antichrist. Another

sacrificially naked girl climbed onto the stage, and six Angels leaped on her at once to toss her from the stage like so much human rubbish.[91]

Nietzsche, as we have already indicated, did not invent the Bacchanal, but, to give him credit, he did propose it as the religious ritual of our age. That he did not describe in detail the modalities under which the Dionysiac sacrifice would take place should not prompt us to deny his assertion that it would have something to do with Africa. Whether voodoo and what Euripides describes in *The Bacchae* are two streams of water flowing from the same subterranean spring is a question worth pondering. However, the white cultural revolutionaries who were eager to draft the Negro to serve in their war on Christian values left no doubt of the connections they saw. "Jazz and rock 'n' roll," according to Michael Ventura,

> would evolve from Voodoo, carrying within them the metaphysical antidote that would aid many a twentieth-century Westerner from both the ravages of the mind-body split codified by Christianism [sic], and the onslaught of technology. The twentieth century would dance as no other had, and through that dance secrets would be passed. First North America and then the whole world, would—like [sic] the old blues says—"hear that long snake moan." [92]

White boys like Elvis Presley, Jerry Lee Lewis, and his cousin Jimmy Swaggart probably did believe that this Negro music came from the devil. Hadn't Robert Johnson, the blues guitarist, after all sold his soul to play that way? By playing that music, nonetheless, they were simply saying how willing they were to accede to the transvaluation of values that Nietzsche had proposed as the aesthetic and moral project for this century. "The voodoo rite of possession by the god," Ventura opines approvingly,

> became the standard of American performance in rock 'n' roll. Elvis Presley, Little Richard, Jerry Lee Lewis, James Brown, Janis Joplin. Tina Turner, Jim Morrison, Johnny Rotten, Prince—they let themselves be possessed not by any god they could name but by the spirit they felt in the music. Their behavior in this possession was something Western society had never before tolerated.[93]

Dionysiac reality turned out to be a lot closer to what was described in the Book of Wisdom than the polite version that Nietzsche proposed. An eighteen-year-old Negro was stabbed to death at the Altamont concert. It seems that you could not have Dionysiac frenzy after all without children getting killed. Western society was about to enter on a debauch that would end as it had for Agave in *The Bacchae*, with her son's dismembered body lying around her and her son's head in her lap. Was this too high a price to pay for ecstasy? The question has yet to be answered. "So the postwar years," Huggins writes of the twenties, when it seemed that Dionysiac ecstasy could be confined to places like the Cotton Club,

> found traditional values in disarray. A very articulate and sophisticated segment of white society appeared ready to stand everything on its head. Where industry, frugality, temperance (including moderation and decorum) had been the touchstones, now exuberance, spontaneity, irresponsibility (to be crazy) and sexual

freedom, were the new norms. The Negro, who had long fought a white-imposed stereotype, found that those very traits which he had denied were now in vogue. One need merely rework the old minstrel model, and one had a new Negro image that both conformed to contemporary values and laid claim to a distinctive Negro self.[94]

Modernity was simply the imposition of Nietzschean values on the Negro race by people who sought to repudiate Christian sexual morality. Negro music—first jazz, then rock 'n' roll—was the musical vehicle for this transvaluation of traditional values. Jazz was the Dionysian expression of this world as the cultural revolutionaries' will and their *Vorstellung*. With the rise of the United States as the world's primary cultural power after World War II, the American cultural revolutionaries' reading of the Dionysian/Apollonian struggle took on a racial tinge. Now their cosmic drama of Gnostic liberation entailed the black instinctual noble savage pitted against a white "fascist" moral order. Because America had won the shooting war and then the cultural war, the background music for this cultural revolution would be first jazz and then rock 'n' roll, but in any event, something Negro.

Notes

1. Martin Gregor-Dellin, *Richard Wagner: His Life, His work, His Century*, trans. J. Maxwell Brownjohn (San Diego and New York: Harcourt Brace Jovanovich, 1980), p. 331.
2. Gregor-Dellin, p. 331.
3. Gregor-Dellin, p. 336.
4. Robert W. Gunman, *Richard Wagner: The Man, His Mind, and His Music* (New York: Harcourt, Brace & World, 1968), pp. 393-96.
5. Ronald Hayman, *Nietzsche: A Critical Life* (New York: Oxford University Press, 1980), p. 107.
6. Friedrich Nietzsche, *Werke in Drei Bänden* (Munich: Carl Hanser Verlag, 1954). vol. 3, p. 1091.
7. Nietzsche, vol. 3, pp. 1091-92.
8. Thomas Mann, *Pro and Contra Wagner*, trans. Allan Blunden (Chicago: University of Chicago Press, 1985), p. 67.
9. Mann, *Pro and Contra*, p. 83.
10. Hayman, p. 63,
11. Hayman, p. 64.
12. Thomas Mann, *Doktor Faustus: Das Leben des deutschen Tonsetzers Adrian Leverkühn erzahlt von einem Freunde, in Gesammelte Werke* (Frankfurt am Main: S. Fishcer Verlag, 1980).
13. BK (10 January 1889): [Nietzsche] "Gibt an, dass er sich zweimal spezifisch infiziert habe" (D. 15), cited by Pia Daniela Volz, *Nietzsche im Labyrinth*

seiner Krankheit: Eine medizinisch-biographische Untersuchung (Wurzburg: Könighausen und Neumann, 1990), p. 188.

14. Hayman, p. 97.
15. "*Denken wir uns jetzt das eine grosse Zyklopenauge des Sokrates au die Tragödie gewandt, jenes Auge, in dem nie der holde Wahnsinn künstlericher Begeisterung geglüht hat—denken wir uns, wie es jenem Auge versagt war, in die dionysischen Abgründe mit wohlgefallen zu schauen. . . .*" Nietzsche, vol. 1, p. 78.
16. Nietzsche, vol. 1, p. 18.
17. Nietzsche, vol. 1, p. 91
18. Richard Wagner, *Prose Works*, trans. William Ashton Ellis, vol. 1, *The Artwork of the Future* (New York: Broude Brothers, 1966), p. 37.
19. Gregor-Dellin, p. 444.
22. Gregor-Dellin, p. 381.
21. Nietzsche, vol. 1, p.71.
22. Wilfrid Mellers, *Caliban Reborn: Renewal in Twentieth-Century Music* (New York: Harper and Row, 1967), p. 31.
23. Hayman, pp. 131-32.
24. Nietzsche, vol. 1, p 26-27.
25. Hayman, p. 111.
26. Volz, p. 254.
27. Nietzsche, vol. 1, p. 47.
28. Nietzsche, vol. 1, pp. 56-57.
29. Nietzsche, vol. 1, p. 87.
30. Nietzsche, vol. 1, p.90, (my translation).
31. Hayman, p. 141.
32. Hayman, p. 145.
33. Nietzsche, vol.3, p. 1152.
34. Hayman, p. 103, *Aus den Jahren 1868-69*.
35. Hayman, p. 143.
36. Hayman, p. 143.
37. Hayman, p. 143.
38. Hayman, p. 141.
39. Hayman, p. 142.
41. Nietzsche, vol. 2, p. 1092.
41. Nietzsche, vol. 1, p. 131.
42. Nietzsche, vol. 1, p. 133.
43. Nietzsche, vol. 1, p. 133.
44. Shakespeare, *Troilus and Cressida*, I, iii, 108-24.
45. A.E. Hotchner, *Blown Away: The Rolling Stones and the Death of the Sixties* (New York: Simon and Schuster, 1990), p. 17.
46. Hayman, p. 192.
47. Hayman, p. 178.

48. Gregor-Dellin, p. 443.
49. Gregor-Dellin, p. 444.
50. Gregor-Dellin, p. 455.
51. Gregor-Dellin, p. 455.
52. Hayman, p. 205.
53. Nietzsche, vol. 2, p. 1052,
54. Nietzsche, vol. 2, pp. 1052-53.
55. Gregor-Dellin, p. 454.
56. Nietzsche, vol. 2, p. 1054.
57. Nietzsche, vol. 2, p. 906.
58. Nietzsche, vol. 2, p. 906.
59. Nietzsche, vol. 2, pp. 930-3 1.
60. Nietzsche, vol. 2, p. 1049.
61 Norman Lebrecht, *Mahler Remembered* (New York: W. W. Norton & Company, 1987), p. 292.
62. Thomas Mann, *Der Tod in Venedig*, Text, Materialien und Kommentar mit den bisher unveröffentlichten Arbeitsnotizen [bearbeitet von] T.J. Reed (Munich: Carl Hanser Verlag, 1983), p. 60.
63. Mann, *Venedig*, p. 79.
64. Michael Ventura, "Hear the Long Snake Moan," part 2, *Whole Earth Review* (Summer 1987), p. 87.
65. Ventura, part 2, p. 87.
66. Allan Bloom, *The Closing of the American Mind: How Higher Education Has Failed Democracy and Impoverished the Souls of Today's Students* (New York: Simon and Schuster, 1987), p. 79.
67. See E. Michael Jones, "The Beloved Community Gets Down: How the Civil Rights Movement Chose the Ghetto," *Fidelity* (September 1991), pp. 20-38.
68. Nathan Irvin Huggins, *Harlem Renaissance* (New York: Oxford University Press, 1971), p. 7.
69. Huggins, p. 11.
70. Huggins, p. 13.
71. Huggins, p. 89.
72. Huggins, pp. 91-92.
73. Langston Hughes, *The Big Sea: An Autobiography* (New York: Hill and Wang, 1940), p. 325.
74. Huggins, p. 95.
75. Huggins, p. 99.
76. Nancy Cunard, ed., *Negro: An Anthology*, edited and abridged (New York: Frederick Ungar Publishing Co., 1970), p. 214.
77. Cunard, p. 214.
78. Cunard, p. 216.

79. Anne Chisholm, *Nancy Cunard: A Biography* (New York: Alfred A. Knopf, 1979), p. 14.
80. Chisholm, p. 29.
81. Chisholm, p. 29.
82. Chisholm, p. 159.
83. Chisholm, p. 159.
84. Cunard, p. 217.
85. Cunard, p. 218.
86. Cunard, pp. 218-19.
87. Michael Ventura, "Hear That Long Snake Moan," *Whole Earth Review*, part 1 (Spring 1987), pp. 28-43; part 2 (Summer 1987), pp. 82-92.
88. Ventura, part 1, pp. 37-38.
89. Nietzsche, vol. 1, p. 113.
90. Mann, *Venedig*, p. 75.
91. Tony Sanchez, *Up and Down with the Rolling Stones* (New York: William Morrow and Co, 1979), p. 184.
92. Ventura, part 1, p. 36.
93. Ventura, part 2, p. 90.
94. Huggins, p. 156.

Chapter 3

Arnold Schönberg
Craving the Law and the Totalitarian Reaction

> I crave the law.
> —William Shakespeare
> *The Merchant of Venice*, IV, i, 206

On May 2, 1879, Friedrich Nietzsche submitted his letter of resignation to the president of the University of Basel. Nietzsche had been at the university for ten years. During that time his health in general and his eyesight in particular had deteriorated rapidly. When his sister met him that May, she hardly recognized him. She described him as "an exhausted man, prematurely aged." Nietzsche received a small pension from the university, and with that he would spend the next ten years of his life moving back and forth from the German-speaking world to Italy in a fruitless search for whatever would cure or at least ameliorate his ever-deteriorating condition. The search was in vain. What he did find, though, and this itself is remarkable, was the time, in spite of the debilitating effects of his illness, to write virtually all of his published works. During his ten years as a professor he had only been able to complete *The Birth of Tragedy* and part of *Human, All-Too-Human*. Nietzsche had hoped that *The Birth of Tragedy*, his book on Wagner and music, would usher in the Dionysian age, but instead it did little more than ruin his reputation as an academic. Ritschl called it claptrap, and soon Nietzsche found it difficult to attract students. So it must have been with some sense of relief that he left his duties at the university and began a ten-year immersion into a loneliness so profound it could have driven a healthier man insane. He was fond of saying that no one had ever experienced this sort of loneliness before. Before, there had always been two people when one man stood alone, that man and God. Nietzsche, however, had set himself the task of annihilating God.

It was in May of 1882 during this period of creative negativity that he met Lou Salome, then a twenty-one-year-old Russian student at the University of Zurich, on vacation in Italy with her mother because of bad health. Lou would eventually become one of the great literary ladies of the modern period, something on the line of Alma Mahler. She would go on to become Rilke's mistress and a confidante of Freud. At the time Nietzsche met her, however, this was all in the future, and she was just another young lady in Italy for her health, fascinated by the intellectual extravagance that poured forth from the mind of the ex-professor from Switzerland. It proved to be a meeting of the minds; but, although Nietzsche would have liked it to become more than that, it did not. *Thus Spake Zarathustra* is the unacknowledged protocol of his failure to win her. "Thou goest to women?" Nietzsche wrote. "Do not forget your whip." A photograph from the period provides an ironic commentary on this famous statement from *Zarathustra*. Nietzsche and his friend Paul Ree are posing in a photographer's studio, spanned in front of a small cart like two horses. In the cart sits Lou Salome holding a whip. Misogyny was probably the only logical outcome of Nietzsche's situation at the time. In poor health, infected with syphilis, and yet at the same time hopelessly drawn toward a woman who rejected him, it was easy to slip into the mode of someone who could only scorn what he could not have. Given his physical condition, marriage as an integral linking of two bodies and two minds had become an impossibility for Nietzsche. He was struck by Salome's intelligence, but, in this instance, union of these two bodies would mean extinction of the mind, as Nietzsche himself was learning. His episode in the brothel had forever severed the sexual drive from its fulfillment in one object of permanent affection. Permanent union would have meant the destruction of the loved one. The only feasible alternative was the indiscriminate rutting of the Dionysiac orgy, and Nietzsche dedicated himself to bringing this about as a pan-cultural sacrament. It was only through the forgetfulness that arose from intoxication that he could escape from the terrible isolation he had imposed on himself. It was a dedication that began with Wagner's music and developed through the infection in the brothel to the complete rejection of God, and finally ended in madness, which may have been psychological conditioned or may have been simply the result of venereal infection, but which was at any rate self-imposed.

By the late 1880s, Nietzsche's identification with Dionysos was becoming all but complete. In a note to Strindberg in which he expressed the desire to have the young Kaiser shot, Nietzsche signed himself "Nietzsche Caesar." It was the last time he used his real name in a letter. Thereafter he was either simply "Dionysos" or "The Crucified One." On the morning of January 3, 1889, Nietzsche had just left his rooms in Turin when he saw a cab driver beating a horse on the Piazza Carlo Alberto. After throwing his arms around the horse's neck and bursting into tears, Nietzsche collapsed on the street and had to be carried back to his room. When he came to, he began acting in a peculiarly manic way, singing, shouting, and pounding on the piano. After a lifelong struggle against reason and what he perceived as the corrupting legacy of Socrates, Nietzsche had finally achieved his goal. His was a partial success initially. He had succeeded in routing reason from his own life. He had driven himself insane. It was, in a way, the logical outcome of the program he had had presented to him by Wagner in the second act of *Tristan und Isolde*. Like Isolde, Nietzsche was willing to extinguish the light of reason in order to satisfy inordinate sexual desire. "*O lösche das Licht nun aus!*" Isolde sings in Act Two, "*Lösche den scheuchenden Schein!/Lass' mein Liebsten ein!*" Brangäne warns Isolde not to extinguish the light of reason, but Isolde can only reply that the goddess of love wants night to come: "*Frau Minne will/es werde Nacht.*"

As Apuleius knew, the only kind of union that exists in the dark is the indiscriminate, instinctive couplings between gods and animals. A truly human union involves not only the union of bodies but also, and more importantly, the union of personalities, of minds. As a way of symbolizing this essential fact about the human condition, Apuleius has Psyche, the soul, uncover a lamp during one of her encounters with the god Amor. Human love requires light, the light of reason. When Psyche uncovers the lamp in their bedroom, Amor, the god of love, flees. Truly human sexual union requires the human individuation which can take place only in the light. In the dark, there is a meeting of bodies but not of minds. Sexual union is not a human activity under such conditions. Perhaps this is why it remained attractive to Nietzsche. Nietzsche recognized in sexual activity an incredibly potent, destructive force. If it had threatened the social order in Thebes under Pentheus, it could threaten the social order in a Europe growing tired of Christian morals as well. If sexual activity could ruin Nietzsche, then why could he not distill the lesson he had learned into an incredibly powerful social solvent that would dissolve the order he hated so passionately? Sexual intercourse liberated from the bonds of morality and the confines of the family was the only force in nature powerful enough to be turned against the Christian West and to bring about the transvaluation of all values. "Whenever the subject was the power of demons over human life," reasons Serenus Zeitblom in *Doktor Faustus* when pondering Adrian Leverkühn, the Nietzsche character,

> sex always played a prominent rule. How could it have been otherwise? The demonic character of this sphere was a chief appurtenance of the "classical psychology," for there it formed the favorite arena of the demons, the given point of attack for God's adversary, the enemy and corrupter. For God had conceded greater magic over the venereal act than over any other human activity....[1]

It was Nietzsche's evil genius to see that no social revolution can proceed in the presence of a stable sexual morality. Wagner wanted social revolution because he wanted sexual liberation; Nietzsche, his disciple, wanted sexual liberation because he wanted social revolution. Wagner's sin was primarily sensual, Nietzsche's intellectual. Wagner was weak, of two minds, and always, as the evidence in *Tannhäuser* and *Parsifal* indicates, flirting with repentance. Nietzsche, on the other hand, had little sexual contact during his life. The little he did have, however, was transmuted into an ideology of rebellion against God and the social order. Sexual license was the means to this end. Given the human condition, given sexuality as the crucial nexus between body and soul, between one generation and the next, sexuality was the only force potent enough to bring about the revolution Nietzsche foresaw. As Homer knew when he described Odysseus' victory over his wife's suitors, the foundation of the entire social order is the faithful sexual union between husband and wife. When that bond is disrupted, no social order can stand. Pentheus recognized the same thing in *The Bacchae*. He has the full power of the state at his disposal when he captures Dionysos, but those armies never get used. Nietzsche, inflamed by the possibilities of infinite sensuality he had heard in Wagner's music, made an irrevocable commitment to sexual disorder when he deliberately infected himself in the brothel. His genius, and I think we can call it that, was to take that act and formulate out of it a philosophical weapon that would bring down the society he hated. The vehicle for the transvaluation of all values was sexual liberation made plausible by the music of Wagner, or Bizet, or something "African," whose outline he perceived in a dim but uncanny way. The culmination of this project was the intoxicated Dionysiac orgy, where all consciousness of individuation, and guilt, and all that had been lost by bad choices could he extinguished in a quasi-religious sexual intoxication and frenzy. In proposing the Dionysian, Nietzsche gave us the blueprint for our age. He, and not Marx or Lenin, was the true revolutionary father of our age. Just what executing that blueprint would cost is still not apparent, but the bill is becoming increasingly impressive. Virtually all the modern ideologies from Nazism to Gay Liberation would have been unthinkable without the superstructure that Nietzsche proposed in his project of transvaluing all values. How much did World War II cost? How much will the AIDS epidemic cost? The ghettos in American cities? Communism is now universally regarded as an *ignis fatuus*, but the ideology that preceded it and succeeded it shows no signs of abating. Fascism as an ideology would be impossible without the philosophical superstructure proposed by Nietzsche. Woodstock Nation and the subsequent wave of sexual liberation and drug use that rolled over the United States in the sixties and, with the help of rock music, over the rest of the world thereafter is just as unthinkable without Nietzsche's philosophical justification of the Dionysian transvaluation of the moral law. The years 1968-1969 brought in a revolutionary reign that is still with us.

By the late 1890s, Nietzsche was finally catching on among the bohemians of the Austro-Hungarian and German empires. His nagging doubts about the audience he worried about reaching (the sales of his books were depressingly low) were now being resolved as word spread among bohemian circles of the man who was so adept at expressing their longing to be free from the burdens of Christian civilization and sexual morality. Just as Wagner had provided the impetus for Nietzsche's commitment to the transvaluation of all values, so Wagner's music, specifically at the music festivals at Bayreuth, was providing a vehicle for the dissemination of Nietzsche's ideas. James Webb describes Wagner as "the Grand Master of the idealistic Underground in the German Speaking countries." [2] By the time Nietzsche's sister returned from the failed racist colony her late husband, Bernard Förster, had founded in Paraguay—he committed suicide—she found that she could live quite well on the royalties from Nietzsche's books. She set about establishing the Nietzsche archives and, to help her, eventually hired Rudolf Steiner, one of the leading lights in the occult revival of the time, a man who had just published a book on Nietzsche. Steiner was just one influential member of the occult avant-garde that found himself drawn to both Wagner and Nietzsche's semi-mystical views of sexual and social liberation. The Nietzsche archive run by his sister, Elizabeth, would eventually become a magnet attracting the Grand Magus of the occult avant-garde, Adolf Hitler himself. By then Nietzsche was dead. But even during the last years of his life, it is doubtful that Nietzsche was at all cognizant of his growing fame. Elizabeth dressed her brother in a white pleated robe. When Steiner saw him, he had the impression of being with a holy man, someone "who could not die." [3] Visiting Nietzsche in 1895, his friend Overbeck saw him in his room,

> half-crouching like a wild animal mortally wounded and wanting only to be left in peace. He made literally not one sound while I was there. He did not appear to be suffering or in pain, except perhaps for the expression of profound distaste visible in his lifeless eyes.... He had been living for weeks in a state of alternation between days of dreadful excitability, rising to a pitch of roaring and shouting, and days of complete prostration.[4]

Peter Gast, the composer who would take daily walks with Nietzsche, had the impression that Nietzsche did not want to be cured. "It seemed— horrible though this is—as if Nietzsche were merely feigning madness, as if he were glad for it to have ended in this way."[5] In this, Nietzsche was like others of his class. Strindberg ended one of his letters to Nietzsche with the Greek inscription "it is a joy to be mad." [6] If so, Nietzsche was enjoying himself immensely, something that left a lasting impression on Gast. "I cannot escape the ghastly suspicion," he wrote, "that his madness is simulated. This impression can be explained only by the experiences I have had of Nietzsche's self-concealments, of his spiritual masks."[7] His madness, self-willed or not, evidently did not affect Nietzsche's piano playing. He would improvise at the asylum's piano, "interweaving," in Gast's words, "tones of Tristan-like sensitivity."[8] Thomas Mann describes a similar episode in his short story "Tristan." Detlev Spinell, a writer, falls in love with a married woman at a spa. Together on a snowy evening, they listen to a piano version of *Tristan's* "intoxicated music of the love-mystery":

> Oh, tumultuous storm of rhythms. Oh, glad chromatic upward surge of metaphysical perception! How find, how bind this bliss so far remote from parting's torturing pangs?[9]

It was music that had intoxicated more than one generation of Germans, and by the 1890s, as Nietzsche sank deeper into syphilitic dementia, a new generation formed by the ideas of Nietzsche and Wagner was coming into being. It was the first modern generation. One member of this rising generation was a young Jewish bank clerk by the name of Arnold Schönberg. Schönberg had received virtually no musical training during his youth. In his biography, H. H. Stuckenschmidt claims that Schönberg's mother taught piano, but this was not true. Reports on his musical ability after that vary. Some claim that he picked up the ability to play instruments without effort, others that his inability to play the piano caused him severe difficulties after he had accepted the directorship of a workingmen's choir. Schönberg was clearly enamored of the musical world of his time, and that meant being enamored of *Tristan und Isolde*. Schönberg, like his contemporary Thomas Mann, never missed an opportunity to hear performances of this work. He would later claim to have heard it performed twenty or thirty times.

Tristan was one part, albeit a major part, of the cultural atmosphere in the capital city of the Austro-Hungarian empire at the turn of the century. In 1896 Brahms died, and the Munich Secession art exhibition that had been successful there in 1892 was restaged in Vienna. Schönberg found himself drawn into the artistic ferment. He was, after all, someone who had done a number of paintings and even had his work included in the famous *Blaue Reiter* exhibit a few years later. Gustav Mahler, who referred to Schönberg and his musical alter ego Alexander von Zemlinsky as "Eisele und Beisele," even bought one of Schönberg's paintings to help out the perennially impecunious artist.

Zemlinsky not only taught Schönberg musical theory and introduced him to the musical world, including invitations to the Mahler household; he also introduced Schönberg to his sister Mathilde, with the result that the whole latter part of the last decade of the last century, when Schönberg was in his early twenties, is suffused with what Stuckenschmidt terms an "erotic glow."[10] The general atmosphere of enhanced artistic possibility probably goes hand in hand with the loosening of sexual mores. One wants, after all, to express all of the strange and wonderful new feelings one experiences, and those in the same cultural situation will pay handsomely to those better equipped to do the expressing. Either way, the two go hand in hand. If there is the sense that the old values are passing, there is a need to see how the new values are going to be fulfilled. In *fin-de-siècle* Vienna there was a whole generation working on the problem.

At some point around the end of the last century, Schönberg became aware of the writings of Richard Dehmel, a disciple of Nietzsche and an advocate of free love. Dehmel's poetry was full of the feeling that a new era of relations between the sexes had dawned. Stuckenschmidt, in attempting to assess the influence of Dehmel on Schönberg, describes the poetry as concerned with "problems of workers' marriages, free love and so-called erotic companions."[11] He goes on to describe Dehmel as "a passionate yes-sayer, an enlightened man trained in socialism who also published metaphysical and religious ideas with increasing maturity."[12] In his poem *Welt und Weib*, Dehmel describes a young couple walking at night in the woods. The woman declares that she is pregnant by another man; her companion accepts the child and promises to raise it as his own. Those who are less sympathetic to the enterprise of sexual liberation as practiced in Vienna at the turn of the century take a correspondingly dim view of Dehmel's literary reputation. Vogel claims that Dehmel was "an author who dwelled mostly in the debased atmosphere of pornography, someone of whom it was recommended to fathers of families who were concerned about their children to leave their daughters and wives at home when dealing with him." [13] J. Meyerowitz, who was friendly with Schönberg's son-in-law Greissle, saw a close connection between Dehmel's unhealthy sexual outlook and *Verklärte Nacht*, Schönberg's major work of the period, which is based on the Dehmel poem:

> The form (or non-form) of the piece follows no musical-architectonic schema, but rather the lines of certain extramusical events, erotic experiences, which Schönberg found represented in a poem by Richard Dehmel, a poem, by the way, that makes a terrible impression today and someone whose books one should avoid at all costs, unless one wants to ruin whatever pleasure there is in the music.[14]

Schönberg was obviously of another opinion. As late as 1912, he wrote a letter to Dehmel, effusive in its praise of the man and his theories. Schönberg's earliest and arguably most famous work, *Verklärte Nacht*, is suffused with all of the elements surrounding the *Wiener Sezession* mood of the time. The poem, written by a devotee and popularizer of Nietzsche, casts adultery in a romantic light. Suddenly there are other possibilities in dealing with the situation of finding oneself confronted with infidelity.

Everything is reconciled in the end. The abolition of the law of reason in the realm of morality, what Wagner symbolized in the night, which found its apotheosis in Act Two of *Tristan*, is "*verklärt*," which is to say, transfigured or illuminated from within. Now we are no longer faced with the necessity of linking death and impossible adulterous love, as Wagner had done in *Tristan*. It seems as if things can he worked out according to reasonable and yet erotically exciting new possibilities. The husband takes the erring woman home. The sexual revolution is on, but everything's going to be okay:

> Be not a burden
> To the soul of the child
> You have received.
> Look at how clearly the universe gleams!
> Splendor surrounds us all,
> You, like I, float on a cold sea,
> Yet warmth flickers
> From you unto me
> And from me unto you.
> This warmth will transfigure
> This alien child
> Which you will bear,
> You have created a splendor in me;
> You have transformed me myself
>   into a child.

The mood here is unmistakably Christian. The poem is in its way a variation on the prodigal-son theme. The man forgives the woman: he accepts the illegitimate child as his own. However, that granted, the Dehmel poem is at the same time a severely naturalized version of the prodigal son. There is no father here, representing God, just a man and a woman working things out on their own. Actually, the real agent of reconciliation is "a unique warmth glimmering from you unto me and me unto you"; this mysterious feeling is the agency that brings about the reconciliation and "transfigures" the child and, by extension, the night as well. Just as the child is transfigured by the warmth flowing between the man and woman in the poem, the night is transfigured, or illuminated, from within as well. No one has mentioned the fact that *Verklärte Nacht* is an oxymoron. "*Verklärte Nacht*" means night illuminated from within. It is precisely this autonomy being granted to human emotion in the poem. The night, the darkness resulting from the extinguishing of the torch of reason in *Tristan*, is now illuminated from within by the mystical warmth emanating from us all. *Verklärte Nacht* is a musical and sexual advance over *Tristan* in that it advocates the liberating ideology of free love. It bespeaks an ideology that says all the tragedy associated with sexual longing is now over. The warmth in you and me will henceforth conquer all jealousy, all social constraint. Night is "*aufgehoben*," to use the Hegelian term. It is simultaneously transcended, exalted, and maintained. Transposed to the sexual realm, this now means that we can both have our cake and eat it, too. We can satisfy the impossible longings that Tristan and Isolde felt without the tragic consequences they experienced. This was the deeply held hope that ushered in this century and grew out of the German romantic tradition as commandeered by Wagner fifty years earlier. *Verklärte Nacht* was the self-contradictory symbol for the sexual aspirations of *fin-de-siècle* Vienna.

Stuckenschmidt traces the erotic musical atmosphere surrounding Schönberg's rendering of the Dehmel poem to his love for Mathilde von Zemlinsky. Schönberg was not only falling in love, he was buying into a whole new *Weltanschauung*, which included, in Stuckenschmidt's words, "a new orientation of literature and ethics and a changed idea of musical form."[15] *Verklärte Nacht* is

> a characteristic Dehmel subject, full of the expression of a new, antibourgeois morality, and carried along entirely by the idea of love, which overcomes everything and sweeps all conventions aside.[16]

All of progressive Vienna was ready for a change, and Schönberg in this regard was no exception. On March 21, 1898, Schönberg renounced Judaism. Four days later he was baptized into the liberal Protestant Dorotheer community, with Walter Pieau, the opera singer, as his godfather. On October 7, Schönberg married Mathilde von Zemlinsky at the Dorotheer Church. It is always difficult to assess motives in any conversion, but the situation in Vienna at the time was complicated by the fact that advancement in the university and the arts was tied to being a Christian. Sigmund Freud, whose medical career at the university was stalled at the time because he refused to convert, was subjected to the same sort of pressure. Gustav Mahler did convert. Schönberg, who was certainly aware of Mahler's career as well as of his music, perhaps saw conversion as a necessary step in fostering his musical career. However, just as it is unfair to Mahler to say that he converted only because of his career, it is just as unfair to claim the same thing of Schönberg. Schönberg was swept up into *fin-de-siècle* bohemia, and that, as Dehmel's poem indicates, was a decidedly Christian enterprise. But if so, it was Christian with a peculiar spin; *caritas* had become free love. The notion of love expressed in the poem had made a deep impression on Schönberg, and that notion was Christian in its inception and modern in its application in a way that fit the times perfectly. Schönberg had been swept away by bohemia, Mathilde, Dehmel, and a loose reading of Christianity that emphasized "warmth" as the thing that was going to transfigure the Wagnerian night and illegitimate children as well. Christ has abolished the law, said Saint Paul, another, Jewish convert. Antinomianism has been a perennial hazard for Christians ever since. "Love and do what you will" seemed like a plausible maxim for personal behavior in an empire whose institutions were firmly embedded in the Christian moral law. However, as is usually the case, the emphasis on love in this context took on a distinctly sexual tinge, and the more that love was liberated from the moral law, the less benign the consequences would become. It was a lesson that Schönberg would learn the hard way.

The music, in keeping with the mood of sexual *Umbruch*, was unmistakably Wagnerian. It was, in fact, Zemlinsky himself, Schönberg's brother-in-law, who referred to *Verklärte Nacht* as a "smeared" version of *Tristan*. "It sounds," he wrote, "as if you had taken a still wet version of the *Tristan* score and smeared it."[17] Vogel notices a preference for the diminished seventh chord in both Schönberg and his model, Wagner:

> One sees as well as hears that Schönberg not only shows a preference for the diminished seventh chord (the Tristan chord), but also, parallel to the Prelude of *Tristan*, uses it as the high point of this ever increasing crescendo three full times. The reader will remember that Wagner allows the massively growing crescendo of the full orchestra to culminate in the Tristan chord three full times. Schönberg does the same thing in his sextet of 1899, *Verklärte Nacht*.[18]

From a musical point of view, Vogel sees the whole rise of modern atonality as flowing from Wagner's use of chromaticism in *Tristan*. Wagner, as we have already noted, was not unaware of the dangers associated with the liberties he took with the diatonic scale. In "Art and Revolution" he talked about sailing out of the safe streams of tonality into a huge chromatic sea with nothing to guide him. The prospect of being absorbed by an ocean of undifferentiated sound was enough to drive the most stalwart musical explorer back to the shores and safe havens of tonality. One major difference between Wagner and the moderns is that "Wagner possessed the musical genius to see his way through the storms of chromatic passion he deliberately incited. The moderns, however, unlike Columbus, sailed off bravely in their experimental boats and eventually reached the end of the musical world, where they fell off its edge into the abyss. Vogel, like virtually everyone else, sees atonality beginning with Wagner. However, Wagner had a way of bringing it off; the moderns did not.

> Just about everyone who writes about music is unanimous in the verdict that the demise of tonality was begun by Richard Wagner in his *Tristan*. In this work, chromaticism has already reached such an advanced state of development that only a master like Wagner can succeed in getting it to adhere to a specific tonal center. The further development of this principle leads ineluctably to a complete disintegration of tonality, causing chromaticism to lose itself in a bottomless tonal pit and the music itself to lose all definition as a result. At this point the twelve-tone technique comes into play by taking this development one step further and creating a complete break with tonality. "If one wanted to write a comprehensive history of modern music," writes Schönberg's pupil Zillig, "one would have to begin it with Wagner, because *Tristan* is already, to use the phrase of Thomas Mann, an atonal work." It is nonetheless noteworthy that on this crucial point the Schönberg pupil, composer, and conductor feels compelled to rely on a literary source, on Thomas Mann, for support.[19]

It is interesting to speculate how Wagner's return to tonality is related to his return to morality. The association is clear in *Tannhäuser*, especially the 1845 Paris version, and in *Parsifal* as well. The moderns, having learned at Nietzsche's feet, were determined to take Wagner one step farther. This entailed a step that was both moral and musical. In fact, the two were inextricably related. Just as the free love proposed in Dehmel's poem was the answer to the tragic bind that adulterous desires created in *Tristan*, so chromaticism would develop beyond tonality in its own way as well, but not in *Verklärte Nacht*, a piece both derivative and, at the same time, musically accessible. The theme of reconciliation at the heart of Dehmel's poem naturally lends itself to tonal resolution as well. A composer who felt that reconciliation between the sexes (or with his own wife) was no longer possible might have doubts about the order of reconciliation implicit in the diatonic scale as well.

At least a composer like Schönberg might. Joan Peyser makes a strong case that

> The method which solidified Schönberg's position in the history of music can best be understood—in terms of the personal dynamics that motivated it—by investigating the life that Schönberg began to give to letters and numbers about 1912, just before he set about creating his new system.[20]

The statement is true in a sense but problematic as well, especially in light of more recent evidence about the real origins of the twelve-tone system. Schönberg is, nonetheless, and in this we agree with Peyser, resolutely autobiographical in even what appeared to be his most abstract works. Peyser cites Thomas Mann, who has written that Schönberg told him that the seemingly abstract Trio, op. 45, "depicted a recent illness and included musical references to a male nurse and hypodermic needle."[21] However, Schönberg was at the same time deeply ambivalent about these personal revelations. He was possessed by something we have elsewhere called the Dimmesdale Syndrome. He simultaneously wants to confess and to cover his tracks. So, in *Style and Idea*, Schönberg calls his music a "language in which a musician simultaneously gives himself away" and goes on to claim that

> one day the children's children of our psychologists will have deciphered the language of music. Woe, then, to the incautious who thought his innermost secrets carefully hidden and who must now allow tactless men to besmirch his most personal possessions with their own impurities.[22]

If he was thinking of the Freudians, Schönberg need not have worried. Freud, who had treated Mahler as a result of Alma Mahler's affair with Walter Gropius, had secrets of his own to conceal. Besides, he was tone-deaf as well and took virtually no pleasure in music at all. In describing Schönberg's state of mind in the early years of this century, Stuckenschmidt cites a female acquaintance of Schönberg who claimed he was "suffering from inexhaustible Bohemianism."[23] The reference is as much to the hours Schönberg spent in Vienna's cafés and *Kneipen* as it is to the intensity of his aesthetic beliefs and the general sense that a new day was coming. "Every night," Stuckenschmidt writes, describing Schönberg and his circle, "they discussed their problems until dawn and then went home drunk."[24]

At some point during 1906, Zemlinsky introduced his brother-in-law Arnold to a shy, young artist by the name of Richard Gerstl. Gerstl was nine years Schönberg's junior and so withdrawn he refused to sign his paintings on the front of the canvas. Alma Mahler had met him at one of her soirées, which were the magnetic north of Viennese cultural life at the time, but never knew that he painted. Zemlinsky, who taught Alma Mahler and later had an affair with her, was living next door to the Schönbergs at the time on the Liechtensteinerstrasse. Gerstl got on so well with the Schönbergs that he moved in with them during the summer of 1907. He began to teach Schönberg painting, and then he began to teach Schönberg's wife. Mathilde von Zemlinsky Schönberg, for her part, went in short order from being Gerstl's pupil to being his model and finally to becoming his lover. Then in the fall of 1908 Mathilde left the then thirty-three-year-old Schönberg and moved in with Gerstl. Mutual friends, most notably Schönberg's student and fellow composer Anton von Webern, appealed to Mathilde's maternal instincts and eventually persuaded her to return to Schönberg. Mathilde eventually got over her adulterous infatuation, but Gerstl did not. On November 4, 1908, Gerstl piled his paintings underneath him in his studio and, in an act that must have been as acrobatic as it was brutal, simultaneously plunged a knife into his heart and hanged himself over the burning canvases.

Within a period of less than a decade, the promise of free love so lushly evoked in *Verklärte Nacht* had turned into a nightmare of suicide and betrayal. There was no more "unique warmth" suffusing the contours of adulterous betrayal, nor was there any musical resolution now into a final chord of decadent Christian-*cum*-free love reconciliation. The breakup of Schönberg's marriage was a moment too dissonant for any chord to resolve. At least he seems to have perceived it as such. It brought about a fundamental change in his personality and, what is more important, a fundamental change in the music he was writing. Tonality collapsed under the weight of his wife's betrayal. Schönberg the erstwhile devotee of Dehmel and free love, had just been hoisted with his own sexual petard. Atonality was Schönberg's response to the empty promises of sexual liberation. "Schönberg," writes Vogel of this intersection of personal and cultural history, "had dedicated himself to atonality. Out of his inner crisis he fashioned a crisis for modern music." [25]

Schönberg's first response to the crisis in his marriage was his String Quartet in F-sharp minor, op. 10. It is a work full of literary and musical allusions. The second movement cites the popular song, "*Ach, du lieber Augustin*," a song that had special meaning for Gustav Mahler, but whose refrain, "*Alles ist hin* [Everything's gone]," probably had reference to Schönberg's marriage. As Vogel notes, it could also refer to the demise of tonality. Tonality and marriage, as Shakespeare knew, were both predicated on reconciliation and resolution of dissonance. The last movement of the Second String Quartet contains the Stephan George poem "*Du lehnest wider ein Silberweide*," whose lines refer directly to Mathilde, to whom the quartet is dedicated:

> Kill the longing, close the wounds!
> Take my love from me, and give me your blessing!

In another line he says that "the shrines are all empty, full of torment only." Schönberg's student Alban Berg described the Second Quartet as an "echo of a crisis in personal life whose sorrow, hardly ever mastered, brought to Schönberg's work its full creative weight." [26] Theodor Adorno said that during the second movement of the Quartet "demons shredded tonality." [27] Schönberg himself was equally precise on dating the end of tonality: "This moment—I can speak out of my own experience—this moment in which we all took part, happened in the year 1908. . . ." [28] In the second movement of the Second Quartet, "passages arise in which the independent movement of the individual voices take no notice of whether their resolution follows in 'recognized' harmonies." [29]

This movement for musical independence continued into Schönberg's next work, his "Three Pieces for Piano," op. 11, which, more than the Second String Quartet, strikes the listener as a full-blown modern work. Schönberg completed the work in early 1909 and described it later as "the first publication of music of this kind." [30] When it was finally performed, the piece caused a sensation of the sort that has been the ardent wish of the musical avant-garde ever since. The uproar in the concert hall was certainly provoked by Schönberg's music, but, much more than that, it was a touching testimony to the fact that the concert-going public took music seriously enough to get upset at those who abused it. By the time Stockhausen, Cage, et al., got around to staging the same sort of thing in the fifties, no one took music seriously enough to get upset about their pompous banalities. Walter Dahms described the "Three Pieces for Piano" as "a scorched-earth policy

Arnold Schönberg

waged against music [*einen Vernichtungsfeldzug gegen die Musik*]."[31] He was more correct than he knew. With the rise of Schönberg as the representative modern after World War II, the music world was subjected to one pulverizing barrage after another. By the time the public emerged from their sonic bunkers, everyone was too shell shocked to complain any more. Schönberg succeeded beyond his wildest dreams. By the 1960s, it was quite possible to make any sort of sonic disturbance, including a Cage piece that consisted of four minutes of silence, and have it be considered music by someone who had access to sonic musical outpost of the aging avant-garde. The scorched-earth policy that began in 1908 as Schönberg's recoil from domestic betrayal and later-reached its apogee as a result of cultural/political exigencies after World War II was a complete success. The liberation of dissonance had annihilated music.

The new-found freedom of what would come to be known as Schönberg's second or atonal period was not without its perils, though. As Wagner had predicted, casting off from the shore of tonality would deprive the composer of any musical orientation. Since nothing now necessarily followed from anything else, musical form became a nagging and eventually unsolvable problem. As a result, the works of this middle period became shorter and shorter. And over the period of the next fifteen years, from the time he was thirty-three until he was forty-eight years old, the meridian of creativity in a man's life, Schönberg's musical production slowed to a trickle and eventually dried up. The First World War, of course, took place during this period, a not insignificant event for Austrians of the time, and Schönberg was for a short period called up for service. During this time, he was even more impecunious than usual and had to exist on the fees he got from students, a fact of economic life that would follow him to the end of his days. He complained about having to teach in California as well. "My work," he said, referring to the teaching he was doing at UCLA, "is as much a waste of time as if Einstein were to have to teach mathematics at a secondary school."[32]

Modesty was never Schönberg's strong suit. But modest was the only word that could describe his production during his middle, atonal period. Schönberg eventually came to the same solution Wagner had found and described earlier in *Art and Revolution*. When musical architectonics failed, there was always the written text to give some organizing principle to his works. This device allowed Schönberg to write longer pieces, but it never really overcame the problem with musical organization that is inherent to the notion of atonal music. Music, quite simply, has to go somewhere. It is organized in time. If there is no reason why one note should follow another, there is no way of organizing that time in any coherent fashion. Atonality meant a freedom analogous to taking down all signs and abolishing all roads. The freedom it instituted was self-defeating and quickly led to a situation in which the composer had less and less to say. This increasingly painful silence lasted until 1923, when Schönberg announced that he had made a discovery that would guarantee the dominance of German music for the next

150 years. (Schönberg would sometimes more modestly restrict this hegemony to the next 100 years.) His discovery has come to be known as dodecaphony (dodecacaphony, to the less admiring), or the twelve-tone system. Before long, legends would arise to surround its birth, legends which had to be propagated by music professors, since by then the concert halls were all but empty of people interested in contemporary music.

Ethan Haimo's book *Schönberg's Serial Odyssey: The Evolution of His Twelve-Tone Method*, 1914-1928, turns Schönberg into a sort of musical Thomas Edison, laboring alone in his laboratory, coming up with an invention that will benefit future generations. Haimo claims that Schönberg

> had set out on a lonely compositional odyssey with nothing but his own imagination to light the way. That he persisted through the first difficult period is a testament to both the persuasiveness of his vision and the indomitable nature of his spirit. That the eventual results include masterpieces like *Moses und Aron* should vindicate his perseverance.[33]

Well, if *Moses und Aron* is a masterpiece, then I suppose Schönberg was vindicated. But the claim that Schönberg came up with the twelve-tone system "with nothing but his own imagination to light the way" can only be maintained by ignoring a large segment of musical history. The fact that there is a term in musical history known as the *Wienerprioritätsstreit* ("the Viennese priority controversy") should be some indication that there was more than one claimant to the authorship of the twelve-tone system. "In 1921," Haimo informs us, Schönberg "was in the process of inventing a method of composition that had not, as yet, even been imagined."[34]

This is complete nonsense, every bit as nonsensical as Haimo's claim that "German music. . . was destroyed as a vital force by the Nazis, who perverted the arts with their political and racial ideology."[35] The fact is that, no matter how much it is obligatory to dislike Nazis, they did nowhere near the damage to German music that Schönberg and the postwar ideologues who appropriated him for their own purposes—Stuckenschmidt, Strobel, Adorno, et al.—accomplished. Can anyone seriously maintain that Hitler did more damage to music than Karl Heinz Stockhausen or John Cage? If Hitler was responsible for the debacle that became modern music, then he did so only by legitimatizing anyone whose artistic credo was set up in reaction to him. Haimo's dragging Hitler into the matter is an indication that the postwar cultural politics of the *Bundesrepublik* still have force in academe, if nowhere else. Haimo's sterile formalism, his analyzing one twelve-tone row after another, reminds one of what Mark Twain had to say about Wagner: "His music is not as bad as it sounds." Haimo's book is an attempt to prove that Schönberg's music is better than it sounds. The adherents of the twelve-tone system have retreated to the safe enclaves of academe, and, like the last Japanese soldiers in the caves of Okinawa, they hunker down to defend a system that not only has been moribund for quite some time but has been emptying concert halls ever since the first performance of Schönberg's *Three Pieces for Piano*. As Schönberg himself recognized, the main attraction of this system is not its musical appeal but rather its claim to originality, as well as its ability to provide composers who lack inspiration a schema for deciding which note should follow which.

However, Haimo not only seems to have failed to learn the fact that other people were not only imagining a twelve-tone system in Vienna at the time (working with twelve tones was only the logical outcome of Wagner's chromaticism), he is likewise ignorant of the fact that another person had invented it ten years before Schönberg arrogated authorship to himself in 1923. Or perhaps, like other members of the Schönberg school, he knows about Josef Hauer, but does not want other people to know about him.

In the spring of 1913, Schönberg received a letter from an eccentric Austrian music teacher by the name of Josef Hauer, who had just composed two works entitled *Nomos*, op. 1 and 2. *Nomos* is the Greek word for law, and the "*Nomos*" of Hauer's music "consisted in the fact that again and again all twelve tones of the tempered scale had to be played out."[36] Pure atonal music, according to Hauer, meant "playing or singing to an end repeatedly the twelve notes of the tempered scale in one voice, without any emphasis, each with the same length and intensity."[37]

Schönberg was unimpressed by Hauer's ideas, which he found both arcane and offputting at the same time. Beyond that, Schönberg gave the impression that he had run out of ideas and had lost interest in composing. In a letter dated June 23, 1913, Schönberg informed Hauer that he saw no point in meeting with him and recommended that he contact instead his students Webern and Berg, because, as he put it, "I myself am at the moment so unclear about everything artistic and especially the technical aspects that I am hardly in a position to give you a half-way decent opinion [of your work]."[38] Schönberg was devoting himself to painting at the time, a sure sign that the springs of musical creativity had dried up. Schönberg's paintings were among those in an exhibit of the *Blanc Reiter*.

Hauer, however, refused to give up in his desire to work with Schönberg. He approached him again in July or August of 1917. Hauer, who was in financially straitened circumstances at the time, visited Schönberg at his apartment at Gloriettengasse 43 and proposed founding a school for the fostering of twelve-tone music. Schönberg, who had already founded the small group that was responsible for the performing of modern music, a group that had performed Hauer's works as well, made a counter-suggestion that they coauthor a book on the twelve-tone system. Neither project ever got off the ground, perhaps because of the disruption the war was causing, perhaps because of the growing rivalry between the two men.

Hauer, however, continued working on perfecting the twelve-tone system during a time period (1917-1920) when Schönberg produced virtually nothing. Beginning around Christmas 1918, Hauer went back to the works he had already composed and tried to formulate in a more precise manner the ideas that had inspired him. By August 1919 he was on his way to finding the "twelve-tone law,"

> the most basic law of music and melody, the law of (noiseless and unobstructed) movement, the "pure Melos," the one real and true "Law of Music" against which every music on earth, the past, the present and the future, can be measured.[39]

In an article in *Musikblätter des Anbruch*, which appeared in 1924 when the whole question of who invented the twelve-tone system was at its most contentious, Hauer gave a detailed account of what he had done during the summer of 1919:

> In August of 1919 I arrived at the idea of examining my works, which had earned so much opprobrium, with a view to finding the empirical, practical law of their being. Up till that tune I had operated more out of instinct than anything else, without the slightest external orientation, following only my own inspiration. As a result, the presentation and formation of my ideas proceeded in a painfully slow fashion, not to mention the fact that my contemporaries, so enmired in outmoded forms and formulae, would often accuse me of "mistakes" in my compositions. I was at that point determined to change horses with the hope of discovering certain rules of thumb for composing. . . . After much back and forth, I came to what seemed to me the simple formulation. I counted the various notes of the individual building blocks and discovered that there were always more than the seven notes which made up the major or minor scale, mostly nine, ten, eleven, or even all twelve notes in the enclosed fifth and quarter cycles without any modulation whatsoever. When I looked at the works of Schönberg and Webern, I found the same results.[40]

Hauer states emphatically that he began the whole attempt to discover the universal law of music empirically, but he seems to have smoothed over the irregularities he found by recourse to the mystical properties he felt were inherent in the number twelve. Hauer was anything but modest about his accomplishment, and, as the foregoing passage indicates, he saw the twelve-tone systems as part of a mystical revelation that encompassed the music of the spheres and the mystical numerology in the Book of Revelation. Hauer was fond of citing the passage from the Apocalypse in which the heavenly city of Jerusalem is described as having twelve gates with twelve angels sitting over them. Vogel speculates that, given his garrulous nature ("*Geschwätzig wie er war*"), Hauer could not have kept so momentous a discovery to himself. Since he was still in contact with Schönberg's circle and had been in contact with Schönberg since 1913, trying to achieve some sort of collaboration on twelve-tone composition, it seems unlikely that Schönberg would not have heard about Hauer's newly discovered "Law of Music."

The chain of events speaks for itself. In March 1920, after virtually a three-year hiatus, Schönberg began writing music again, this time ten bars of a twelve-tone Passacaglia for Orchestra. According to Vogel, Schönberg broke off after ten bars because "Hauer and his people would have immediately found out that Schönberg had become a disciple of Hauer's."[41] In 1923, Schönberg sent his opus 23 and 24, not to his usual publisher, the Universal Verlag in Vienna, but rather to Hansen in Copenhagen in order to forestall letting it be known that he had switched over to the twelve- tone system. On December 1, 1923, Schönberg wrote Hauer a letter in which he informed him,

> Approximately one and a half to two years ago. I realized by reading one of your articles that you were looking in similar fashion for the same thing that I was looking for. After dealing with the painful feeling that someone else was grappling with the same problems which I had been involved in for going on fifteen years now, that this endangered my reputation for originality, something which could force me to renounce the presentation of my ideas, if I don't want to he considered a plagiarizer—a painful feeling, you must admit—after I thought this over and recognized wherein we differ, and as a result was able to prove the independent character of my own ideas. I came up with the following suggestion: We should write a book together.... [42]

When the circumlocutions were over and done with, Schönberg came up with the formula that "we are looking perhaps for the same thing and have in all probability found something related." [43] Vogel claims that the letter was written long before with an eye for publication later. According to the official version, the one passed on to posterity by Stuckenschmidt, members of the *Verein für musikalische Privataufführungen* assembled at Schönberg's house in Modeling and listened as he announced that he had "made a discovery which will ensure the supremacy of German music for the next hundred years." What he meant was the method of composition with twelve-tone technique. Stuckenschmidt even back-dates the meeting to 1921.[44]

Thus began a battle over the authorship of the twelve-tone system, a battle that Hauer quickly lost. Hauer is the subject of at least two novels. He is the main character in Otto Stössl's *roman à clef*, *Sonnenmelodie*, and he appears as Matthias Fischbock in Franz Werfel's *Verdi*. In neither is Hauer portrayed as particularly adept socially. In fact, during his stint in the Austrian army during the First World War, he was taken to be insane. In his memoirs, the Viennese musicologist Egon Wellesz described how one day a soldier in a dirty uniform showed up at his house with a note from the military authorities, who wanted to know Wellesz' opinion as to whether Hauer, the man in the dirty uniform, was really a musician as he claimed or just insane. Wellesz, even after convincing himself that the man was indeed musically literate, had to concede that in his speech and mannerisms, Hauer did give the impression of being odd.

Once Schönberg laid claim to authorship of the twelve-tone system, Hauer found himself frozen out of his circle. Hauer complained, "When the critics realized that Schönberg (in his *Serenade*) had lifted my twelve-tone technique, they became spiteful and malicious and refused to grant me my rights as originator."[45] One of the malicious critics was Theodor Wiesengrund Adorno, who was later to become one of the significant promoters of the Schönberg school after World War II through his influence on Thomas Mann and the composition of *Doktor*

Faustus. Adorno spoke disparagingly of "the other attempt which bears the name of twelve-tone composition alongside Schönberg's and with which it is sometimes confused and which sometimes claims priority."[46]

Schönberg, like Freud and Gropius, was more of a political organizer than he was a thinker. Given the work he had done with the Viennese club for musical private performances and with his students Webern and Berg, it was easy to see who was going to win out. The socially inept Hauer was quickly marginalized as the author of the twelve-tone system. If Haimo's book is any indication, it is possible to mention the twelve-tone system as the possession of Schönberg alone. However, as Vogel indicates, the evidence points to Hauer as its creator.

If we look to Hauer's life, we find many similarities with what Schönberg was experiencing at the time. Common to both, there is, first of all, the early experience with *Tristan und Isolde*. In *Sonnenmelodie*, a young Johann Körrer, the protagonist and stand-in for Hauer, listens to those a few years older than himself talk of Wagner as a "god" and whistle the various Wagnerian leitmotifs. Virtually everyone the young Körrer/Hauer meets is "driven by a common but enormous lust of undiminished enthusiasm over [Wagner's] work":

> The musicians found in Wagner a meta-music, the Germans, their many singing and misty tribal gods, the Catholics, their incense and their redemptive magic, and the Jews found the supernaturally penetrating sensuality of the Orient.[47]

Körrer/Hauer, on the other hand, finds in Wagner, specifically *Tristan und Isolde*, "something mighty and knowing but also something deeply confused":

> A new life calls for the first time to an unwary youth, who blushes with shame because in some way he had just eaten from the forbidden fruit of paradise. It's not that the talk was simply about love and the power of its magic and that the sounds of this possession and of this confused struggle repeated themselves so tumultuously.... It was rather this Love and spell that made people both mad and perspicacious at the same time that lay beneath the music, which evoked it and echoed it.[48]

Körrer/Hauer's musical awakening coincides with his sexual awakening, and as the novel progresses, it becomes clear that Hauer does not like what he hears. He is deeply offended by what he perceives as the sensuality of the huge Wagnerian orchestra of the time. After his marriage, he is just as offended by the sensuality or, more precisely, the corporeality of the people he comes in contact with, including his wife. When he learns that his wife is expecting a child, she becomes as a result "doubly alien" to him. "What an unbelievably violent act of life," he muses, thinking about the propagation of the human race through sexual intercourse, "to bring two people together so that the race continues and then to put them apart again just so another being comes into existence with its own rights and will and with its own need as well."[49]

Körrer/Hauer's crisis comes in mid-novel, when he is playing cello in a string quartet with a number of prominent citizens from Wiener Neustadt, Hauer's home town. In the middle of the quartet, "disgust crept over all of his limbs."[50] Instead of encountering the spiritual in music, all Körrer/Hauer can hear is "longing or lust for love, or craving."[51] The tonal instruments themselves remind him of human bodies, their sounding boards resemble stomachs, and all Hauer can think of as he is playing the cello is: "my stomach is growling."[52] Finally, Hauer can take it no more. This music is nothing more than "lewd thoughts" ("*Unzucht mit Gedanken*").[53] He breaks off in mid-concert, excuses himself from the governor's company, and goes home. It is the beginning of his downfall, but also the beginning of his discovery of the twelve-tone system. Hauer gradually withdraws from the world, sitting alone in his room with a piano, not a sensuous tonal instrument, playing one note after another, over and over again. At one point, he listens to the buzzing of a fly in the room and muses that its motion and sound are "more important to him than a human being, more important than he is to himself."[54] When his wife announces that they are going to have a baby, Hauer withdraws within himself even more, "appalled at a future full of his child's crying and the smell of dirty diapers."[55]

When Körrer/Hauer finally gets to give a concert featuring his new twelve-tone music to the home-town crowd in Wiener Neustadt, the evening is a disaster. The musicians haven't the faintest idea how to play their instruments; the audience walks out in disgust; his reputation is ruined. Hauer, however, almost oblivious to his career going up in smoke, dwells on the gross corporeality of his audience: "girls longing for a husband, and people in general who wallowed in the nether world of their own bodily organs and needs."[56]

According to the Austrian writer and psychologist Ferdinand Ebner, who knew Hauer from childhood, Hauer was psychologically disturbed. "Erotic longing," Ebner claimed in his memoirs, was completely alien to Hauer's make-up. When Ebner psychoanalyzed a water dream Hauer had brought to him, Ebner was able to trace the problem to Hauer's marriage.[57] Ebner also testified that he noticed a marked improvement in Hauer's disposition when the latter, who was a devout Catholic, went to confession.

Thus, at the heart of both Hauer's system and Schönberg's appropriation of it, as well as of Schönberg's turning away from tonality in 1908, we find personal and marital problems. Schönberg appropriated the chromatic scale in *Verklärte Nacht* as a way of taking the sexual liberation he found in *Tristan und Isolde* and Dehmel's poem one step further, but ended up getting burned when his wife ran off with Richard Gerstl. On the rebound, he turned away from tonality but could find no musical organizing principle to replace it. As a result, he found himself running out of things to say by 1917. Hauer was similarly affected by the mammoth sensuality of *Tristan und Isolde*, but he, unlike Schönberg, never espoused the cause of free love. Instead he seems to have been put off by Wagnerian sensuality, to the point where he sought out a music from which all sensuality of this sort had been banned. His *Nomos* symphonies were pure music of the spheres. In this "cosmic music" one detects a perhaps psychologically unbalanced reaction to the musical sensuality of the times, as well as perhaps neurotic reaction to his own introduction to sexuality and the impending birth of his child. Interestingly enough, both Hauer and Schönberg saw the essentially rigid and unmusical twelve-tone system as the antidote to the hypersensuous Wagnerian orchestra, which had become the musical norm at the time. The musical pendulum, it seemed, was determined to swing from one extreme to the other. From the overly sensual music of *Tristan*, we move to the overly intellectual *Nomos* of Hauer and Schönberg. The same transformation had occurred in other spheres as well. The sensuality of the Weimar Republic was replaced by the totalitarianism of the Third Reich. Using the twelve-tone system as an antidote to fight the extravagant emotions evoked by Wagner was an apt symbol of the way that fascism followed license in Germany and the Soviet Union as well. Stalin followed the decadence of the Lenin years. If there is an inner logic connecting *The Magic Flute*, *Tristan und Isolde*, *Verklärte Nacht*, and *Moses und Aron*, it is the trajectory of disgust that follows liberation from the moral law. The defeat of the Queen of the Night—the Catholic Church in Masonic parlance—led to a darkness in *Tristan*, which was supposedly transformed from within through Dehmel's ideology of free love in *Verklärte Nacht*, but which in fact led to the totalitarian imposition of the law we find in *Moses und Aron*.

Interestingly, both Hauer and Schönberg saw the twelve-tone system as the *pis aller* that was to rescue music from its hypersensual captivity. Both saw the twelve-tone system as the "*Nomos*," the law, the iron-clad alternative to a world dissolving into sensual chaos. Like most of his contemporaries, Hauer had to confront Richard Wagner as the primary musical presence of his age. Unlike most of his contemporaries, who found in *Tristan und Isolde* an erotic stimulus, Hauer was appalled at the musical world being proposed. Listening to *Tristan*, Körrer/Hauer is reminded of "a thousand pictures in a thousand dark rooms that gleamed boldly like molten metal or the sheen on synthetic tar."[58] The man who wrote this music was "a master of all guilt, someone who knows, someone who is deeply implicated, someone incapable of redemption."[59] But, Körrer/Hauer wondered, listening to *Tristan*, "Was this really music?"

> Was this movement so exhausted after a few motifs and yet at the same time turned round and round on all sides with the various noises emanating from the tortured bodies of the various instruments and then taken up by the human voice, these obliterated and yet reassembled melodies in the midst of an increasingly intoxicating flood of sounds, which sought the mortification of a final resolution to calm the nerves which were being tortured beyond endurance? Was this really music? Noise, sound, tormenting confusion, pictures, words were all less than pure peaceful thought. The chaos of a ruined reality, not the idea and image, but rather the raw doing and being and suffering itself. The individual notes no longer spoke their own unconfused language but instead every possible sound....[60]

Arnold Schönberg

Standing at the back of the concert hall with his *Tristan* score open in front of him, Körrer/Hauer hears in Wagner's music "the fate of an entire age revealed in the one man and his work."[61] Looking at the score with his tired eyes, the music could only appear to him as an "evil temptation."

> When after many years and sorrows even these luxurious colors had paled and the artificial stimulation they achieved had become faded and spoiled and dated, then a mature person would recognize that this music damned an entire age to its own ineluctable hell. . . . This insurmountable evil of human confusion peered out of shining, feverish eyes. The restlessness of bad conscience and guilt-ridden anxiety spoke forth in their gestures and waved to them from hypersensual pictures and forms.[62]

It reminds Körrer/Hauer of "the wandering Jew forced to travel from one tortured melody to another with an unquenchable yearning for Christ. . . . driven with a terrible craving for love and redemption."[63] When the concert is finally over and the audience breaks into applause, Johann/Josef "crept confusedly into the cool night, as if having suffered a beating over his entire body, like a malefactor reacting to an Epiphany of secret guilt."[64] It was obvious that Hauer would now have to confront the diabolical foolishness and shamelessness of Vienna alone, since he alone understood how sensual and corrupt the modern orchestra had become.

Few people would claim that Josef Hauer was a balanced person. Yet part of his critique of the music at the time is valid. *Tristan* was hypersensual. As music it missed the mark by being excessively emotional. There is something unsatisfactory about it because the emotions are incited to the point where they can no longer be ordered in some musical resolution. It was the perfect analogue to the sexual excitement of the times; in fact, it probably did more than anything else to bring about this mood of yearning for sexual liberation. However, even granting all that, one notices a disturbing tendency in Hauer to throw out the baby with the bath. We see it in his description of the "tortured bodies" of the musical instrument. Hauer generalized from his time too broadly. Wagner was not only the man of his age; he was also the representative of the music of the West and of the tonal system as well. In reacting to Wagner, Hauer overreacted. Ebner recounts a conversation with Hauer in which the latter demanded "literally that I abandon this music, and especially Beethoven—whom he hated as much as he hated Richard Wagner—and that I honor his music as the only spiritual value."[65]

Hauer was very clear on this point. It was only with the advent of his twelve-tone system, based on half-tones that chastely abstained from any sort of sexual attraction to each other, that "music could begin to become art and liberate itself from coarse natural desires, and from the coarse imitation of nature."[66] For Hauer, the half-tone scale was nothing less than "the highest stage of spirituality in music."[67] Essential to this "spirituality" is the fact that individual notes in the twelve-tone scale maintain an equal distance from each other on the scale. Each half-tone remains independent of every other note; they hang freely suspended in mid-air, so to speak; they are free of any tonal connection. As a result, it is only through the twelve-tone system that the "sweet swamp of sound" that the modern orchestra has become can be purged of its noise and sensuality. In the twelve-tone system, the individual notes, according to Hauer, lead a "spiritual, higher life rather than a sensual one."[68]

Hauer's reaction to music is analogous to his reaction to sex. In order to be spiritual, Hauer's notes have to be asexual. They live like celibate monks in their half-interval cells, showing no attraction to each other. Hauer could have with justification rejected *Tristan* as hypersensual, but he goes beyond that by rejecting the whole diatonic scale as too "sexy". The attraction of one note to another sets up a longing for a tonal center, which is in Hauer's view the antithesis of spirituality. It is in many ways a deeply platonic view, in which the soul stands in opposition to the body. According to this view, propagated by many Gnostic cults throughout history, and by the Cathars in medieval Europe, sex is bad per se because it is of the body. In Hauer's view of things, corporeality is a threat to spirituality. The body with its urges, sexual and otherwise, is the antithesis of the spiritual, which is construed in essentially platonic/angelic tents. It is no wonder, then, that Hauer would describe his music as the music of the spheres. At the heart of Hauer's system, arising perhaps from the ascendency of Wagnerian sensuality at the time, we find a sweeping condemnation of all sexual activity as somehow demeaning and animalistic, just as Hauer confuses lust with marriage in his recoil from human sexuality, he also confuses *Tristan* with the diatonic system, which marked the departure from the tonal system. In his zeal to purify the music of his time of its excessive attachment to passion, Hauer throws out the baby with the bath. The tonal system is entirely too sexy for him, as are all nontempered instruments, such as the cello. Hauer prefers instead "spiritual" (that is, tempered) instruments, such as the piano, the organ, the chromatic harmonica, and the celesta. In his twelve-tone system, Hauer is proposing the exact opposite of what Wagner proposed in "Music and Drama." There *Tristan* found its justification in a system where the individual notes "climbed the barriers of the patriarchal family, to knit alliances with other families."

> The Key of a melody is that which presents to Feeling its various included tones in their earliest bond of kinship. The incitement to widen this narrower bond to a richer, more extended one, is derived from the Poetic Aim, insofar as that has already condensed itself in the speaking-verse to a moment-of-feeling; while this extension is governed by the particular expressional character of single chief-tones, which have themselves, in turn, been prompted by the verse. These chief-tones are, in a sense, the adolescent members of the family, who yearn to leave its wonted surrounding for an unhindered independence: this independence, however, they do not gain as egoists but through encounter with another being, a being that lies outside the family. The maiden attains her independence, her stepping beyond the family, only through love of the youth who, himself the scion of

another family, attracts her over to him. Thus the tone which quits the circle of the Key is a tone already prompted and attracted by that other key, and into the latter must it therefore pour itself according to the necessary law of Love.[69]

If Wagner erred by excess in discussing the musical/sexual connection, Hauer erred by defect. If Wagner's sexual analogue for what goes on in music is adultery, Hauer's is a cenobitic celibacy of the sort practiced by fanatical Cathar heretics. Wagner's notes are amorous and adulterous, scorning social convention and the social order, bopping over tonal walls to achieve their desires. Whereas Wagner's notes try to seduce notes belonging to another key, in such the same way that Wagner tried to seduce his patrons' wives, Hauer's notes have no natural sexual attraction to each other at all. Hauer's notes are Gnostic: they are all celibate in a weird and neurotic way. (The connection between Wagner's and Hauer's antithetical use of the twelve-tone scale—one seeing it as musical lust and the other seeing it as the renunciation of all sexuality—makes for fascinating comparisons with Albigensianism in other ways as well. The Albigensians were sterile, because they renounced procreation, but not chaste, and in many instances they were perverse. Rev. Eduard Perrone claims that the "purity" of the "detached" notes in the twelve-tone system permits and, in fact, necessitates the promiscuous vertical "coupling" of any tones with any others, even those which result in unnatural discord.) According to Hauer, the erotic had to be banned from music completely, not just conformed to reason, before inspiration was possible.[70]

Interestingly enough, both of these sexually disturbed musical systems are dependent on the twelve-tones of the chromatic scale. If the Wagnerian system is musical adultery, and Hauer's system, musical Albigensianism, then the diatonic scale corresponds to matrimony. In order to corrupt music with their ideologies, both Wagner and Hauer/Schönberg had to dispense with nature, which in this instance corresponds to both matrimony and the diatonic scale. Just as matrimony, which was raised to the status of a sacrament by Christianity, is the natural ordering of sexual desire so that it can flow productively into offspring, the care of offspring, and the continuation of society, so the diatonic scale is an ordering of sound that is both reasonable and dynamic. It does not crush emotion beneath an absolutely iron-clad law, as the twelve-tone system does, nor does it liberate it to the point of irrational sensuality, as happens in Wagner's chromaticism. The diatonic scale with its irregularly spaced half-intervals has a beginning, a middle, and an end. It is intrinsically dramatic, which means it strikes a balance between human emotion, which it does not crush, and human reason, which orders that emotion, and thereby creates a cathartic effect in the listener. In the diatonic scale, emotions gets aroused and resolved, as is evident in virtually every piece of tonal music. This ever-increasingly sophisticated development of tension and resolution lies at the heart of Western music as its crowning achievement. In twelve-tone music we have order without emotion; in Wagner's *Tristan und Isolde*, we have something perilously close to emotion without order. In order to have either extreme—music that errs by either excess or defect of emotion—modern composers have to dispense with the diatonic scale. To the extent that they dispense with it completely, they destroy what music is. Diatonic morality is the sexual/musical mean between these two extremes. It is a "natural" order and, so, incapable of being destroyed. Since the human will is free, we can ignore that order and create others that ignore it, but to that extent we will stop doing music. The price one pays for ignoring nature is the abolition of all order and, as both the music and the polities of the twentieth century have shown, self-annihilation as well.

Which leads us again to the fascinating connection between music and the social order. Wagner's deeply deranged music was born out of his contact with Bakunin and flirtation with the revolution in Dresden in 1849. Shakespeare was more correct than he knew. As in music so in politics, sexual license, when socially accepted on a wide scale, necessitates totalitarian reaction to reestablish at least the image of social order. In Germany, Weimar preceded the Third Reich. In England, Bloomsbury and the "higher sodomy'" (to use Lytton Strachey's term) practiced by the Cambridge Apostles led to the Cambridge traitors, Maclean, Burgess, and Blunt. Stephen Spender, in *The God That Failed*, described the prime attraction of totalitarian communism as "the Soviet Conscience machine." The guilt aroused by the sexual liberation of the twenties was harnessed by the sense of moral purpose that flowed from involvement in the rigors of communism.

The same thing happened in Russia in the 1920s. The free-love bohemia that was established in Russia under Lenin disappeared with his death and was replaced with the oriental despotism that flowed from Stalin's increasingly totalitarian reading of Marx and Engels. Max Eastman, the libertine editor of the American socialist magazine *The Masses*, arrived in Russia on the fifth anniversary of the Bolshevik revolution in time to attend the fourth congress of the Third International. What he found there was the fulfillment of the deepest desires of socialist throughout the ages, a world in which the prohibition against adultery had been revoked. He wrote in his memoirs:

> No ghost of the Seventh Commandment [that is, Thou shalt not commit adultery, in the Jewish interpretation], no wraith of a marriage vow, not even, I think, the memory of a talk about fidelity between Nina [a Russian woman he picked up in the Crimea] and her husband, haunted the sky-covered scenes of our embraces. The October revolution, whatever it was going to do for the proletariat, had already done some liberating for the cultured classes. It had cut down a number of artificial barriers between the beautiful and the good—one of them the habit of putting on clothes to go swimming.[71]

The workers of the world might have had nothing to lose but their chains, but the intellectuals who supported the communist revolution were looking forward to losing their bathing suits. According to Eastman, not wearing a bathing suit "in the new land of freedom... became symbolic of a kind of candid realism, a living in the truth, that I thought the abolition of class status might bring into the whole world."[72] By the time Stalin came to Power, Eastman was on his way to renouncing communism. He could see that what Stalin was proposing was the antithesis of what the Western intellectuals like himself had sought when he went to the Soviet Union in the twenties, but he was unable to see how what Stalin proposed was the culmination of what he had sought. Once the moral law, what Lincoln Steffens called "old exploded ideas like right and wrong," is abolished in the name of sexual liberation, it cannot be resuscitated on demand to ensure the guarantees that civilized people had taken for granted, legal niceties like *habeas corpus*, and so on.

As in politics, so in music. As in morality, so in tonality. The abolition of the natural law leads to tyranny. Just as inexorably as free love leads to the Gulag, so *Tristan* led to the musical totalitarianism that was the twelve-tone system. Libertinism and fascism are two sides of the same coin, and in cultural terms that coin was known as modernity. Rage against the natural order led to a pendulum swinging from sexual liberation to totalitarianism and back again. *Tristan* led to the Third Reich as its cure. The Dionysiac sixties led to the politically correct campuses of our day. Just as the movement from license to totalitarianism, which we see in the development of the twelve-tone system is the movement of sexual disgust, so the opposite movement is sexually conditioned as well. The aridity which the twelve-tone system brought to classical music found its core when the educated classes turned to Dionysiac jazz. This happened, as we have already indicated, in the twenties, in such people as Nancy Cunard and Carl Van Vechten. It happened again in the sixties. With the triumph of the Schönbergian modernism in people like Stockhausen and Cage, emotion took its musical revenge by going African once again. Rock 'n' roll was the protest of a generation that could find no emotional sustenance in the classical tradition that Schönberg and his followers had succeeded in destroying. By the 1960s, the victory over tonality was all but complete in sophisticated circles—but nature, as Aesop knew in describing the woman who once was a cat, will opt out. Offered the choice between a musical straitjacket (the beautifully appropriate title of Alois Melichar's book on twelve-tone music, *Musik in der Zwangsjacke*) and Muddy Waters, Brian Jones, the founder of the English pop group the Rolling Stones in the early sixties, knew which alternative was more musically compelling. The choice eventually killed him, as it did many of his generation; however, nature always did have a way of forcing the issue—But we get ahead of ourselves.

Schönberg was not Hauer. Schönberg did not invent the twelve-tone system; Hauer did. But Schönberg saw something in Hauer's system that satisfied some deep need of his own—so deep, in fact, that he was willing to risk his reputation with the blot of plagiarism to appropriate it. Schönberg, like Hauer, was having marital difficulties. Unlike Hauer, who was appalled by Wagnerian sensuality from the first time he heard it, Schönberg was a good bohemian, which meant espousing *Tristan* and Dehmelian free love and all the other occult "isms" circulating in Vienna at the time. That's how Schönberg ended up hoist with his own petard. The liberation promised by Richard Dehmel, by liberal Christianity and Bohemia, turned out to be a lie, and Schönberg was severely wounded by the betrayal his wife inflicted on him. It was a wound that never healed. Schönberg's Second Quartet, according to his student Alban Berg, was an "echo of a crisis in personal life whose sorrow, hardly ever mastered, brought to Schönberg's work its full creative weight." [73]

Atonality was Schönberg's revenge on the music of the West. But it was not a cure for the problem Schönberg now faced. He repudiated the sensuality of *Tristan* and the free love of Dehmel, but now he was faced with a world torn apart by emotional chaos and irrational forces. What was the antidote to that? Christianity? That had already been tried and found wanting. From Schönberg's imperfect point of view, it was Christian love (bohemian free love was its derivative) that had burned Schönberg in the first place. Faced with a world threatening to dissolve into the chaos that resulted from the rebirth of Dionysian fertility cults, Schönberg drew on his Jewish heritage and chose the law. He appropriated Hauer's *Nomos*. There was to be nothing but unresolved dissonance, now that he had been betrayed not only by his own wife but by bohemia and Christianity as well. Schönberg was in many ways a very unattractive personality. He could hate with the best of them. He could hold a grudge to his grave. He was morbidly sensitive to affront. What he saw in Hauer's system was a way to control chaos. After his wife's infidelity, Schönberg became not only a deeply suspicious man: he became a deeply superstitious one as well. The twelve-tone system was a neurotic numerological attempt to assert control over a chaotic world. Peyser calls Schönberg a deeply religious man; however, upon closer analysis, much of what she terms religious sentiment was indistinguishable from superstition of the most arrant sort:

> Before 1912, Schönberg's ritualistic behavior was not apparent. The names of his first two children, Gertrude and George, appear to have been chosen on an arbitrary basis. Several decades later, after Schönberg married a second time, he chose Ronald as the name of his first son by this marriage and Roland as the name of the second, both anagrams of his first name. Upon discovering adverse numerological implications in the name Roland, he changed the child's name to Lawrence Adam, which contains all the letters of Arnold except the o.[74]

In addition to his penchant for anagrammatic names for his children, Schönberg was obsessed with numerological superstitions. He was obsessed with the number thirteen, which he associated with death. So obsessed, in fact, that he dropped one letter off Aaron's name in his magnum opus *Moses und Aron* (sic) so that the total number of letters would not equal thirteen. In preparation for his sixty-fifth birthday (5 x 13), Schönberg asked a friend and fellow composer Dane Rudhyar to prepare his horoscope. On Friday 13, 1951, Schönberg was so frightened at the numerological confluences of this date that he refused to get out of bed. When shortly before midnight his wife attempted to reassure him that everything was going to be all right, Schönberg looked up at her and died. Peyser connects Schönberg's "mystical beliefs," that is, his numerological superstitions, with psychological problems but draws no conclusions about his attraction to the twelve-tone system from her otherwise acute analysis. "One is struck," she writes,

> with what psychiatry would consider to be obsessional behavior, a carefully ordered system that influences one's every thought and action. Psychiatrists generally attribute such behavior to the belief that one has the power to control events. Drawn to a belief in this kind of magic Schönberg attempted to control his powerful inner drives as well as what happened during the course of his life and possibly even the moment of his death.[75]

The twelve-tone system was just such a neurotic attempt to control musical reality. Faced with what he perceived as the failure of religion, Schönberg sought solace in occult numerology. Schönberg's connection with the *Blaue Reiter*, which exhibited his paintings, has already been mentioned. The *Blaue Reiter* (and especially Kandinsky) was one of the prime promoters of the occult in art. A recent exhibition "On the Spiritual in Art" documents this connection effectively. James Webb links Kandinsky to Rudolf Steiner, an early promoter of Nietzsche and theosophy, and claims that the "coincidence of art and occultism was. . . a definite part of the idealistic Underground, which drew its sustenance from the same revolt against reason as had inspired the Symbolists."[76] Kandinsky's book *On the Spiritual in Art* was influenced by Steiner's theosophy and influenced Schönberg's *Harmonielehre*, which was published around the same time. Peyser notes some of the many similarities.

> Schönberg and Kandinsky followed remarkably similar paths in their moves away from representation to abstraction and from the single focuses of perspective and tonality in painting and music to the subsequent afocal attributes of both. Both artists had received the initial impulses in these directions as early as the last years of the nineteenth century, and neither one achieved the full realization of his purpose until many years later. . . . As Kandinsky formulated the principles of an abstract style for the first time in 1910 in his treatise *On the Spiritual in Art*, so Schönberg first set down the theory of the emancipation of the dissonance in his *Theory of Harmony* (*Harmonielehre*) published in 1911.[77]

Hauer saw his music as a struggle between the musical and the mathematical within him. He saw his theory as the revelation of the deepest secrets of the universe as well. However, there is nothing really mathematical in the twelve-tone system at all. There is, on the other hand, the sort of thing that would appeal to the numerologically superstitions, which is exactly what Schönberg was. Lichtenfeld finds it striking "that especially among the adepts of the twelve-tone technique one finds a definite preference for numerological speculation, for astrological convergences and an inexhaustible affinity for discovering parallel twelve orders in other cultures and in other cultural disciplines."[78] Hauer saw his system as the secret law of the universe, and Schönberg appropriated his cosmic music as a way of asserting numerological mastery over the chaos he found around him.

The convergence of all these forces is nowhere more apparent than in Schönberg's *Moses und Aron*. Virtually everyone who comments on it sees it as a personal allegory portraying Schönberg as a Mosaic lawgiver. Peyser refers to Schönberg as "a profoundly religious man" and sees *Moses und Aron* as "a musical translation of an idea which, in its origin, was the Word of God." [79] The evidence in the libretto, however, indicates something else again. When Moses refers to the law, he describes it as "*meinen Gedanken*," that is, my thought. When Aron pleads with Moses to make his message more accessible to the emotional Israelites—"*ein Volk knann nur fühlen*," "Kein Volk kann glauben, was es nicht fühlt"—Moses insists not on the immutability of God's law, but rather on the importance of his own ideas, "I love my thought and live for it." If Schönberg is referring to the twelve-tone system here and the world's inability to comprehend it, then the testimony of Moses is doubly suspicious. Not only is the law of God not the thought of Moses, the twelve-tone system was not the thought of Schönberg either, although he claimed that it was. On both counts, Moses/Schönberg doth protest too much.

The significance of the twelve-tone "law" becomes apparent, however, when Moses/Schönberg comes down from the mountain and confronts the bacchanal surrounding the golden calf. Toward the end of his life, Schönberg expressed doubts that *Moses und Aron* would ever be performed, and the main reason for those doubts was the bacchanal scene, which culminates in the murder of "four naked virgins." According to the stage directions: "The priests embrace and kiss the maidens. Behind each pair, a girl stands holding aloft a butcher's knife and a jug for catching the blood." As the seventy elders shout "Blood sacrifice!" the priests take the knives and "seize the virgins' throats and thrust the knives into their hearts. The girls catch the blood in receptacles. The priests pour it forth on the altar."

After that, what Schönberg terms an "Erotic Orgy" takes place on the stage: "A naked youth runs forward to a girl, tears the clothes from her body, lifts her high and runs with her to the altar." "In your godly image," the youth says addressing the golden calf, "we shall let our passions live." Then, again according to the stage instructions, we are told that "many men follow this example, throw their clothes aside, strip women and bear them off the same way, toward the background, pausing at the altar," where they shout, "Holy is fertility! Holy is desire!"

What Schönberg/Moses discovered when he came down from the mountain was the Wagnerian-inspired Dionysian bacchanal that Nietzsche had proposed as the prime religious rite of the new age. A younger Schönberg might have been more amenable to its charms, but Schönberg/Moses had been deeply wounded by his wife's betrayal. Now, instead of naively going along with Dehmel's ideas of sexual liberation, Schönberg is possessed with an overwhelming desire to reimpose order on a musical/sexual cosmos gone mad with lust and unrestrained emotion. Schönberg/Moses now has the law, the *Nomos* he had appropriated from Hauer, which he refers to as "my thoughts." Moses/Schönberg's deepest wish is not to proclaim the law of God, which in musical terms would have been analogous to the diatonic scale and, therefore, not "his" idea. His deepest wish is rather to impose his "idea" on reality in a purely arbitrary and violent way. Just as Hauer's use of the twelve-tone system bespeaks a kind of sexual squeamishness, Schönberg's bespeaks revenge on what Gerstl and his wife did to him. Schönberg's solution is to kill the dancing girls, kill harmony, reimpose the law, which is Moses/Schönberg's "thought." Like Shylock, Schönberg can say, "I crave the law." Like Shylock, Schönberg applies the law in a maximally dissonant way, as musical revenge on the Christian system, which betrayed him with false promises of love. Schönberg's "law" is nothing more than a superstitious desire to impose order on chaos. It is not an attempt to discover an order in nature, because the experience of the past half-century had convinced the moderns that there was no order in nature. The only order in the universe is the one we impose. In this sense, *Moses und Aron* is not a religious work at all; it is a profoundly occult work. It is the work of a man who spent his entire life trying to impose his will on musical reality, no matter how grotesque the consequences, no matter how much music suffered in the process. In a letter to Paul Stefan, who wanted at one point to be his biographer, Schönberg gave his opinions of criticism. "Criticism," Schönberg opined,

> is extremely obnoxious to me and I have nothing but contempt for anyone who criticizes in the least anything that I have produced. That . . . is my pedigree, that I believe in what I do and only do what I believe, and woe to the man who dares to lay a finger on my beliefs. I consider this man an enemy that is to be hunted down without mercy.[80]

So much for Schönberg's "religious" beliefs! No more Mr. Nice Guy. In reaction to the hurt he sustained at the hands of Wagnerian sensuality as a young married man, Schönberg turned to musical Stalinism as a way of reasserting control over a musical universe gone mad. Schönberg the bohemian had become Schönberg the despot.

The composition of *Moses und Aron* corresponded with Schönberg's renunciation of Christianity and reconversion to Judaism. It also corresponded, in a way, with the beginning of the Third Reich, the rise of the totalitarian state in Germany. Part of the reason for Schönberg's reconversion to Judaism was his hope to find wealthy Jewish backers who would support him in his composing. That hope never really materialized. But there seem to have been deeper reasons as well. Schönberg did not take hurt well. He was, according to Berg, deeply hurt by his wife's betrayal. Although he took her back, there seems to have been no reconciliation. Peyser mentions that Mathilde von Zemlinsky Schönberg died alone in 1923, the same year that Schonberg appropriated the twelve-tone system. Ten years later, in May 1933, Schönberg was dismissed from the Prussian State Academy as part of the Nazi program of purging Jewish influences from the German state. Schönberg had reasserted his Jewishness in 1923, the crucial year when his wife had died and he had claimed authorship of the twelve-tone system. "Do you think someone like myself lets himself he rejected?" he asked Kandinsky.

Schönberg was in many ways a revenant of Shylock. He was a Jew who had been treated badly by Christians, a Jew who sought his revenge against what he saw as Christian society through the law. For Shylock it was the law of Venice, for Schönberg it was the twelve-tone system. "The Americans have the atom bomb," Hauer said in his typically blunt way, "we have twelve-tone music."[81] Hauer saw his system as some sort of purifying fire poured down on the decadent post-Wagnerian orchestra, purging it of all erotic impurities. Schönberg, who was not insensible to the toxic dissonance of twelve-tone music, saw it as an instrument of revenge against a society that rejected him. Schönberg's willingness to associate the twelve-tone system as the vehicle ensuring the ascendency of German music for the next 150 years could just as easily turn to revenge when that society turned against him. The first betrayal was domestic, when his wife left: the final betrayal was political, when the Nazis expelled him from the Prussian Academy. Between the two, Schönberg turned his back on his decadent European heritage:

> I have learned at last the lesson that has been forced upon me this year [1933] and I shall never forget it. It is that I am not a German, not a European, indeed, perhaps, scarcely a human being (at least, the Europeans prefer the worst of their race to me), but I am a Jew! I am content that it should be so! Today I no longer wish to be an exception. . . .[82]

Moses und Aron was Schönberg's revenge on the West. As we have already indicated, this work is not particularly religious. Moses is more interested in his own thought (*"Ich liebe meinen Gedanken und lebe für ihn!"*) than he is in God's law. His thought is, in effect, God's law. "You are bound to your idea," Aaron says. And Schönberg/Moses responds, " Yes, bound to my idea as these tablets set it forth." Moses brought God's law to the Jewish people; Schönberg brought his own recently appropriated twelve-tone system to his followers as a way of punishing them for worshiping the Wagnerian golden calf. The religious aura surrounding *Moses und Aron* is only tangentially Jewish. Its spirit is primarily a manifestation of an anti-European attitude, something we have become more familiar with of late. When Schönberg identified himself as a Jew, he showed an almost eager willingness to adopt Nazi categories and apply them to himself. He saw the Jew as Goebbels saw the Jew, which is to say, in primarily negative terms, as someone who was "not a German, not a European." The final straw was most certainly his expulsion from Nazi Germany. Immediately upon leaving Berlin in 1933, Schönberg went to Paris and at a synagogue there reconverted to Judaism. However, the seeds of his discontent had been planted earlier. In his *Harmonielehre*, written in 1911, while the betrayal of his wife was fresh in his mind, he described the diminished seventh chord, one of the key tonal elements in *Tristan und Isolde*, as "not really at home in any key, living on its own. Rather it has so to speak a right to live where it wants and yet it never settles down. It is a cosmopolitan or a hobo. I call this sort of chord a vagabond chord." [83] At another point in the same work, Schönberg characterized the diminished seventh, "Tristan" chords as

> homeless wraiths which travel back and forth between the keys, possessing an unbelievable ability to fit into any situation and yet lacking all independence, spies which publicize your weaknesses and use the occasion to foment unrest, turncoats, for whom the relinquishing of personality is its own end, troublemakers in every relationship, but above all highly amusing fellows.[84]

It is worth wondering whether Schönberg had Richard Gerstl in mind when he wrote this description of the hallmark of Wagnerian music or whether he perhaps had the whole Viennese bohemian scene in mind. It is hard not to hear Schönberg the disappointed Christian speaking here. Schönberg found that the culmination of this "Christian" culture was free love and that its necessary corollary was betrayal. He never got over the betrayal, which was both domestic and national. The recoil from it sent Schönberg back to his superstitious redaction of Judaism and back to the "law," in his instance the musical law of the twelve-tone system, which was his attempt to subdue the anarchy that *Tristan* and its chords, "*Kosmopolit*," "*Landstreicher*," "homeless. . . spies," "*Unruhestiftern*," but "highly amusing fellows, nonetheless," had called forth. The twelve-tone system was Schönberg's attempt to get the genie back into the lamp.

Moses und Aron was Schönberg's expression of disgust at the sensual license of the Wagnerian age, both musical and sexual. His solution was the return to an earlier age. It was, first of all, a return to Judaism, but also in a strange sort of way a return to the tradition of world harmony. After killing off the dancing girls in *Moses und Aron*, Schönberg attempted to reimpose the law, which in this case is a superstitious numerological parody of the Pythagorean classical view of world harmony. What the classical music tradition got instead was a pseudo-Mosaic musical totalitarianism; it made dissonance the norm in music and virtually guaranteed its destruction. Schönberg's music triumphed after his death in 1951, but it was a pyrrhic victory. By the time his music found access to the world's concert halls, the cultured world had turned its attention elsewhere for the expression of its aspirations. Schönberg/Hauer's terrible attempt to purge music of its sensuality had succeeded beyond their fondest hope, but patient Musica had expired on the operating table during the operation, and no one seems to have noticed.

Notes

1. Thomas Mann, *Doktor Faustus: Das Leben des deutschen Tonsetzers Adrian Leverkühn erzählt von einem Freunde*, in *Gesammelte Werke* (Frankfurt am Main: S. Fischer Verlag, 1980), p. 104.

2. James Webb, *The Occult Establishment* (LaSalle, Ill.: Open Court, 1976), p. 43.
3. Ronald Hayman, *Nietzsche: A Critical Life* (New York: Oxford University Press, 1980), p. 349.
4. Hayman, p. 348.
5. Hayman, p. 341.
6. Hayman, p. 334.
7. Hayman, p. 341.
8. Hayman, p. 341.
9. Thomas Mann, "Tristan," in *World Masterpieces Revised*, Maynard Mack, general editor, vol. 2, *Literature of Western Culture since the Renaissance* (New York: W. W. Norton & Co., 1965), p. 1421.
10. H. H. Stuckenschmidt, *Schönberg: His Life, World, and Work*, translated from the German by Humphrey Searle (New York: Schirmer Books, 1977). p. 40.
11. Stuckenschmidt, p.37.
12. Stuckenschmidt, p.37.
13. Martin Vogel, *Schönberg und die Folgen: Die Irrwege der Neuen Musik* (Bonn: Verlag für systematischen Musikwissenschaft, 1984), p. 192.
14. Vogel, p. 192.
15. Stuckenschmidt, p. 40.
16. Stuckenschmidt, p. 40.
17. "Das klingt ja, als ob man über die noch nasse Tristan-Partitur darüber gewischt hätte!" Vogel, p. 191.
18. Vogel, p. 189.
19. Vogel, pp. 45-46.
20. Joan Peyser, *The New Music: The Sense Behind the Sound* (New York: Delacorte Press, 1971), p. 10.
21. Peyser, p.9.
22. Peyser, pp. 9-10.
23. Stuckenschmidt, p. 102.
24. Stuckenschmidt, p. 31.
25. Vogel, p. 196.
26. Peyser, p. 23.
27. Vogel, p. 49.
28. Vogel, p. 49.
29. Vogel, p. 49.
30. Vogel, p. 196.
31. Vogel, p. 197.
32. Peyser, p. 56.
33. Ethan Haimo, *Schönberg's Serial Odyssey: The Evolution of His Twelve-Tone Method, 1914-1928* (Oxford: Clarendon Press, 1990), p. 6.
34. Haimo, p. 5.
35. Haimo, p. 1.

36. Walter Szmolyan, *Josef Matthias Hauer* (Wien: Verlag Elisabeth Lafite, 1965), p. 30.
37. Szmolyan, p. 32.
38. Szmolyan, p. 40.
39. Vogel, p. 73.
40. Vogel, pp. 73-74.
41. Vogel, p. 104.
42. Szmolyan, p. 45.
43. Szmolyan, p. 45.
44. Stuckenschmidt, p. 277.
45. Vogel, p. 117.
46. Vogel, p. 117.
47. Otto Stössl, *Sonnenmelodie: Eine Lebensgeschichte* (Berlin and Leipzig: Deutsche Verlags Anstalt, 1923), pp. 158-59, my translation.
48. Stössl, pp. 163-64.
49. Stössl, p. 412.
50. Stössl, p. 346.
51. Stössl, p. 345.
52. Stössl, p. 345.
53. Stössl, p. 346.
54. Stössl, p. 411.
55. Stössl, p. 414.
56. Stössl, p. 382.
57. Ferdinand Ebner, *Schriften* (Munich: Koesel Verlag, 1963-1965), vol. 2, p. 1062, my translation.
58. Stössl, p. 165.
59. Stössl, p. 165.
60. Stössl, pp. 165-66.
61. Stössl, p 167.
62. Stössl, p 167.
63. Stössl, p 167.
64. Stössl, p. 168.
65. Ebner, p. 1065.
66. Szmolyan, p. 21.
67. Szmolyan, p. 23.
68. Szmolyan, p. 23.
69. Ellis, p. 291.
70. "*Alles Schroffe, Gegensatzliche, Affektiose, die Stimmungen, das Sinnliche, Erotische, mussen ausgeschaltet sein, damit die Intuition moglicht ist.*" Vogel, p. 77.
71. Max Eastman, *Love and Revolution* (New York: Random House, 1964), p. 325.
72. Eastman, p. 325.

73. Peyser, p. 23.
74. Peyser, p. 10.
75. Peyser, p. 12.
76. Webb, p. 422.
77. Peyser, p. 27.
78. Vogel, p. 87.
79. Peyser, p. 8.
80. Vogel, p. 526.
81. Vogel, p 84.
82. Peyser, p. 52.
83. Vogel, p. 174.
84. Vogel, p. 174.

Chapter 4

Sympathy for the Devil
Theodor Adorno, Aleister Crowley, Mick Jagger

> Erotic politicians, that's what we are. We're interested in everything about revolt, disorder, and all activity that appears to have no meaning.
> —Jim Morrison
> *The Doors*

> I see horror. I see suffering. I see grief.
> —Euripides
> *The Bacchae*

During 1941, a Japanese submarine surfaced briefly off the coast of California, fired at an oil refinery, and just as quickly got away. The attack did virtually no damage, but it did unleash a mood of panic among the local inhabitants. Japanese-Americans were interred in camps; there was fear in the air of an imminent invasion. The fears, it turned out, were unfounded. California was slated for invasion, not by the Japanese, but by the Germans. Beginning with the Nazi seizure of power in 1933, a steady streams of German artists and intellectuals—many, but by no means all, of whom were Jewish—made their way to the land of unlimited possibility. Freud, like some of the other émigrés, was too old to make it farther than England, where he died by requesting that his doctor kill him. Some émigrés, including Walter Gropius and Paul Tillich, made it to the United States but got no further than the East Coast. But an unusually large number ended up in, of all places, Hollywood.

It is said that politics makes strange bedfellows, and, in this instance, cultural politics was no exception. The grey eminences of high European culture had all assembled in the mecca of lowbrow American kitsch to congregate, to ruminate, and to continue their Nordic musings under the benign and sybaritic spell of places like Brentwood and Pacific Palisades. Franz Werfel had escaped from Austria immediately following the *Anschluss*, first to France, and then, when the Nazis arrived there in 1940, through France to Portugal and eventually California. He brought with him his wife, Alma Mahler-Gropius-Werfel, who was thirteen years older than he and had enough cultural patrimony just from the people she had slept with to keep a colony of exiles going single-handedly. (Oskar Kokoschka and Schönberg's mentor von Zemlinsky were included in this illustrious company.) One of Werfel's stops on his escape from the Nazis was the French village of Lourdes, where he learned the story of Bernadette Soubirous, to whom the Blessed Mother had appeared in 1859. Werfel was impressed by the story, and that, combined with the desperate nature of his plight, compelled him to make a vow to the Blessed Virgin that if she got him and Alma safely out of the clutches of the Nazis, he would tell Bernadette's story in his next book. It was an unusual vow for a Jew, but the Blessed Virgin evidently granted him his wish. After a series of miraculous escapes, Werfel found himself comfortably ensconced in Hollywood, writing a book that would go on to become not only a best-seller but the top-grossing movie of 1943. There are, I suppose, many strange concatenations of literary and religious fate, but the scene of the Jewish former anarchist writing a novel on the Blessed Mother to be filmed in Hollywood Babylon is one of the strangest. In a way, however, it was not untypical of the times. Goebbels was determined to show the world that German culture could exist without Jews and representatives of "degenerate art," and Hollywood was determined to profit from his mistake. The film *Casablanca* was one notable artifact of this cultural exchange. Hollywood had become in a way Rick's *Café Américain*, the place where the Germans went when Germany did not want them any more.

On May 7, 1943, Thomas Mann had dinner at the Werfels' house, as he often did. On that evening he spent time talking with another émigré guest of the Werfels, Arnold Schönberg, pumping him for information on his music and the life of a composer. Schönberg had arrived in California nine years earlier with his second wife and family. From 1936 to 1944 he held a teaching position at the University of California. It was not a particularly lucrative position, and Schönberg had to supplement his music by teaching composition to students. But as a visiting foreign dignitary and representative of German culture and member in good standing of the exile community, he had rights not normally granted to someone of his financial standing. Schönberg was aging and in bad health but an avid tennis fan (his children would go on to excel at the game), and during his stay in Hollywood he would get to play on George Gershwin's court. From this period dates the probably apocryphal anecdote about a conversation between Schönberg and Gershwin. When Gershwin asked Schönberg for composition lessons, Schönberg responded by asking how much money Gershwin made a year. Upon hearing that not inconsiderable sum, Schönberg is said to have replied, "Perhaps I ought to take lessons from you."

Mann had met Schönberg three years earlier, on September 21, 1940, in a "soirée" at the home of Mrs. Salka Viertel, née Salome Steuermann, wife of the film and stage director Berthold Viertel and sister to the pianist Eduard Steuermann. Steuermann had been the pianist for Schönberg's "Club for musical private performances" and had been in Schönberg's apartment in Modeling in the fall of 1923 when Schönberg announced that he had discovered the twelve-tone system, thereby ensuring the hegemony of German music for the next century.¹ Steuermann had also performed one of Hauer's pieces at the "Club," but so badly that Hauer and his small entourage walked out in the middle of his performance. Salka Viertel had come to Hollywood in 1928 as an actress but before long turned to script writing and wrote most of the scripts for her friend Greta Garbo. The "soirée" at her house on September 21, 1940, included a performance of Schönberg's *Pierrot Lunaire*, which left Thomas Mann singularly unimpressed. It struck him as "antiquated modern" ("*veraltet modern*," he wrote in his journal), a vestige of *fin-de-siècle* Vienna, which must have seemed eons in the past to the German émigrés in their brave new world in Lala Land. But that was before Mann had decided to write his Nietzsche novel about the creation of modern music. By the time of their meeting three years later, Mann was at work writing *Doktor Faustus*. On October 24, 1942, while m the final stages of writing the last of his Joseph tetralogy, Mann noted in his diary that he had been reading Erich Podach's book on Nietzsche's collapse. By the mid-forties, Mann was deeply involved in the work he considered his *Parsifal*. In many ways, *Doktor Faustus* was the culmination of the prescription for disaster he had sketched out almost 40 years earlier in his novella *Death in Venice*. Germany had taken Nietzsche's Dionysian challenge to heart. In *Death in Venice*, the Dionysian orgy had just been Aschenbach's dream: by the 1940s, it had become the world's nightmare. In his *Faustus* novel, Mann conflates what he considered to be three periods of especial importance for Germany: the time of the Protestant Reformation; Nietzsche/Leverkühn's life and pact with the devil, which corresponded to the twenty-four years during which syphilis brought on insanity; and the events of World War II, which Mann followed from California while writing the novel. The Protestant Reformation found its culmination in Nietzsche, and Nietzsche's pact with the devil found its culmination in the apocalyptic destruction visited on Germany in World War II. "I know my lot," Nietzsche had written in the "Why I Am a Fate" section of *Ecce Homo*:

> There will come a time when my name will be associated with the memory of something abominable—with a crisis the like of which has never existed on earth, with the deepest collision of conscience, with a decision, conjured up against everything, everything which up until that time had been believed, encouraged, and called holy.²

Mann was watching the fulfillment of Nietzsche's prophecy from his sybaritic retirement in Hollywood as the Nazi armies rolled out over Europe and then rolled back again in a backwash of destruction of the sort the world had never seen. It was as if Gustav Aschenbach had made a slight miscalculation. Those who longed for the destruction of the social order as a cover under which they could pursue forbidden desire got more than they bargained for as city after German city, the culmination of a thousand years of Christian culture, succumbed to the Allies' saturation bombing. Aschenbach's wish in Venice had resulted in the firebombing of Dresden. When Mann, the literary man, was writing *Death in Venice*,

Dionysos Rising

Adolf Hitler, fourteen years younger, was a down-and-out bohemian and aspiring architect in Vienna, absorbing the combination of artistic theory that found expression in Schönberg's *Harmonielehre* or Kandinsky's *On the Spiritual in Art* and the occult racist ideology that Alfred Rosenberg was promoting in the Thule Society. Things had not worked out according to plan. Even the ambivalence Mann expressed in *Death in Venice* could not have prepared him for the cataclysm that was being visited on Germany. *Doktor Faustus* was Mann's way of sorting things out, and, in doing the sorting, Mann was faced with the inextricable connection between German music and German philosophy. Nietzsche, he knew, might have become a musician had the training been available. As it was, his philosophy was born out of music, Wagner's music, and music stayed with Nietzsche long after his mind had become incapable of any other sort of discourse. Music, specifically Wagner's *Tristan und Isolde*, was the matrix out of which Nietzsche's philosophy arose; it was the closest approximation to Dionysian intoxication—the characteristic emotional state of the new age. It was the device that made the attitudes of the new Dionysian age humanly plausible. Yet, *Tristan* was not the music of the new Dionysian age. Had Nietzsche been a composer, he might have written that music himself As it was, he could only propose guidelines and leave the work to others.

That Mann saw Schönberg as the musical heir to Nietzsche is indicated by the conflation of both philosopher and modern musician in the hero of his *Faustus* novel. Adrian Leverkühn lived Nietzsche's life, but he produced music that sounded like that of Schönberg or Berg. When he heard *Wozzeck*, Mann described its sound as "*leverkühnisch*." The similarity lay primarily in the use of dissonance, which is the characteristic emotion of modern music. The twelve-tone system may have allowed composers to write without reference to tonal centers; however, from the point of view of the listener, the crabs and inversions of notes beloved by the twelve-toners were virtually inaudible. What was heard was dissonance. The notes were now all individuals with their own right not to be merged into each other according to musical analogues of love. There was no harmony now, and the resulting disharmony and ugliness "was an artistic game in which the will, in the eternal plenitude of its lust, played with itself."[3] Nietzsche, in his way, had remained true to the tradition of world harmony. He was proposing, not its abolition, but its inversion. Disharmony would be the goal of society now, brought about by the apotheosis of human will. It was as if Nietzsche were proposing as good everything Ulysses had proposed as bad in Shakespeare's *Troilus and Cressida*. Just as musical harmony was a means to bring about social order in *The Merchant of Venice*, so musical dissonance would bring about the destruction of that order and the advent of the Dionysiac era of unrestrained will:

> This most basic phenomenon of the Dionysian art, so difficult to grasp, becomes easily understood once one grasps the wonderful meaning of musical dissonance—just as music juxtaposed with the world can alone give some inkling of how the world can be justified as an aesthetic phenomenon. The lust that tragic

myth creates has the same home as the lustful perception of dissonance in music. The Dionysian, with its lust perceived in pain, is the common womb of both music and tragic myth.[4]

Up until the time of Nietzsche and Wagner, according to Nietzsche's view as expressed in *The Birth of Tragedy*, the Germanic genius had been alienated from its true home by its servitude to "malicious dwarves," that is to say, Romans, which is to say, Christianity. Wagner's resuscitation of Germanic myth had set up the cultural machinery whereby Germans could now liberate themselves from the Mediterranean hegemony of Christian faith and lead themselves back to an era of Germanic myth. The music of that past and future era was dissonance: "Both music and tragic myth," Nietzsche writes in *The Birth of Tragedy*, "illuminate [*verklären*, that word again] a region in which lustful chords, dissonance as well as the terrible cosmos corresponding to it, sound attractive; both play with the goad of revulsion, relying on their mighty magical arts."[5]

Mann was intimately familiar with Nietzsche and the German musical tradition and also smart enough to make the connections for himself between the music Nietzsche had proposed in *The Birth of Tragedy* and the music that Schönberg and his students produced as its fulfillment. However, the fact was that he was not alone in making the connection. During the same time that Mann was mulling over the consequences of Nietzscheanism being fulfilled in the catastrophe of World War II, he was reading the manuscript copy of a work of another German émigré, a professor, who was also a part of the exile community in Hollywood in the forties. Theodor Wiesengrund Adorno, who was twenty-eight years younger than Mann, was associated with the leftist Frankfurt school, which would bequeath the theoretician of the sixties' counterculture, Herbert Marcuse, to the university system in California as well. Adorno's manuscript version of *Zur Philosophie der neuen Musik*, which appeared in German in 1948, one year after the publication of *Doktor Faustus*, was to have an enormous influence on Thomas Mann and then, as the reputed source of Mann's musical theories, in its own right, on the formation of the musical ideology that became one of the pillars of *Kulturpolitik* in the nascent *Bundesrepublik* after the war.

Schönberg was in many ways a creation of Adorno, and Thomas Mann's novel *Doktor Faustus* was the chief publicist of this creation. Mann's diaries throughout the forties are peppered with references to Adorno's manuscript, which Mann described as "something important. I found here an artistic-sociological critique of the situation which was of the greatest elegance and profundity as well as deeply progressive; it possessed the closest affinity to the idea of my book, to the 'composition' on which I lived and which I was in the process of weaving."[6] Once Mann met Adorno, he was convinced, "that's my man."[7] Peter de Mendelssohn saw Adorno's manuscript as possessing "inestimable importance" in the completion of *Faustus*. What began as a Nietzsche novel grew, under the influence of the émigré community in Hollywood, into a novel in which Schönberg was the culmination of what Nietzsche aspired to in *The Birth of Tragedy*. Mann in Hollywood "appropriated" both Schönberg and Adorno for his own ends.

Adorno's reading of Schönberg, as well as his apodictic adjudication in Schönberg's favor of the controversy over who had created the twelve-tone system, was an essential ingredient in creating the ideology that would rule over and eventually ruin the German classical music tradition in the period following World War II. The first step in this transformation was a firm linking of Schönberg with Nietzsche, which Mann, then in the throes of a music/Nietzsche novel, must have found especially compelling. "Not until Schönberg," Adorno wrote in his apodictic fashion, "has music accepted Nietzsche's challenge."[8] Adorno saw in the rise of atonality, as practiced by Schönberg, "the fulfilled purification of music from all conventions."[9] Adorno, like Mann in *Death in Venice*, saw in this "purification" the "elements of barbarism" but seemed to be willing to take the risk because liberation could take place only when conventions had been abrogated:

> In Schönberg's outburst—often hostile to culture—this purification repeatedly causes the surface to tremble. The dissonant chord, by comparison with consonance, is not only the more differentiated and progressive; but furthermore, it sounds as if it had not been completely subdued by the ordering principle of civilization—in a certain respect, as if it were older than tonality itself.[10]

Adorno, as this and other passages indicate, appropriated the Schönbergian system for his own purposes. Schönberg was interested in subduing tonal reality to a completely superstitious totalitarian system. His dissonance is in reality the application of the system Hauer created, in which, in Hauer's words, "Everything crude, opposed, and affectionate, including moods, the sensual and the erotic, have to be eliminated so that intuition is possible."[11] If Adorno had granted Hauer authorship of the twelve-tone system, Adorno would have been confronted with a system that was the polar opposite of the liberationist primitivism being proposed by Adorno and the cultural left. So Hauer had to he dismissed from the scene as the necessary preparation for Adorno's ideological takeover of dissonance. With Hauer as the author of the twelve-tone technique, we are confronted with a system that is anti-Wagnerian, anti-Dionysian, and radically anti-sexual. The original twelve-tone system is the reaction of a sexually troubled Catholic to what he perceived as a tonal universe that had become too sensual. (This may also explain the otherwise perplexing involvement of Webern, another devout Catholic, with the twelve-tone system.) Hauer's solution was to take the music out of this world and remove it to the "celestial spheres" where it could reign in angelic corporality. Schönberg was attracted to the system because of his numerological superstitions. Hauer's system promised him occult control of the universe.

What Adorno saw was something else again. Taking his cue from Nietzsche, Adorno saw in dissonance an antidote to the order of nature, which for all three men—Adorno, Schönberg, and Hauer—was symbolized by the diatonic scale. Whereas Schönberg saw in the twelve-tone "law" the escape from the Dionysian excess that Moses found among the Israelites upon his return from Mount Sinai, Adorno appropriated the system and imposed on it the opposite meaning. The twelve-tone system was one more blow for liberation. Like Nietzsche, Adorno saw dissonance as a blow against the established social order, the way of establishing a new social order completely independent of nature and totally at the service of human will. Dissonance means that no tone is absorbed into any other to form "harmony." The twelve-tone technique assures that noise of the chromatic half-tones will ever return to some natural order, that is, to something approaching the tonal organization of the diatonic scale. Each note remains autonomous, which is to say, its own law, a law unto itself immune to the persuasions of both reason and musical reason—that is, tonality. "The predominance of dissonance," Adorno tells us, expressing in his round-about way its attraction to the cultural left,

> seems to destroy the rational, "logical" relationships. Dissonance is nevertheless still more rational than consonance, insofar as it articulates with great clarity the relationship of the sounds occurring within it—no matter how complex—instead of achieving a dubious unity through the destruction of those partial moments present in dissonance.[12]

The subjection of musical reality to the arbitrarily imposed law of the twelve-tone technique brings about, according to Adorno's view, a twofold "emancipation":

> The conscious disposition over the material of nature is two-sided: the emancipation of the human being from the musical force of nature and the subjection of nature to human purposes.[13]

If Adorno had simply been interested in "emancipation" from a political system, then Wagner would have sufficed; in fact, Bakunin thought that Beethoven would do the trick. Emancipation from nature requires a more potent system. The interesting thing about Adorno's project is how quickly it became fraught with ambivalence. The only system strong enough to dominate and/or destroy nature is a system even more domineering than nature itself at least according to Adorno's perception. The devil, it seems, is the only one who has a system strong enough to hold out against the power of nature. We can free ourselves from nature only by becoming imprisoned in a completely alien and inhuman system. No wonder Mann came up with the pact with the devil as the source of modern music, even though there is no evidence of any such pact in Schönberg's life. The evidence comes from Adorno's appropriation of Schönberg. According to Adorno, virtually the only justification for twelve-tone music is that—to paraphrase Milton—it is better to reign in an atonal hell than to serve in a diatonic heaven. The new order is much more rigorous and unpleasant than the old one, but at least it is not God's order. The paradox has been expressed well in C. S. Lewis's *The Abolition of Man*. Man sells his soul for power over nature but finds that when the power arrives he has no control over it. The devil wins both coming and going. Something similar happens in the twelve-tone system. Like Marxism, it can be powerful enough to abrogate nature only by enslaving those who dedicate themselves to it. Both are essentially demonic in their orientation. The only thing good about hell is that it is not heaven, which is where God's reign is too painfully apparent. The diatonic scale, which Adorno identified with nature, produces music that is pleasing but "heteronomous," which is to say, according to a law not of the composer's own making. In twelve-tone "rationality," Adorno found the triumph of the will. In order to be truly triumphant, the will must destroy all heteronomous order—first the destruction of music and then the destruction of the self. This is precisely what Mann saw as the consequence of Nietzsche's and Germany's pact with the devil, culminating in the devastation of World War II. Complete emancipation from heteronomy leads to complete annihilation. Adorno liked the twelve-tone system because it was the musical expression of this completely nihilistic emancipation:

> This technique further approaches the ideal of mastery as domination, the infinity of which resides in the fact that nothing heteronomous remains that is not absorbed into the continuum of this technique. Infinity is its pure identity. It is, however, the suppressing moment in the domination of nature, which suddenly turns against the subjective autonomy and freedom itself, in the name of which this domination found its fulfillment. The number game of twelve-tone technique and the force it exercises borders on astrology, and it is not merely a fad of those adept in the technique who have succumbed to its appeal.[14]

The only consolation that Adorno could derive was that of rebellion against nature. "Twelve-tone rationality approaches superstition per se in that it is a closed system—opaque even onto itself—in which the configuration of means is directly hypostatized as goal and as law." [15] Beyond that, twelve-tone technique is "the fate of music":

> It enchains music by liberating it. The subject dominates music through the rationality of the system, only in order to succumb to the rational system itself. . . . From procedures which broke the blind domination of tonal material there evolves a second blind nature by means of this regulatory system. The subject subordinates itself to this blind nature, seeking protection and security which it indicates in its despair over the impossibility of fulfilling music out of itself.[16]

Adorno here simply substantiated something we stated earlier. *Tristan's* erotic chromaticism leads directly to the totalitarianism of the twelve-tone system. The rebellion against the natural law implicit in adultery and *Tristan's* erotic chromaticism leads directly to the Gulag in both music and politics. Mann appropriated Schopenhauer as "his" philosopher, according to Erich Heller, because both Mann and Wagner saw in the sexual drive the true focal point of the will. Its 1858, in a letter to Mathilde Wesendonck, Wagner "corrected" Schopenhauer "by the discovery that there exists a way 'leading to the perfect appeasement of the Will' that is much simpler and more direct than Schopenhauer's strenuous renunciation: namely, the love that 'has its roots in sex.'" [17]

"This," according to Heller,

is how Schopenhauer became the patron philosopher of *Tristan und Isolde*, of the *Liebestod*, the most paradoxical and ravishing consummation of the erotic will, both in its triumph and in its defeat. About a year later, Wagner knew better and told the lady in Zurich: "Longingly I often turn my eyes toward the land Nirvana. Yet Nirvana always becomes Tristan again. . . ." *Death in Venice* is, on a miniature scale, the Tristan and Isolde of European Decadence, showing in an even more drastic manner the essential incompatibility of "reality" with that magical love.[18]

If the defeat of reality or reason ("*O sink hernieder Nacht der Liebe*") is a means to a sexual end in *Tristan*, with the twelve-tone system it becomes a demonic end in itself. The need to defeat nature and nature's God becomes so all-consuming that the threat of self-annihilation is no longer a deterrent. Adorno was clear in seeing a continuum leading from Wagner to Schönberg. The twelve-tone technique was "the executor of a tendency stemming from Romanticism":

> The manner in which Wagner interpolates motives—which are so defined that they contradict the procedure of variation—is a precursor of Schönberg's compositional procedure. It leads to the decisive technical antagonism of music since Beethoven: the antagonism between traditional tonality which is in constant need of reconfirmation—and the substantiality of the individual. If Beethoven developed a musical essence out of nothingness in order to be able to redefine it as a process of becoming, then Schönberg in his later works destroys it as something completed.[19]

We are left, in other words, with this "terrible discipline as an instrument of freedom,"[20] but the freedom it offers is indistinguishable from self-annihilation. "*Zwölfton macht frei*," Adorno might have said in a parody of the slogan *Arbeit macht frei* over the entrance to Auschwitz. In either case, the freedom promised turned out to be that of the concentration camp. "The new ordering of twelve-tone technique," Adorno asserted at another point, "virtually extinguishes the subject."[21] Vogel takes note of the connection between the destruction of the heteronomous musical world and self-destruction, especially as evidenced in Adorno's musical aesthetic. "Others," he writes, have understood Berg's "death chord" in the same way: not only Lulu dies as a result of it, but all music as well."[22]

When Adorno wrote that "the twelve-tone music is inseparable from dissonance, and the death chord is therefore a cipher of its fulfillment" (all twelve tones taken together in one chord are "deadly because all movement finds rest in them without any resolution"),[23] he arrived at the heart of the twelve-tone system. It is complete rebellion against the natural order, which is frozen in a moment of death, so that there is no possibility of ever going back on that fateful decision. It is indistinguishable from suicide, whereby the subject makes his rebellion against God permanent and irrevocable. No wonder, then, that Thomas Mann, influenced by Adorno's *Zur Philosophie der Neuen Musik*, would look upon that music as something essentially diabolical. Adorno saw this music as the fulfillment of Nietzsche's prophecy.

Dionysos Rising

Twelve-tone music was not only the fulfillment for his longing for cosmic dissonance; it was likewise the means to bring that world into existence. Like Orpheus, the moderns would call the stones into life, a life indistinguishable from death. It was the vehicle for the transvaluation of all values. It was the magic act that would conjure up the arrival of the Dionysian age. Vogel sees an unmistakable link between Adorno's idea of harmony and his *Weltanschauung*. "The longing of the chords is nothing other than the longing for death. Just as Lulu longs for her murderer, so the chords long for the composer who will murder music and then carry it to its grave. The composer is the murderer of music."[24]

One could plausibly say that Theodor Adorno was the creator of modern music. By drawing on Nietzsche, he gave meaning to a point of view that, by the 1940s, had come to seem old-fashioned even to someone as sympathetic as Thomas Mann. Adorno took a Schönberg who was at the end of his life and, to a great extent, already passé and infused him with an ideology once again attractive to the avant-garde, which had largely abandoned his music in the years following World War I for the aurally more attractive and sensually more compelling American jazz. Jost Hermand, in his recent history of cultural politics in the *Bundesrepublik*, confirms Schönberg's musical insignificance toward the end of his life. During the 1940s, Schönberg was considered hopelessly old-fashioned; he was, to use Hermand's term, "a strange and bizarre eccentric."[25] He was also considered too formalistic. By the time the war ended, Hindemith, not Schönberg, was considered the prominent German composer of the modern era.

However, Adorno was smart enough to see that Schönberg's aesthetic was remarkably well-suited to the political situation in the nascent German Federal Republic after World War II. The Germans were completely prostrate after the war; the world's premier cultural power, certainly in music, now had to struggle with the evil legacy of the Third Reich, with its essentially racist and nationalist ideology associated with a glorification of pagan German myth, primarily created through Wagner's operas. Culture in the Third Reich had become the project of the state; its function was to promote racial unity, racial purity, and anything that glorified German blood and soil.

In such a climate, where art had been degraded to propaganda for an intellectually bankrupt racial ideology, Schönberg's formalism suddenly was a virtue. Indeed, throughout the entire early postwar period, formalism dominated most of the arts. Probably the best example was the rehabilitation of the Bauhaus school of architecture. In order to compensate for their earlier rabid racism and nationalism, the Germans now began promoting the "international" school of architecture. It was a style particularly in tune with the needs of the time. In reaction to the Nazi emphasis on "*Boden*," Bauhaus buildings were elevated into the air on piers. In order to counter the dark secrets in the German past, the Bauhaus facade was more taken up with panes of glass, as if to show that the Germans now had nothing to hide. The culmination of this trend was reached in Mies van der Rohe's

Farnsworth House, which was quite literally a glass cube on stilts. Similar public buildings are Crown Hall at the Illinois Institute of Technology and the museum of modern art in Berlin. Buildings of this style became an architectural *mea culpa* for the Nazi period and a testimony to the world that (a) the Germans had nothing to hide and (b) they were just like everybody else now. Their buildings were no different from the *Wohnmaschinen* being erected on the South Side of Chicago and the suburbs of Moscow, not coincidentally the two victors in World War II. Vernacular architecture in the fifties would have been as culturally chic as a beer-hall putsch.

Schönberg's formalism was reassuring in a similar way. There was nothing identifiably German about his music. (The fact, of course, that he considered the twelve-tone technique to be something that would assure the hegemony of German music for the next one hundred fifty years was left conveniently unmentioned.) In fact, the only really identifiable characteristic of the twelve-tone technique was its soul-destroying monotony. It was in many ways the international style in music, and it served the same political purposes in the *Bundesrepublik* as did the international style in architecture. It gave the reassuring impression that Germans were just as progressive as the rest of us. They were no different any more. In this regard, the twelve-tone system was exactly what the doctor ordered. As it gained in ascendency during the fifties, primarily because of the amount of money the German government was willing to pour into having it performed, one by one nearly all of the postwar composers tried their hand at twelve-tone composition, and the technique worked its magic on all of them. From Aaron Copland to Igor Stravinsky, no matter who picked up the technique, it made them all sound the same. Copland, whose best work was immediately recognizable as American, submitted meekly to the twelve-tone system and ended up sounding exactly like everyone else who composed in that mode. The same was true, *mutatis mutandis* of Stravinsky. Twelve-tone technique was the great musical in internationalizer, democratizer, and homogenizer.

It was also remarkably easy to learn. And as a result, the Germans could almost overnight produce a whole new generation of young composers, whose music was all equally opaque, equally monotonous. No one need fear for lack of inspiration or lack of talent now. The twelve-tone system was so rigid that it did away with the necessity for inspiration and ability. Everything that everyone produced was equally unmusical; the system itself made sure of that, so no one needed to feel disadvantaged. Since the music was all of equal value, the musical culture of the postwar period became the domain of the promoters and not, as in an earlier age (for example, the Romantic era), that of the composers. Since all of the music was equally bad, reputations were made or broken by the critics and the publishers and the organizers of the *"Ferienkurse für neue Musik,"* like those held at Schloss Kranichstein or Donaueschingen. The radio stations also began to exercise an enormous influence over what was heard, whether anyone liked it or not.

As a result of the confluence of these needs and forces, one by one the devotees of the new music crossed the street and switched their allegiance from Hindemith to Schönberg, whose music went from being hopelessly dated to being a shining witness against fascism, standing *"in stolzer Einsamkeit"* ("in proud solitude") against the Philistine hoard. The new music demanded "absolute freedom," to use Stuckenschmidt's term. It was completely without content, completely formalistic, completely international. The world had nothing to fear from the good Germans now. "If you want to be performed," became the hot tip among young composers, "you have to go to West Germany." The only catch was that you had to compose according to the twelve-tone system. The result was a government-subsidized corpus of music that was commissioned, heard once, and then promptly forgotten. "During the Adenauer era," writes Hermand,

> the German Federal Republic took upon itself the task of fostering an elite-modern music which just about nobody wanted to hear, as people kept saying then, through the expenditure of untold millions of tax dollars and in the process created fur the so-called "new music" a home, unlike any other country in the world, just about every twelve-tone, serial, and aleatoric instrumental composition as well as most modern operas were performed for the first time in this country (and not in France, Italy, or the USA), as can be shown by the statistics and bibliographies of the time. For both the composers and their coteries of connoisseurs, this was the golden age of new music. But for whom else?[26]

In this as in so many other areas of modern cultural life, the operation was a success, but the patient died. The cultural managers of modern music in the *Bundesrepublik* succeeded in promoting the twelve-tone technique and its successors, but they killed contemporary classical music in the process. The masses of the most musically literate culture in the world simply voted with their feet and over a twenty-year period went over to pop music. The musical tradition was relegated to the classics from the past. The composition of music recognizable as a part of that tradition simply stopped. Contemporaries of Schönberg and his school who composed in the traditional manner were simply dropped from the roles of the living. Those representatives of the German classical tradition living at the time have testified to how ruthlessly this cultural scorched-earth campaign was pursued by the modern elite. Alois Melichar describes the publicity campaign waged against those who objected to the first performance of *Moses und Aron*, three years after the composer's death. Those who objected were stigmatized as anti-Semites. When a rabbi from Berlin objected to the stigmatizing and claimed that the main objections were musical and not religious, he was conveniently ignored.

Both Melichar and Peter Jona Korn have described the ruthless whispering campaigns that went on behind the backs of those who dared to compose in a tonal manner in postwar Germany. The insinuation was, of course, that tonality and fascism went hand in hand. On the two hundredth anniversary of the founding of the music publishing house Schott, the campaign went beyond insinuation. Heinrich Strobel, one of the main promoters of the musical avant-garde in Germany after the war, attacked those who dared to defend tonality, calling them "narrow-minded traditionalists" who "continued to cling to the worn-out stereotypes and epigonal late romanticism like a pack of reactionary nationalists. . . who foam at the mouth slandering anything young or original with the epithet 'cultural bolshevism.'"[27] Korn, suspecting that so much bile was probably an indication of a guilty conscience, found that, as matter of fact, Strobel, writing in *Melos* in 1933, had gone out of his way to praise the "steely romanticism" of Joseph Goebbels.

The musical politics of the postwar era were simply the cultural politics of the Third Reich turned upside down. Whatever counted as "degenerate art" under the Nazis was now promoted by opportunists like Strobel as a way of covering their trails and quieting their consciences. According to Korn, "the Nazi concept of 'degenerate music' was simply turned on its head; the more 'degenerate' a piece of music might have sounded to an audience of true believers in the Third Reich, the more 'relevant' it was now; or, vice versa, anyone who composed in a manner which aroused no protest then was now—regardless of the quality of his work—no longer performed."[28]

According to Korn, the postwar musical world was the creation of three people, the already-mentioned Heinrich Strobel, publisher of *Melos*, Hans Stuckenschmidt, author of the hagiographical but inaccurate standard biography of Schönberg, and Theodor Adorno, whose book *The Philosophy of Modern Music*, along with his collaboration with Thomas Mann in the writing of *Doktor Faustus*, revivified Schönberg's *fin-de-siècle* modernism into something usable for the neo-modern cultural bolshevists of the *Bundesrepublik*. Like Strobel, Adorno was not shy in drawing moral lessons from the cultural debacle of the Third Reich and in condemning those who disagreed with his cultural conclusions as crypto-Nazis. Yet, as in the case of Strobel, beneath Adorno's protest one begins to detect the note of a guilty conscience. Adorno, like Strobel, had written Nazi propaganda and was using the promotion of Schönberg's music after the war as a way of covering his trail.

In the June 1934 issue of the Nazi monthly *Die Musik*, Adorno could be found recommending Baldur von Schirach's chorus cycle *Die Fahne der Verfolgten*, "not only because this volume has a distinctly Nazi character because of the choice of his poetry, but also because of its quality." Later in the same article, Adorno called for "a new romanticism. . . perhaps of the sort that Goebbels has called romantic realism."[29] In 1962, the past caught up with Adorno when a student from Frankfurt published the above-cited words in an open letter, in which he wondered how Adorno could claim that no poetry was possible after Auschwitz when he had written in support of the people who had made Auschwitz possible. Why, the student wondered, had Adorno kept quiet about his own collaboration with the Nazis while so loudly denouncing others? Adorno could only reply lamely that "the incriminating sentences should be placed on balance against my entire *oeuvre* and life." [30]

Twelve-tone music, as the foregoing anecdote indicates, served a number of needs, virtually none of which entailed pleasing the ears of an audience. For cultural politicians like Strobel and Adorno, who were in need of rehabilitation from a politically tainted past, the emphasis of the Schönbergian school of formalism and novelty distracted the curious from thinking about content and any connections with the past. The principle of what Hermand calls the autonomic aesthetic, art having no law other than one dictated by itself, fit nicely into the growing desire for moral relativism and sexual liberation at the time. It relativized the individual work of art to the point where the promoter and not the composer was the main figure of influence. It also gave the impression that the neomodern elite were somehow above the law, a reassuring feeling in a country that had just experienced the Nuremberg war-criminal trials.

The twelve-tone system satisfied deep needs for some young composers of the time as well. The most apparent attraction of the twelve-tone system was that the aspiring musician could he a virtual musical illiterate and still compose in its style. "Everyone knows," claims Korn, "that any student at a music conservatory can learn how to compose twelve-tone music in a matter of hours, even if he is incapable of harmonizing a nursery rhyme." [31] Stuckenschmidt was astounded at how quickly the Japanese caught on: "Just a few years of studying dodecaphonics and serial composition and they master it better than most of the Europeans who taught them." [32] Adorno gave a more ambivalent explanation in his *Philosophy of Modern Music*. The new music provided both freedom and escape from freedom:

> This explains the readiness of so many young musicians—particularly in America, where the empirical roots of the twelve-tone technique are totally lacking—to compose in the "twelve-tone system," and it also explains the jubilation over having found a substitution for tonality, as though it were not even possible to survive aesthetically in this freedom and were necessary underhandedly to substitute a new compliance for tonality.[33]

In other words, the euphoria the novice experiences by his initial easy mastery of the twelve-tone system soon gives way to the sobering realization that the system necessarily determines what is said. We have already described the similarities between this musical experience and twentieth-century totalitarianism. The twelve-tone system is a "machine," like the conscience machine Stephen Spender and his contemporaries found so attractive in communism. The twelve-tone system is either childish in its simplicity or impossibly complex. Either way, it is impossible to listen to and, for those who have to play it, a source of illness. In an uncanny confirmation of Pythagoras, who felt that music had medicinal effects, Korn claims a correlation between higher rates of illness among orchestra musicians and the amount of twelve-tone music they play. Like Saint Augustine, who in his *Confessions* claimed that "even those who set themselves up against you do but copy you in a perverse way," so the twelve-toners in then attempt to destroy the classical musical tradition ended up substantiating the fact that dissonance makes us ill at ease, to the point of just plain illness.

The cultural exchange between Germany and the United States after the war seems to have occurred along the lines discussed above. The talented older generation of Germans driven out by the Nazis came to the United States before and during the war, and after the war, the young and untalented left the United States to take advantage of the cultural opportunities that the government of the *Bundesrepublik* wanted to subsidize. So the United States got people like Adorno, Mann, Marcuse, Gropius, Tillich, Schönberg, and virtually the entire cast of *Casablanca*, and the Germans got soldiers on the G.I. bill and people like John Cage. On the whole, the Germans made out better than we did in the deal. Nobody took Cage seriously, but plenty of people took the "great white gods" (Tom Wolfe's phrase) of German culture seriously when they came over here. The arriving German professoriat soon would have its influence on American higher education by giving an aura of respectability to cultural bolshevism. Bauhaus was installed in Black Mountain College in the woods of the South; Gropius ended up at Harvard, Marcuse in California, and Tillich at Union Theological Seminary—and *Kulturbolschewismus* became our national educational policy.

Paul Tillich is a good example of this transfer of influence. Tillich was given the stamp of moral authenticity by being driven out of Germany by the Nazis. He then came to America and spent his stay at Union Theological Seminary and Harvard undermining the morals of the students with whom he came in contact. As elsewhere in this century, the key intellectual equation had Nietzsche as one of its main components. The German professors injected the Nietzsche virus into the bloodstream of American education, which has had an immune deficiency ever since.

Tillich was immortalized as a pornography addict in a memoir his wife wrote after his death. But before he got into pornography, Tillich cut his teeth on Nietzsche. Hannah Tillich relates how the young Paul was influenced by his friend Dox, who "established a circle of young women with whom he acquainted his friends, encouraging them to get involved with one another. Huysmans' *La Bas*, Baudelaire's *Flowers of Evil*, Nietzsche's *Zarathustra*, and description of black masses circulated in his group." [34] It was Nietzsche, according to Hannah, who "lured Paulus away from middle-class respectability," and *Zarathustra* in particular, "which broke with everything Paulus had learned from [his] Father." [35]

Rollo May described the impact that Tillich's teaching had on him as a young theology student (soon to switch to psychology) at Union Theological Seminary. "A wave of freedom swept over me," May wrote in an affectionate memoir published after Tillich's death, "—freedom from all the futile arguments of undergraduate days." May then went on to enumerate those "futile" undergraduate arguments he abandoned under Tillich's tutelage while ostensibly studying theology.

> Is there a god? I was freed from all that useless controversy. . . . I felt freed also from the nagging inner compulsion to believe. Carried over from childhood, intellectually superseded but still present in some deep corner of my emotions, some compulsion pushed me to believe this or that because my mother and father had believed it. . . . I was here subject to a childish form of what Nietzsche proclaimed, the great eye of God which nobody can stand peering at him all the time. . . . Paulus' statement took away my security, that childish belief to which, against all intellectual development, I apparently still clung. I knew that God for most people was the guarantor of the status quo; he protected them from fundamental upset, from moral anarchy. God guarded the sanctity of marriage, he was against crime, he protected property (especially if you belonged to one of the sects that sprang from Calvinism).[36]

It was precisely the sort of liberation one has come to expect from Nietzschean professors addicted to pornography. Tillich brought Nietzsche and sexual liberation to the theology students, and the students lost their faith. The natural unruliness of the sexual drive was given encouragement by Nietzsche's philosophical transvaluation of all values. Tillich, according to May, represented, "eros," "ecstatic reason," "reason. . . overpowered by. . . ultimate concern," and the Weimar Republik. Whenever May grasps for some expression of Tillich's interaction with transcendent values, he invariably comes up with a Nietzschean formulation. Tillich "had to live Dionysian and think Apollonian. . . like the rest of us," May added. Leaping too quickly to morality causes us to "miss the richness of experience," which one finds in "the abyss," which is "a realm of creative chaos which transcends values. It is transmoral—prior to the ethical. It does not surprise us when he names Nietzsche as the philosopher who most clearly expresses it."[37] Like Gropius in architecture and Schönberg in music, Tillich was proposing the international style in theology. It is, according to May, a "new religious outlook" characterized by "internationalism but by interracism and intersexism as well."[38]

When the Tillichs arrived in New York in the thirties, they had to reorient their lifestyle and readapt their categories to take account of the new surroundings. According to his wife, one of the first things Tillich did when he arrived in a new city was to seek out the local red-light district. New York proved to be a bit disappointing in this regard, but the Tillichs did find Harlem, which they found stimulating in a new sort of way. The Harlem Renaissance was over, finished with the stock-market crash, but there were still sensual compensations for the newly arrived Germans. In her memoir, Hannah relates how

> we found some sort of consolation in Harlem. Somebody must have taken us to Small's Paradise, where one went up a steep staircase, watched by an old pockmarked Negro, whose muddy uniform with gold braid we feared a little. Later we would shake hands with him. Inside the dark, long room, we sat facing clouds that drifted behind an orchestra of Negroes, who played noisily and shrilly. It was as if we had entered a tropical forest with parrots screaming, dark faces peering out of the jungle, falsetto voices, and brilliant colors. A Negro danced with me, a Negress with Paulus.

Sympathy for the Devil

We felt relaxed at Small's and returned there with our friends, grateful voyeurs, taking in the primeval charm of the hearty men and swaying women. We considered it an aesthetic show. We did not think at all in economic, political, or social terms.

Once we dared to go to a show in a basement where there were mostly Negroes. In the dancing space at the center of the room occasional performances were given. A nude Negress painted gold, having danced with a Negro twice her size, leaned her body against a post and masturbated with violent snakelike movements, while her former partner and another girl unmistakably performed the acts of intimate sex. It did not seem vulgar or fleshy. It was filled with the natural vivacity of these beautiful black people.

People at the seminary did not think our adventures such a good idea. They had misgivings about our dancing with Negroes. Later, others objected to our aesthetic attitude concerning Negroes. Paulus and I had talked about the black image from primeval times on, the dark people being considered the least aristocratic... in psychic circumstances, the black or dark one always the devil... the black soul against the white soul... black as a magic color expressing evil or dark, underground powers... in fairy tales, the black princess, submerged under water, reappearing as white and no longer evil.[39]

Once a Nietzschean, always a Nietzschean. When the Tillichs were transplanted to the United States, they simply made the Negro a paradigm of the Dionysian forces they were hoping to act out. In this they were not alone; in fact, as a result of the combined forces of modernity and the northern migration of the rural Negro in the United States, the two categories were hopelessly merged in American cultural politics, and the Negro became in the eyes of the white liberals the paradigm of sexual liberation. The idea was not new. When Nietzsche turned away from Europe in disgust at Wagner, his eyes almost of necessity alighted on Africa with its darker uninhibited races. C. G. Jung, who remembered stories from his childhood about the mad Professor Nietzsche, had the same sort of feeling when he first set foot on the dark continent. "At last I was where I longed to be: in a non-European country where no European language was spoken and no Christian conceptions prevailed. . . ."[40] Jung, of course, let the cat out of the bag. The real attraction of Africa was the fact that Christianity had not taken root there (at least not as of the turn of the century) as it had in Europe.

But it would be incorrect to see the cross-culturalization that was taking place in America's big northern cities as a one-way street. At the same time that the modern Europeans were becoming negrified (Norman Mailer's "The White Negro" is an example of this process), the Negroes, for the most part newly arrived from the farms of the South, were also becoming modernized. This meant almost invariably of course, a loosening of sexual morality. Writing about the Negro family in the thirties before the full impact of northern migration was felt, the black sociologist, E. Franklin Frazier, saw the migration to the northern cities in almost unrelievedly negative terms. In moving to the ghettos of New York and Chicago and Detroit, the Negro "had not only escaped from the traditional subordination to white overlords but had also cut himself loose from the moral support of relatives and neighbors."[41] Family disintegration was one immediate result of the meeting between the Negro and modernity. As modernity's hold over the culture intensified, so did the breakdown in the Negro family. It was just as Mann had predicted in *Death in Venice*; sexual lust and the social order were incompatible. The more these lusts were indulged, the more the social order broke down. When Bauhaus was finally let loose on the Negro in the fifties, as in the housing projects on the South Side of Chicago, the disintegration of the family quickly accelerated to its current catastrophic proportions.

Throughout the postwar period, the cross fertilizations continued: the Negroes were becoming modern, and the moderns were becoming Negro. Ernst Krenek wrote *Jonny Spielt Auf*, and Martin Luther King did his dissertation on Paul Tillich. (The fact that King plagiarized his dissertation lessens the influence somewhat but not completely.) The rise of the Negro through the Civil Rights movement meant the rise of his music as well. The fact that Elvis Presley sang "black" not only caused the stock of people like Little Richard and Chuck Berry to rise, but it also opened the gates for a whole generation of white boys for whom it was now okay to act like a Negro, at least as far as music went. Ahmet Ertegun has claimed that among the working class youth in England in the early sixties

> there was a constant attempt to find out how to play like a black person. But no matter how they tried, it came out English, but it came out like the real thing too. I think the key group was Cream—Eric Clapton was the center of it. And *the* person who really got this the best was Stevie Winwood who, at age sixteen or seventeen, was singing and playing very black.[42]

Eric Clapton was a sort of English dandy version of Robert Johnson, who, having sold his soul to the devil, was a sort of Mississippi delta version of Adrian Leverkühn. Johnson, it must he admitted, did not get a very good deal for his soul, but then again neither did Leverkühn, or Nietzsche for that matter. By the time the real money started rolling in, selling one's soul to the devil had become part of the standard paraphernalia of the rock 'n' roll lifestyle. Black Sabbath even put it on one of their album covers: "We sold our soul for rock 'n' roll."

During the sixties, a number of important cultural transactions took place. The classical musical tradition (that is, new music being composed in the tradition of Beethoven and Mozart) finally collapsed under the weight of its own inanity. The fact that John Cage and Karl Heinz Stockhausen were at all taken seriously was a sign that the Schönberg/Adorno school had finally triumphed in its takeover of classical music. The operation was a success, but, once again, the patient died. It was the same sort of thing that Antheil had described in the twenties. If the intellectuals had listened to one more atonal piece, they would have all committed suicide. So during the sixties a massive shift of allegiance took place, similar to the first shift from Schönberg to jazz that had taken place when the first black jazz band arrived in Paris after World War I. Only this time it took place on a much more massive scale. Faced with a choice between Stockhausen and Muddy Waters, British working-class teenagers in the early fifties had the sense to choose at least some semblance of musical life, and they went with Muddy. Sidcup professor Brian Yates remembers someone bringing a Stockhausen recording to the jam sessions that took place in the empty art-school classrooms that were now the hangouts of the British youth who in another age would have gone into the military or an apprenticeship. There is no indication that anyone listened twice. As the sixties progressed, a massive shift of allegiance took place. The postwar generation coming to maturity in the early sixties converted to rock 'n' roll. The occult avant-garde detached itself from the classical music of the sort being produced by the Schönberg epigone in the *Bundesrepublik* and attached itself to Negro music of the sort coming from the newly modernized blacks from the United States. These were blacks who had grown up in Gropius' *Wohnmaschinen* in places like Detroit and Chicago and whose consciousness of themselves as icons of liberation had been forged from the leftist-dominated Civil Rights movement in the South. John Dunbar, Marianne Faithful's husband before she moved in with Mick Jagger, remembers the advent of rock 'n' roll:

> But in England, it just suddenly—Boom! —one minute it wasn't there and suddenly it was Little Richard and Elvis and Chuck Berry. In the space of a few months, all this music suddenly arrived. Elvis was selling millions of records. And suddenly rock and roll in England appeared as if it were dropped out of the sky. We'd never heard anything like it before.[43]

He also remembers the arrival of the avant-garde who would eventually take that music and appropriate it to their own ends. During the time when all the early bands were forming, Dunbar and his friends heard about Allen Ginsberg, roughly twenty years their senior. In 1962 he held a reading of "Beat Poetry in the Albert Hall" and drew six thousand people. England, however, did not need to import an avant-garde; it had one of its own which, when combined with Negro rock 'n' roll, produced the outburst of decadence and *outré* fashion that was the sixties in England. Mix Oscar Wilde and Muddy Waters, and you ended up with something like Brian Jones, the founder of the Rolling Stones. Mix Robert Johnson, the Mississippi blues singer who reputedly sold his soul to the devil, and Aubrey Beardsley, and you ended up with Eric Clapton and Cream and their electrified, drug-fueled version of the blues. Mix Chuck Berry and Aleister Crowley, and you got Jimmy Page, of the Yardbirds and Led Zeppelin, who eventually went on to buy Crowley's mansion on Loch Ness because both felt it was the ideal place to work magic.

On May 19, 1967, in an interview in the *Daily Express*, the Beatles announced that the bald-headed man with the bags under his eyes in the upper left-hand corner of the crowd of "people we like" surrounding them on the cover of their *Sgt. Pepper's Lonely Heart Club Band* album was Aleister Crowley. Crowley was born in 1875, the same year as both Thomas Mann and Arnold Schönberg, to well-off parents who were members of the Plymouth Brethren sect, which had been founded in 1830. After making a fortune from his brewery, Crowley's father spent his time traveling around England preaching Plymouthist doctrine to anyone who would listen. Among other things, "the Brethren believed that they were the only true Christians; they considered the idea of ordained ministers contrary to the teaching of Scripture; the Bible was literally true; Christ's Second Coming was imminent; the Elect would inherit the Kingdom of God." [44] Crowley's father, who married late, died when Crowley was only eleven. The event seems to have precipitated a complete reversal of values. Now Crowley identified with the devil and with everything that the Plymouth sect had identified as evil in a way he could still not explain when he wrote his autobiography thirty-six years later. Another curiously reactionary effect of his early exposure to the radical Protestantism of the Plymouth sect was a love of ritual, Satanic ritual albeit, which never left him. He was passionately interested in the minutiae of ritual magic; this passion first led him to become a thirty-third degree Mason and then to get involved with the whole occult underground as revivified by the followers of Madame Blavatsky, who had died the same year Crowley was born.

The high point of Crowley's career as a magus came during a working in Cairo, where he encountered not only the gods of ancient Egypt but also Aiwass, his guardian angel. It was from Aiwass that he received the Law of Thelema (Greek for "will"), "Do what thou wilt." Crowley was associated with Steiner and the Golden Dawn and virtually all the occult organizations of the time, but, in spite of the mumbo-jumbo that burdens his "autohagiography" to the point of virtual unreadability, his doctrine is essentially Nietzschean. The will is the ultimate reality. In his autobiography he acknowledges the debt, but the admission is buried under an avalanche of detail, occult and otherwise. "I entirely agree with Nietzsche," he says at one point, "that Christianity is the formula of the servile state; true aristocracy and true democracy are equally its enemies. In my ideal state everyone is respected for what he is. There will always be slaves, and a slave is to be defined as he who acquiesces in being a slave." [45]

In a long passage discussing the Law of Thelema, Crowley explicitly notes his debt to Nietzsche, specifically Nietzsche's critique of Christian morality, which Crowley sees as damaging to a true "moral sense":

> Their [that is, the Christians'] authority rested on definitions of right and wrong which were untenable. As soon as Nietzsche and others demonstrated that fact, they lost their validity. The result has been that the new generation, demanding a reason for acting with ordinary decency, and refusing to be put off with fables and sophistries, has drifted into anarchy. Nothing can save the world but the universal acceptance of the Law of Thelema as the sole and sufficient basis of conduct.... Its truth is self-evident.... In its way it is the logical climax of the idea of democracy. Yet at the same time it is the climax of aristocracy by asserting each individual equally to be the centre of the universe.[46]

Sympathy for the Devil

Not for Aleister the little picture. He was always interested in putting the Law of Thelema into widespread, if not universal, application, but the logical place to start seemed to be Germany, primarily because Nietzsche had come from Germany. Crowley confesses to being a Germanophile from boyhood:

> the German social system was considered by nearly all thinking Englishmen as a sublime model. German thought and action had been made immortal by Carlyle. German social economy had been slavishly adopted by Lloyd George in the Insurance Act. Great lawyers like Lord Haldane and talented errand boys like H. G. Wells mingled their voices (of course, in the latter case, with a somewhat cockney accent) to extol the greatness of Germany and to hold her up as a pattern to all good Englishmen.[47]

Crowley picked up this veneration for things German in his youth and seems to have carried it with him throughout life. At the top of the German heap, in Crowley's view at least, was Nietzsche, whom he describes as "to me almost an avatar of Thoth" and "the god of wisdom."[48] Thus, it should come as no surprise that Crowley would not only travel to Germany but that by the twenties he had a group of followers there as well. In 1925 he went to Thuringia, birthplace of Nietzsche and Wagner, home of the Wartburg, the cradle of Protestantism and *mise en scène* for the sexual crisis in Wagner's *Tannhäuser*. While in Germany, Crowley met with Marthe Künzel, head of the German branch of both the Ordo Templum Orientalis and Crowley's own breakaway organization the Astrum Argentinum, and told her that the first country to adopt Crowley's *Book of the Law* as its gospel would rule the world. Künzel was a friend of Rudolf Hess, who frequented both homosexual and occult demimondes, but Webb, who tells the story, thinks any direct influence unlikely. However, he is struck by the similarities between Hitler and Crowley, as was Crowley himself, who annotated a copy of Rauschning's *Hitler Speaks* some time in the early forties. Crowley, according to Webb,

> marked for attention all the passages where Hitler is reported by Rauschning to have referred to a new world-order of the collapse of the old system of values. These are general apocalyptic expectations with which both might indeed well have agreed. But Crowley saw correspondences everywhere.... On page after page Crowley took Hitler's side against Rauschning, acclaiming the magnetism of the Leader's presence and the rumors that Hitler had a room decorated with "obscene nudes." To Hitler's declaration that it was time to "protect the strong against the weak," Aleister Crowley added an enthusiastic "Yes!" Although, by the end of his reading, Crowley had decided that Hitler had probably become a "Black Brother," he persisted in fostering the legend that the similarities of which he was convinced had been inspired by Marthe Künzel and his own sacred text.[49]

Webb, like most other commentators, tends to get lost in the minutiae of occult doctrine and historiography to the point of losing sight of the obvious fact that virtually all the associations Crowley saw between his own thought and Hitler's came from Nietzsche. The collapse of values, as well as the strong uniting against the weak, is a theme found in Nietzsche in its greatest specificity. It seems undeniable that both Crowley and Hitler picked up these doctrines though their association with occult circles, but here, as in the case of Rudolf Steiner, the medium should not be confused with the message. The transmitter was the occult/bohemian network of organizations that grew up in the wake of Wagner and his festivals, but the source is Nietzsche. Both Count Gobineau's and Houston Stewart Chamberlain's racist theories grew up in the protective shadow of Wagner's music as did *The Birth of Tragedy*. The occult/bohemian network, of which both Kandinsky and Schönberg were a part, was simply the transmission vehicle for Nietzschean theories of transvaluation of values and the Wagnerian music that made them culturally plausible.

Raschke, whose study of the connection between contemporary rock 'n' roll and Satanism is especially compelling, is one of the few people who has noticed the connection:

> Virtually all historians of the occult sidestep the fact that the teachings of Crowley or Aiwass, depending on whether one takes a psychological or a metaphysical slant, were little more than inferior literary imitations of the German philosopher Friedrich Nietzsche, who was a generation younger than the Beast himself. . . . While Nietzschean philosophy vaunted the artistic life as the premier expression of the "will to power," what Crowley termed "magick" with a k on the end promised the unlimited satisfaction of instinctual wishes along with total liberation from both human and divine laws. Crowley, in fact, spent the remainder of his days immersed in every mode of unusual or deviant sexual experiment, not so much to be loose-moraled as to carry out the mandate of *The Book of the Law*.[50]

In Crowley one finds all the themes of the sixties counterculture *in nuce*. He was bisexual and, after World War I, founded what he called a "monastery" for sexual magic in Cefalu, Sicily, which he called the Abbey of Thelema. He was also a tireless propagandist for drug use, and, like Sigmund Freud, particularly fond of cocaine. Paul Vitz, in his recent book on Freud, makes interesting connections between cocaine and the occult. Goethe modeled Mephistopheles on Merck, the German pharmaceutical house that manufactured cocaine for medical use. Freud ordered his cocaine in liquid form and imbibed it in ritualistic fashion on Walpurgisnacht in an aping of Faust's pact with the devil.[51]

It was while using cocaine that Crowley came to his mystical awareness of himself as the Beast of Revelation, the "self-crowned God whom men shall worship and blaspheme for centuries."[52] Raschke also suggests that Crowley introduced Aldous Huxley to mescaline. In October 1960, Huxley met with a Harvard psychology professor by the name of Timothy Leary and urged him, according to the latter's account in his autobiography, to "become a cheerleader for evolution" by pouring "brain-drugs, mass-produced in the laboratories, into the streets of the Western democracies."[53] The title of Huxley's book on drug use, *The Doors of Perception*, got shortened to simply *The Doors* by a California-based rock-group led by Jim Morrison, the son of a U.S. Navy admiral, who became a cult figure for years after his death. His tomb at Père LaChaise cemetery in Paris is currently that city's fourth most popular tourist attraction. Journalists writing for the countercultural *Rolling Stone* magazine have claimed to get phone calls from the dead singer in the middle of the night twenty years after his death. Crowley was perhaps the main conduit by which the occult reading of Nietzsche was introduced into popular culture.

With the inclusion of Aleister Crowley into *Sgt. Pepper's Lonely Hearts Club Band*, the marriage of the occult underground and Negro music was complete. As its dowry, rock music was given hegemony over popular culture. The hegemony began in earnest with a series of Dionysian rituals in 1969 and continues until this day. The Dionysian nature of the rock concert should have been obvious to even the most obtuse observer from the beginning, but it was not. The screaming hysteria of the teenage girls who came to listen to the Beatles was simply written off as something that teenage girls did. But then the energy at the concerts started to increase, and suddenly things did not seem so harmless any more.

Even as early as the Rolling Stones' 1966 concert tour, the music was leading to mayhem almost everywhere it was played. "The opening concert in Lynn, Massachusetts," according to one account,

> was stopped by the police after only minutes, and the audience dispersed with a ferocity that turned mere high spirits into orgiastic mob rage. As the Stones drove away from Lynn Bowl auditorium, their car windows were belabored with wooden planks torn up from the walkways. In Montreal, the Stones stopped playing to boo the stage-front bouncers for punching and judo-chopping at girls who tried to join Mick Jagger at the microphone. . . . In Vancouver, the thirty-six concert casualties included ushers kicked in the groin, policewomen suffering from exhaustion, bouncers with alleged concussions, and fans nursing assorted broken bones. In Montreal, where the police had subdued fans by ramming them head-first into a wood fence, the Stones came offstage through an aisle of fifty prostrate bodies.[54]

When the Stones finally got home that summer, the English fans seemed determined to outdo their American counterparts in mayhem and orgiastic violence. "The final show, at the Royal Albert Hall, was halted after three minutes when Jagger was attacked by three girls simultaneously, and the arbitrary collaring, punching and tossing back of half a dozen more still manifestly could not stem the screaming tidal wave."[55]

Anita Pallenberg, former Stones groupie, remembers the "madness" that emanated from a Stones concert she witnessed in Berlin, as the performance became absorbed into the emotions the performers evoked. Suddenly the emotion the musicians called forth threatened their lives:

> The music was very rebellious that night, very wild, and the atmosphere was really charged up. I was watching from backstage. Mick was doing his sexy number and the girls were throwing their panties on the stage, then quite suddenly it all

began to turn ugly, with the audience pushing and shoving their way onto the stage, and the Stones all dropped their instruments and ran. To get back to the hotel we had to go through the underground concrete bunkers connected by tunnels where Hitler and his staff had operated during the war. That was my introduction to the Stones—escaping that mad mob of wild teenagers by running through Hitler's bunkers.[56]

In an eerie replication of the rites in which the god was torn to pieces by his crazed followers, rock concerts were becoming increasingly frenzied and increasingly dangerous to the fans and the performers alike. In Zurich, Mick Jagger was pulled from a twenty-foot platform and "almost torn to pieces."[57] One musician remembers seeing fan after fan being injured during the concert and then barely escaping with his life after the concert is as over.

> We finally managed to drive a short distance to a helicopter that was waiting, and as we got off the ground we watched the kids attack the car like it was some enemy from outer space and tear it to pieces. I mean, they tore off fenders, the hood, the doors, the trunk, the wheels—it looked like giant beetles devouring a corpse from where we were in the air.[58]

"It wasn't pleasant," the musician concluded, "to see what our music did to people." Mick Jagger, however, was more philosophical (or less compassionate): "Of course, I do occasionally arouse primeval instincts, but I mean, most men can do that. They can't do it to so many. I just happen to be able to do it to several thousand people."[59] Of course, Jagger was probably not being interviewed immediately after one of his performances. Marianne Faithful, who was his girlfriend during the sixties, describes his frame of mind at moments like that:

> He was very violent. He was like somebody possessed. I don't think he even knew who I was. He still had his makeup on, and there was a froth of spittle around his lips. His eyes were violent. He was making sounds, guttural sounds, and he was completely unintelligible. He was a berserk stranger.[60]

One expert in psychology consulted to explain this phenomenon delivers himself of the opinion that

> concert-hall hysteria represents a sudden escape of the kind of emotions which the forces of puritanism, morality and authority—both social and parental—normally seek to contain. When a pop audience blows its top, it is, in fact, indulging in a communal act of defiance against a set of values which it feels to be unnecessarily and intolerably restrictive.[61]

Nietzsche did not invent the Dionysian orgy, any more than the author of the Book of Wisdom in the Bible did; he discovered it by studying Greek literature, specifically *The Bacchae* of Euripides. So, in effect, he discovered something as old as mankind itself The Dionysian orgy was the age-old rebellion, not against "an intolerably restrictive . . . set of values," but, as Mann saw through his much more perceptive reading of Nietzsche, against all reason, all social order, all possible morality, and any sexual restraint. It was, as Euripides himself well understood, a rebellion against the whole idea of state, family, and civilization. This is a rebellion to which we all, as young Pentheus demonstrated so effectively, possess a fatal attraction. Nietzsche had found that Euripides had discovered original sin, and now the syphilitic young philology professor who had gambled his life and sanity on a promise he had heard in the music of Wagner's *Tristan und Isolde* wanted to turn that arcane knowledge into a weapon against the human race in an act of unprecedented cultural terrorism. The history of the twentieth century—from the Nuremburg rallies, to the Stones concert at Altamount, to the destruction of intellectual life at the universities at the hands of his deconstructor epigoni—is a catalogue of his triumphs—triumphs, as Leni Reifenstahl might have put it, of his will.

So the Rolling Stones could have tapped directly into the Dionysian sources every bit as much as Euripides did. But the connections with modern occultism are more direct. Instead of reaching Dionysos in Protestant fashion by a direct link, they did it in more Catholic fashion through a sort of diabolical apostolic succession. The key figure in this connection was a man from Hollywood by the name of Kenneth Anger. Raschke describes Anger as a "'cult' figure in the motion-picture industry." [62] Anger, a follower of Aleister Crowley, joined Anton LaVey's Church of Satan in the sixties. In 1965 he authored the quintessentially trashy *Hollywood Babylon*, which recounted the wild goings-on in Hollywood in the good old days before the arrival of the Hays commission, which was organized by the movie moguls to avert pressure from America's churches. Featured prominently on the cover of *Hollywood Babylon* was Jayne Mansfield, another Church of Satan member who broke with LaVey and ended up being decapitated in a particularly gruesome automobile accident. Anger claimed in *Babylon* that the Hollywood director William Desmond Taylor was a follower of Aleister Crowley and a "high officer" in the Order of the Templars of the Orient, "a secret society whose precepts included the practice of *Magia Sexualis*, 'sex magic,'" Anger translates for the non—Latinists among his readers.[63]

In 1967, Anger was working on what he called his "first religious film," something called *Lucifer Rising*, which included footage of the Rolling Stones, a helicopter touching down in Vietnam, and alchemical tattoos.[64] While in London, he met Marianne Faithful, who introduced him to the Stones. In an interview with David Dalton and Richard Henderson, Anger gives the impression that the Stones were already involved in the occult though their connection with Anita Pallenberg, whom Anger calls "a witch." Brian Jones had met Pallenberg in Munich during the Stones' 1965 European tour. According to legend, it was Pallenberg who persuaded Mick Jagger to goosestep around on stage during the singing of "I Can't Get No Satisfaction" on the German part of the tour, outraging the German press. Anger saw *Lucifer Rising* as a piece of Crowleyan sympathetic magic, which would inaugurate the Luciferian age. At one point he proposed doing the film with the Stones cast in the leading roles: "Mick being Lucifer and Keith [Richards] as Beelzebub. Beelzebub is really the Lord of the Flies, and is like the crown prince next to the King in the complicated hierarchy of demons. Beelzebub is like a henchman for Lucifer. . . . The occult unit within the Stones was Keith and Anita and Brian. You see, Brian was a witch too." [65] When asked what "the active magical element in the Stones' music" was, Anger replied. "It has such strong sexual connotations. It's basically music to f— to." "Which is where rock 'n' roll came from?" the interviewers wonder. "Sure," replies Anger.[66]

Anita Pallenberg in another interview claims that she learned what she knew about black magic from Anger. Brian Jones was especially prone to violent incidents where women were concerned, and, after being on the receiving end of one of these beatings, Pallenberg decided to get revenge by casting a spell on him:

> I decided to make a wax figure of Brian and poke him with a needle. I molded some candle wax into an effigy and said whatever words I said and closed my eyes and jabbed the needle into the wax figure. It pierced the stomach. . . . Next morning when I went back to where I was living with Brian, I found him suffering from severe stomach pains. He'd been up all night, and he was in agony, bottles of Milk of Magnesia and other medications all around him. It took him a day or so to get over it. Yes, I did have an interest in witchcraft, in Buddhism, in the black magicians that my friend, Kenneth Anger, the filmmaker, introduced me to. The world of the occult fascinated me, but after it happened to Brian, I never east another spell.[67]

Whether she did or didn't is a matter for debate. The Stones' factotum Tony Sanchez claimed that Pallenberg used human remains to cast spells against people. At some point in the sixties, Pallenberg went from being Brian Jones' girlfriend to being Keith Richards'. According to Norman, it was through Pallenberg that Richards got involved in the occult.

> At Anita's prompting, Keith himself had grown fascinated by black magic and witchcraft and convinced—as many others had been—that Kenneth Anger possessed the powers of a "magus," or sorcerer. At one point, Keith and Anita even contemplated a pagan marriage ceremony, with Anger officiating. They were deterred—according to Spanish Tony—by an unmistakable warning not to meddle in realms that could become dangerous.[68]

By the late sixties, Anger was involved in a series of "religious" films that were attempts to bring about the dawning of the new age prophesied by Crowley. *Inauguration*, according to Raschke,

> was crafted to celebrate the spring equinox of the year 1966, when Crowleyite prophecies of the "new age" were supposed to be consummated and LaVey would proclaim the "second coming" of Satan. According to Crowley's own notes, *Inauguration* is supposed to be set in Crowley's Abbey of Thelema. The face of the historical Crowley appears in the movie. . . . Film analysts have noted that *Inauguration* is designed to ritualize the raging, psychic elements of the sixties as the epoch of what Crowley termed "force" and "fire." Anger's "Eucharist" was the theatrical murder of the Christian God, in fact, of all civilized values bespoken

in the classical divinities themselves. Anger told the press his film was a major "improvised happening." It was the supreme "communion" with the unfathomable, black abyss of time and history.[69]

After having experienced the "summer of love" in the Haight-Ashbury district of San Francisco during the summer of 1967, Anger felt that the time was right for another attempt to ring in the dawn of the Luciferian age. This version of *Lucifer Rising* featured a twenty-year-old actor by the name of Robert K. Beausoleil in the starring role. Beausoleil had been living with Anger in a house known as the Russian Embassy and was the lead guitarist for a group known as the Magick Powerhouse of Oz, which was to perform the sound track for the film. Under Anger's tutelage, Beausoleil was introduced to the arcana of sympathetic magic as well as the lore of Aleister Crowley. On September 21, 1967, Anger filmed a performance of the band at the Straight Theater on Haight Street, which was billed as a celebration of the Equinox of the Gods. The event was intended to be a celebration coinciding with the completion of the filming of *Lucifer Rising*, but something seems to have gone awry, inducing Anger to fall into a rage, smashing in the process a cane he had inherited from Crowley. Evidently sensing that the time of their collaboration was over, Beausoleil moved out of the Russian Embassy, taking with him Anger's car, some camera equipment, and footage from *Lucifer Rising*. Ed Sanders suspects that the move took place while Anger was in Washington at that year's famous anti-Vietnam war demonstration, during which Anger, stripped to the waist, revealing a tattoo of Satan on his chest, screamed "Out, Demon, out" in an attempt to levitate the Pentagon. A number of the demonstrators were arrested for civil disobedience that day.

Back in England, Anger's other adepts in the occult were having their own problems with the law. On February 12, 1967, the police arrived at Keith Richards' country house in West Sussex and arrested both Richards and Mick Jagger, whose jacket contained four amphetamine pills Marianne Faithful had brought back from Italy. It was the beginning of a series of encounters with the legal system that would continue for years. On June 29, 1967, both Jagger and Richards were convicted on drug charges and sentenced to three months and to one year in prison, respectively. What followed their sentencing was like a replay of *The Bacchae*. There were, of course, public demonstrations against the severity of the sentences, but the really uncanny parallels could be seen in the authorities' reaction to the young Dionysos who was now so manifestly within their grasp. The establishment clearly found itself drawn to what Jagger stood for every bit as much as young Pentheus found himself drawn to his prisoner Dionysos' offer to go and view the rites of the Bacchantes. On July 2, William Rees-Mogg, editor of the *Times*, opined that Jagger should be let off. "If we are going to make any case a symbol of the conflict between the sound traditional values of Britain and the new hedonism," Rees-Mogg wrote in the lead editorial in the *Times* that day, "then we must be sure that the sound traditional values include those of tolerance and equity."[70] Norman saw in this editorial "the new official line that Jagger was to be let off the hook."[71] On the last day of that law term, July 31, the London Appeals Court overturned the convictions of both Jagger and Richards and set them free. Instead of going to jail, Mick, the young Dionysos, with Marianne Faithful on his lap, was on his way by helicopter to a televised encounter with the Establishment, where he could lecture them on the errors of their outmoded ways. Philip Norman refers to the incident as

> Mick Jagger's moment of supreme triumph. The society that had mocked, abused, and finally tried to destroy him now cast itself down before him with all the apologetic reverence due to a misjudged messiah. The editor, the peer, the bishop and the Jesuit earnestly entreated him to reveal "what the young people in this country *really* think."[72]

When, later, Jagger was confronted on another case of moral dereliction, this time getting Marianne Faithful pregnant, the Establishment once again proved singularly ineffective in getting its point of view across. In public debate, Mrs. Mary Whitehouse defended the institution of marriage on Christian principles: "If you're a Christian or a person with faith, and you make that vow, when difficulties come, you have this basic thing you've accepted. You find your way through the difficulties." Jagger, who was probably smart enough to know that the Church of England was founded because Henry VIII wanted a divorce (in case he didn't have time to do the research himself, *A Man for All Seasons* was the Academy Award winner for 1966), replied, "Your Church accepts divorce. It may even accept abortion—am I right or wrong?"[73] From its very inception, the Church of England had a spotty track record when it came to upholding sexual standards. It did eventually go along on abortion, just as it had ratified the society's desire for contraception with the verdict of the Lambeth Conference of 1930. Like Pentheus in the *Bacchae*, the Establishment was having a difficult time condemning Jagger as a reprobate when it seemed intent on reserving to itself the same sort of sexual freedoms he was advocating so openly. It was clear from Rees-Mogg's editorial that appearing tolerant and open were higher values for the Establishment than defending the integrity of Christian marriage. When Jagger flaunted what they acknowledged in private, they found that they did not have the heart to press the issue. Like Pentheus, they let him off, and the social fabric was torn to pieces as a result.

The Rolling Stones did not go unaffected by the Establishment's decision either. Throughout the late sixties, their involvement in both drugs and Satanism grew apace. In what they hoped would be an attempt to cash in on the Beatles' success with *Sgt. Pepper*, the Stones produced *Their Satanic Majesties Request*, which was a drug-soaked, mushy-sounding commercial and artistic failure. As a result, by mid-1969, the Stones were in deep financial trouble. Their agent Allen Klein was embezzling their money, and the Inland Revenue people were now looking for their cut of all the money that had passed so quickly through their hands. In addition to all that, by 1969 the Stones' founder and lead guitarist, Brian Jones, was so consumed by his drug habits that he had become all but worthless to the band. He would nod off at recording sessions, and what he eventually did play had become so musically incoherent that the other Stones had taken to leaving his amplifier unplugged during recording sessions. Jones was generally so stoned he oftentimes did not notice one way or the other.

During this period of crisis, Jagger responded by firing Klein, kicking Jones out of the band, and coming up with an album, *Beggar's Banquet*, and a song, "Sympathy for the Devil," which made them a marketable commodity again. Jagger ostensibly got the idea from Marianne Faithful's reading of Mikhail Bulgakov's novel *The Master and Margarita*, but their previous association with Kenneth Anger probably played a role as well. With Jones out of the band and Klein out of the way as manager, the Stones now had a chance of making some money on their upcoming American tour. On July 3, 1969, Brian Jones was found dead in the swimming pool of his estate, the former home of A. A. Milne and the place where Milne composed the Winnie-the-Pooh stories. Hotchner claimed that Jones had been murdered, but no charges were filed then or later. Jones' death had cleared the way for the Stones' comeback. On July 26, 1969, Jagger's twenty-sixth birthday, Jagger played the newly finished tape of "Sympathy for the Devil" for the assembled well-wishers. (Paul McCartney was there that night and played his new song "Hey Jude" to similar accolades.) When the crowd at Club Vesuvio spontaneously started dancing, Mick Jagger must have known he had a hit in "Sympathy for the Devil."

Satanism had finally made its way out of the arcane and prolix journals of Aleister Crowley. It was no longer just the fixation of the turgid underground films of Kenneth Anger. It was now part of mainstream pop culture. Mick would sing his Satan song to millions of people in the States during his tour that fall. And during his press conferences he would say that he identified with revolutionary youth in America. Having heard about Woodstock, and stung by the charges that he was overcharging for tickets, Jagger decided in a moment of either revolutionary altruism or good PR to announce that the Stones were going to give a free concert. "It's going to be on December sixth in San Francisco. But it isn't going to be in Golden Gate Park. It's going to be somewhere adjacent to Golden Gate Park and a bit larger...."

By the time Anger returned from the anti-Vietnam war demonstration in Washington in the late fall of 1967, Beausoleil was gone, causing the Satanist filmmaker to fall into another rage. This time the result was a road-shaped amulet with Beausoleil's name on it and a corresponding curse. Beausoleil had gone south, to Los Angeles, and both he and his girlfriend Laurie were living with a thirty-year-old graduate student by the name of Gary Hinman at the time. As the summer of love in Haight-Ashbury had shown, it was a time of lemming-like pilgrimage out of the heartland and toward the centers of bohemia on either coast for the nation's disaffected youth. At the mouth of Topanga Canyon in Los Angeles was one such collecting point, a two-story house owned by a lady named Gina and famed for its "light-show" parties. In December of 1967, Beausoleil attended one of these parties and met a diminutive (5'2") thirty-three-year-old ex-con by the name of Charles Manson, who since his first LSD trip had identified himself with Jesus and had the disconcerting habit of falling down in mid-conversation and kissing his interlocutor's feet. Manson was typical of the criminal element then feeding on the drug-fried teenagers who had converged on San Francisco. He had acquired a group of followers known as his "family." The daughter of actress Angela Lansbury was just one of the offspring of the rich and famous and the not so rich and famous who formed part of Manson's entourage in the late sixties. Taking his cue from Ken Kesey and Neal Cassady, Manson purchased a school bus, decorated it with what were termed at the time psychedelic colors, and traveled from state park to state park, picking up the teenage casualties of divorce and broken families. Manson's technique was to use his age to his advantage. After he picked up the then nineteen-year-old Susan Atkins, he took her to her apartment and, while having sexual intercourse with her, asked that she pretend he was her father.

Sanders claims that Manson was introduced to satanism through the work of the Process Church of the Final Judgment, a satanic offshoot of the Church of Scientology, which was proselytizing among the Los Angeles demimonde in general and motorcycle gangs in particular during the late sixties. (In the spring of 1967, the Process Church had rented a mansion in the Mayfair section of London and opened an all-night coffee bar that attracted much of the avant-garde of the time, including Marianne Faithful, whose picture eventually showed up in the third number of their *Process* magazine. Through Faithful, the Process Church attempted to make contact with both the Beatles and the Rolling Stones.) However, it is more plausible to attribute Manson's connection with the occult to his contact with Beausoleil, who got what he knew from Anger, who was a disciple of Aleister Crowley. Manson's contact with Beausoleil antedated the efforts of the Process Church in Los Angeles by at least a year. In late 1967, Manson, who could quote the Bible chapter and verse, identified himself as Jesus, working the hippie love-scam in a way palatable to the sensibilities of America's runaways. Beausoleil at this time identified himself as Satan, and gradually, through their mutual association, Satan and Christ began to merge their identities—with the former, as one might suspect, gaining the upper hand.

Manson's deepest aspiration was to become a rock musician. Given the times, it was not an implausible aspiration. Manson's entourage or sexually willing teenage girls (Manson had been a pimp in the fifties) provided a sure entrée to the wealthy sybarites of the Los Angeles music and film colonies, including Dennis Wilson, drummer of the Beach Boys, whose house was eventually taken over by the Manson family, forcing Wilson to relocate. The "family" appropriated Wilson's gold records, which eventually began showing up as objects of barter in various places in Southern California. Manson recorded his song "Cease to Exist" at head Beach Boy Brian Wilson's recording studio. Renamed "Cease to Resist," it later became the B-side of a Beach Boy single. Manson was also in contact with Terry Melcher, the wealthy son of Doris Day and, at the time, producer of her television series. Melcher was at one point interested in recording Manson's music and in producing a *cinéma vérité* film on hippies' mores but backed away when the general weirdness became too much for him. It was a fateful decision, if not for Melcher, then for the people who were living in what Manson thought was his house.

No one has ever claimed that Charlie Manson was a deep thinker. Yet he is perhaps all the more interesting as a sign of the times for that very reason. Much of Southern California was seized with an apocalyptic mood in the late sixties, fearing and/or hoping for an insurrection that would begin in the Negro ghettos and spread to the general population, carried by white youth alienated by the country's increasing involvement in the war in Vietnam. Such was the gospel preached in the circles of left-wing, occult bohemia, and gradually the music of the times began to switch from singing the praises of surfing and fast cars to expressing the concerns of this group of people. Manson was interested in social change, and being a product of his times he saw in music its most potent agent. Everyone had the sense that an old age was ending and a newer, more liberated one beginning, and that somehow rock music would play a role in its advent. The new age was going to be Dionysian; even the people who did not know what the word meant and had never read Nietzsche were convinced of that. And as Nietzsche could have told them, music is the characteristic Dionysian art, and intoxication its primary effect. Southern California in the late sixties was awash with Dionysian music and new and more complicated agents of intoxication. Manson was no intellectual innovator; he was simply a con man trying to put the currents he found all around him together into some coherent scam. In this regard, Manson's attempt to work the occult bohemia of California in the late sixties is remarkably similar to Adolf Hitler's attempt to do the same in Vienna in the period before World War I.

Vincent Bugliosi, the prosecuting attorney who eventually got Manson convicted and sentenced to death (the death sentence was commuted to life imprisonment when California abolished the death penalty) and got to know Manson as well as anyone, saw "substantive parallels between Hitler and Manson":

> Both were vegetarians; both were little men; both suffered deep wounds in their youth, the psychological scars at least contributing to, if not causing, their deep hatred for society; both suffered the stigma of illegitimacy, in Manson's case because he himself was a bastard, in Hitler's because his father was.
>
> Both were vagrant wanderers; both were frustrated, and rejected, artists; both liked animals more than people; both were deeply engrossed in the occult; both had others commit their murders for them.[74]

According to Bugliosi, the two men had an uncanny ability to influence others based on personal magnetism and a philosophy that rationalized any action no matter how monstrous. The philosophical source for both men was Nietzsche. The debt Hitler owed to Nietzsche is obvious; Manson, according to his own testimony, claimed to be equally indebted, and Bugliosi sees in both a commonly shared philosophy:

> Both Manson and Hitler believed in the three basic tenets of Nietzsche's philosophy: women are inferior to men, the white race is superior to all other races, it is not wrong to kill if the end is right.
>
> And kill they both did. Both believed that mass murder was all right, even desirable, if it furthered the attainment of some grand plan. Each had such a plan, each had his own grandiose obsession: Hitler's was the Third Reich, Manson's was Helter Skelter.
>
> At some point parallels become more than coincidence. How much of this was conscious borrowing on Manson's part, how much unconscious emulation, is unknown. I do believe that if Manson had had the opportunity, he would have become another Hitler. I can't conceive of his stopping short of murdering huge masses of people.[75]

"Helter Skelter" was the phrase smeared in blood on the walls of the victims murdered by the Manson family. It was Manson's occult term for the general apocalyptic uprising that these murders were to presage and provoke. Helter Skelter was Manson's term for the new Dionysian age.

Helter Skelter was the Book of Apocalypse as interpreted by the Beatles. In keeping with the tenor of the times, Manson claimed he got his inspiration from the Beatles, specifically the song of the same name from their so-called "white" album, which was released in December 1968. Manson was convinced that the Beatles' song "Revolution No. 9" referred to Revelation 9 and that the four angels referred to there were the Beatles. The angels had "hair as the hair of women," and out of their mouths "issued fire and brimstone," which, according to Gregg Jakobson, who explicated Manson to Bugliosi, "referred to the spoken words, the lyrics of the Beatles' songs, the power that came out of their mouths."[76] According to Manson's interpretation of the song "I Will," "the Beatles were looking for JC [Jesus Christ] and he [Manson] was the JC they were looking for. He also told them that the Beatles knew that Christ had returned to earth again and that he was living somewhere in Los Angeles."[77] According to Manson's plan, the Beatles' white album had set up the expectation for the revolution, but Manson's album, soon to follow, would actually set it off. Charlie's music would "blow the cork off the bottle. That would start it."[78] Bugliosi gives the impression that the music was simply appropriated by Manson's deranged mind. However, the lyrics of George Harrison, the one Beatle who would not grant Bugliosi permission to quote his material, also ended up in blood on the wall of the house Sharon Tate rented. The lyrics, from his song "Piggies," refer to "piggies" in starched white shirts who need a damned good whacking. In a culture suffused with threats of terrorism and of revolution ruled over by rock stars, it was tantamount to a permission slip for mayhem.

The Manson family murder of Sharon Tate and the people staying at her house was seen by Manson as the ideal event to unleash the coming revolution. One week later, at the other end of the country, five hundred thousand drug-zonked teenagers and musicians gathered for an orgy of music and intoxication that seemed to be everything Nietzsche could have asked for in terms of Dionysiac excess. Much was made of the fact that no one was murdered at Woodstock. (One person died after being run over by a tractor.) The event was a harbinger of a new age of peace and love. But the age didn't last long. It ended before the year was out at the follow-up concert the Stones held at an abandoned race track in Livermore, California, forty-some miles southeast of San Francisco. Stung by the charge that they were gouging their fans for inflated ticket prices on their American tour, the Stones decided to give a free concert at Sears Point as their tribute to the spirit of the age. When the conditions for using that site proved unacceptable, Melvin Belli, the famous San Francisco trial lawyer, was called in to negotiate another venue, eventually at the Altamont raceway. Belli, in a touch of Dionysian symmetry, was at the time involved in the Charles Manson trial, then taking place in Los Angeles. The Maysles' documentary of the Stones' tour, eventually released under the title *Gimme Shelter*, shows footage of Belli interviewing people with suitably large plots of California property while witnesses in the Manson case cooled their heels in another room.

Just who invited the California Hell's Angels to act as bodyguards at the free concert is a matter of dispute. In light of what happened there, it is not difficult to see that no one would want to claim responsibility for the decision. However, the fact was that virtually all the rock bands in the area considered the Hell's Angels cultural heroes and an integral part of the scene. One of Janis Joplin's albums sported the official Hell's Angel seal of approval. Jefferson Airplane, who would play at Altamont, regularly invited the Hell's Angels to their concerts, apparently feeling that the Angels' outlaw image and paraphernalia of leather and violence enhanced the band's image as cultural revolutionaries.

When the Hell's Angels arrived at 10:00 A.M. on the morning of December 6, 1969, one hundred thousand spectators had already arrived, most of them having abandoned their cars on the traffic-clogged access roads. In order to increase the drama of their entrance, the Angels rode through the crowd up to the stage. Those who did not get out of the way were in danger of being run over. When one female spectator complained, one Hell's Angel stopped and dispatched his female companion to punch her in the mouth. By the time the music started that afternoon, the sun had gone behind a veil of hazy cloud-cover, suffusing the gritty and auto-wrecked moonscape with a grey light. If this was the Woodstock of the West, the future did not seem as promising as it had that summer.

Santana, a Woodstock alumnus, was the first group to play, and the Latin rhythms of that band seemed to dispel the encroaching gloom for a bit. However, with the music came the increasing violence that the music inspired. On top of that, the sound system was not functioning particularly well, and a sort of desultory moodiness settled over the crowd. Throughout the day the temperature fell, until by nightfall the crowd had taken to burning what wood there was from a fence and their own trash in order to derive some fleeting warmth from the acrid smoke that swirled over them. By the time Jefferson Airplane took the stage, a pattern had been established for the day. The band would bellow out some incitement to revolution and then stand back in befuddlement as the crowd actually acted on what they were saying. Jefferson Airplane, a group that had always billed itself as front men for the encroaching anarchy and disorder, now seemed at a loss, if not genuinely terrified, as the understanding dawned on them that what they had been preaching in their songs was now happening before their very eyes. When Jefferson Airplane sang the refrain to their song "Revolution," "Up against the wall, m—f—," a swarm of their culture heroes, the Hell's Angels, started pounding on a young black man in the audience with their lead-filled, sawed-off pool cues. This conflict of cultural icons provoked acute cognitive dissonance among the band members. Marty Balin, the group's lead vocalist, jumped off the stage to intervene and was pounded into unconsciousness for his troubles, while Grace Slick, the female lead singer, could only register lack of comprehension over the PA system. "Hey," she pleaded impotently, "we're cool. We can be cool. Hey, down there. Why are we hurting each other?"[79]

By the time the Rolling Stones took the stage, it was dark and the crowd had already been incited to riot by the music and been beaten by Hell's Angels when they did riot, for hours. If the Stones had been capable of appraising the situation and responding to it in a musically appropriate fashion, they would have gone out and played a Brahms' lullaby. But the Dionysian festival has its own rigorous protocols, and as a result of that and the Stones' very limited musical repertoire, the disaster went on as if preprogrammed by forces beyond their control. The crowd seemed programmed, too. In spite of the chill in the air, the spectators determinedly kept taking off their clothes and crawling toward the stage, there to be bludgeoned by the Angels' leaded pool cues. "Does it take five of you to handle that?" Jagger asked over the PA system as a swarm of Hell's Angels bludgeoned a naked girl in front of the stage.[80] Spanish Tony Sanchez gave the best account when he said that the rock fans acted like sacrificial victims, "impelled, as if by some supernatural force, to offer themselves as human sacrifices to these agents of Satan."[81]

The festivities reached their apogee when Mick Jagger broke into the by now wildly inappropriate "Sympathy for the Devil." Even Jagger seemed shocked and appalled at the violence his song began to unleash. He broke off in mid-verse and pleaded pathetically for everyone to "just cool out now." For the first time since the beginning of the whole neo-rock movement of the sixties, the performers seemed completely intimidated by the violent forces their music unleashed. Suddenly they recognized they were not in control of these forces. Thinking that the crowd was heeding his injunctions, Jagger started "Sympathy for the Devil" once again, and once again the violence broke out. Once again Jagger broke off in mid-song. "We always have something very funny happen when we start that number," he told the crowd. If the comment was intended as a joke, no one was laughing. Jagger now found himself squeezed into a little box of space on a stage occupied by a phalanx of Hell's Angels who wanted to be the center attraction and star of the show. Their particular form of performance art was clubbing spectators. The Stones were about to be overwhelmed by mayhem. Their only defense was their music. "We knew that if we stopped playing there really would have been a riot," said Mick Taylor later. Taylor was the late Brian Jones' replacement and would later drop out of the band, claiming the dubious distinction of being the only guitarist to leave the band alive. Unfortunately the only music the Stones knew how to play was precisely the sort that would incite even more mayhem. In the middle of the confusion over whether they should continue with "Sympathy for the Devil" or try something else, a young black man wearing a green suit started running toward the stage with what looked like a gun in his hand. He was met half-way to the stage by the usual cohort of Angels, one of whom this time had a knife instead of a pool cue. Eighteen-year-old Meredith Hunter was stabbed to death in front of the stage. The supernatural forces mentioned by Tony Sanchez, as if now placated by human sacrifice, allowed the Stones, who either could not tell what was going on or would not admit to knowing it, to finish their set and run for the waiting helicopter:

> As the Stones bolted from the stage, the Angels moved in on the remaining beer supply, howling that now "the party" could really begin. Across in the asphalt pit area, fourteen people threw themselves into the Stones' eight-seat helicopter. Before the door closed, it was lifting off, its plastic bubble crammed like a cookie jar with bodies and leather lapels and boots and Mick Jagger's sweat-smeared, frightened face.[82]

The fact that the revolution would start with music was a genuinely Nietzschean concept. Nietzsche had always insisted that the new age would be born out of the spirit of music. He had even indicated that Africa might be the source of this new music. Now it seemed that his prophecy was going to be fulfilled. Charles Manson was hardly the only one thinking in terms of Dionysian revolution. The more well-read the revolutionary, the more explicitly Nietzschean/Dionysian the project.

Anger's films had been full of interspersed shots of motorcyclists and rock groups. Mick Jagger had written the film score for Anger's *Invocation of My Demon Brother* on a Moog synthesizer. Now it seemed that life was going to imitate art.

Dionysos Rising

Those who knew about the Dionysian mysteries in an explicit way set about replicating them according to the tenets of the sixties' avant-garde. Sometime during the modern age the work of art ceased to be an act of mimesis, of imitation of nature, as Aristotle would have called it, and became instead a work of sympathetic magic, something that enhanced the power of the "artist" and brought about the type of world he and his demonic supporters found congenial. Art became a sort of occult/bohemian terrorism, and the people associated with that milieu noticed the connection themselves. "Drugs," said Marianne Faithful in retrospect, after having kicked a heroin addiction,

> kept me from being a terrorist—by that I mean there came a point where I think I felt that either I was going to have to explode out out into something, into actual acts of violence in some way, or I was going to have to implode and contain it. And I decided to keep it in. So I turned the violence against myself by taking drugs, which did violence to me. But that destructiveness could easily have gone the other way. If I had fallen in with Erika [sic] Meinhof, for example, I can see I could have readily joined my terrorism to hers and exploded in violence against society. I could have. I really could have.[83]

The fact is that Miss Faithful and her friends did explode in violence against society in a way that was much more effectively destructive than anything that Ulrike Meinhof or Andreas Baader or the Rote Armee Faktion did. Herr Baader and Frau Meinhof are dead, and their followers were dispersed when their safe houses in the DDR disappeared in the wake of the fall of communism in 1989, but the aesthetic terrorism (to use Raschke's term) of the Rolling Stones is still the regnant religious rite at rock concerts throughout the world—a rite, it should he noted, that still culminates in human sacrifice on a disconcertingly regular basis. Along the way, the similarities between rock music and other Dionysian festivals in this century crop up, but no one seems to take them very seriously. Albert Goldman, for instance, wrote in a quasi-humorous vein about the similarities between the Nuremberg rallies and a Rolling Stones concert in *The New York Times*:

> Ja wohl! Mein friends dot's right! Dot good old rock 'n' role could warm the cockles of a storm trooper's heart. OK—they don't give you a torch and an armband, like in the real old days, and send you down the Rhine to swing with the summer solstice. But you can still squeeze in hip by haunch with thousands of good kamerads; still fatten ears, eyes and soul on the Leader; still plotz out while he socks it to you in stop time, and best of all, boys and girls, you can get your rocks off, no, with that good old arm action that means . . . well, you know what it means. . . . No question about it, Der Fuhrer would have been gassed out of his kugel by the scene at the Forum. . . .[84]

The evolution that took place within a matter of three years in the Manson family from peace and love to murderous insurrection replicated itself in rock music in general. "Heavy metal" rock music became the heir to the cutting edge in cultural terrorism. Before long, people other than Albert Goldman began to recognize the connection between Nuremberg and Woodstock. "Heavy metal rock videos and heavy metal magazines," according to Raschke,

> are often nothing more than crude but ruthless commercials for what in Nazi speech was called the "triumph of the will." The aesthetics of heavy metal videos are often copied from Nazi propaganda films. And heavy metal is by and large propaganda.[85]

Like Charles Manson, Nikki Sixx of Mötley Crüe saw in Hitler a paradigm of social organization. Just as Hitler's spectacle at Nuremberg was a working of sympathetic magic that organized the brown-shirted youth of his day, so Mötley Crüe concerts function in the same way for the black T-shirt crowd: "The one thing I got from Hitler," says Mr. Sixx, "was the idea of the Nazi youth. I believe in the Mötley youth. The youth of today are the leaders of tomorrow. They're young, they can be brainwashed."[86] If anything, the rock concert is a more effective implementation of what Nietzsche foresaw in *The Birth of Tragedy* than anything Hitler put on in Nuremberg. For one thing, Hitler's extravaganzas were much too controlled compared to the more Dionysian rock rites. Raschke cites the testimony of a security guard at a Scorpions' concert—"It was wild. . . . There was vomit and blood everywhere. . . . This band drives the kids into an uncontrollable frenzy"—and concludes that "drugs go with heavy metal as wine flowed, of necessity, through the Dionysian frenzy."[87] Both Hitler and the heavy metal crowd are attempting to implement the ecstasy that Nietzsche proposed in *The Birth of Tragedy*.

The rock concert is this age's institutionalization of Nietzsche's Dionysian festival, complete with fornication, intoxication, and death. It was honed into an art form by the explicitly satanic overlay provided by Crowley and Anger and the African music composed by the Rolling Stones. By the 1970s it had all become formalized in what Raschke calls "aesthetic terrorism," which is by now indistinguishable from satanism:

> "Magic" in Crowley's sense of mastery of the world by the will, or what Nietzsche called "the will to power as art," became extraordinarily fashionable, if only at a sophisticated and self-conscious level. Aesthetic terrorism was the notion derived from avant-garde artistic work, and applied to the occult, that power over things ultimately requires social revolution, which in turn demands a subversion of symbols. . . . For the supreme "knowledge of good and evil" in the occult sense to dominate over what Nietzsche dubbed the "slave consciousness" of the Christian believer, a campaign of terror must he waged. Bourgeois and Christian values must be ambushed, trampled down, eviscerated, and tossed aside by creating a universal sense of the invincibility of evil. Aesthetic terrorism is a blunt instrument in the war of values. It slices to the heart of what we mean by satanism.[88]

In another scene reminiscent of *The Bacchae*, the Dionysiacs of the sixties took over one after the other of our cultural institutions behind the backs of the conservative guardians of law and order, who were concentrating on a military and economic confrontation with a communist empire that would collapse under its own weight roughly twenty years later. The guardians of the social order had been trying to understand Marx while the revolutionaries were all reading Nietzsche. When the revolutionaries played the sexual card, the guardians of the social order all found themselves compromised or in possession of a cultural Maginot line whose weapons were an inadequate response to their opponents' strategies. Like Mr. Rees-Mogg of the *Times*, the Establishment preferred "openness and toleration" to the moral order. Dialogue was the ploy whereby the revolutionaries captured the high cultural ground. The guerilla theater of the sixties was followed by the tenure battles of the seventies, as Dionysiac sexual liberation and its adherents made their march through the institutions. The turn inward always seems to be the aftermath of failed political revolutions. After the failures of 1849, Wagner wrote *Tristan*. After the failures of 1968, Rudi Duetschke and Daniel Cohn-Bandit proposed the "march through the institutions," of which we are still suffering the consequences. However, the cultural revolution beginning in the sixties seemed more than just that. It seemed to be a conscious effort to implement the vision Nietzsche sketched out in *The Birth of Tragedy*. In the early sixties in Vienna, the playwright Hermann Nitsch organized the performance of what he termed "OM," or "orgy mysteries," during which the performers became intoxicated with alcohol and drugs and then dismembered live animals and smeared themselves with their blood. The object of the Dionysian revel was to render the participants "divine" and bring about "the liberated joy of strong existence without barriers."[89]

In New York City in the late sixties, Richard Schechner, a professor of drama at New York University, was involved in a similar project. During much of 1968 and 1969, Schechner directed *Dionysus '69*, a nude group grope, complete with animal blood, based loosely on Euripides' play *The Bacchae*. Schechner was unaware of Nitsch's orgy mysteries at the time he initiated *Dionysus '69*, but he was aware of Nietzsche, and it is in light of his sympathetic reading of the Dionysiac forces (an interpretation Euripides did not share) that Schechner saw the parallels between New York in 1969 and Thebes under Pentheus.

> The analogues between the situation in the *Bacchae* and our own times are obvious. The logic of the *Bacchae* is inescapable and unconsoling. The state cannot recover its youthful virility. And the young blond, effeminate god offers nothing but his politics of ecstasy Dionysian demands gratification here and now. He overturns the traditional values which have become oppressive and only apparently strong (Pentheus' army never marches and it is made clear that if it were to fight it would lose).The state is worse than weak—it is silly, controlled by a young, prurient king, old men disguised as women and women driven mad.[90]

Professor Schechner is an instructive example for a number of reasons. One was his role in directing *Dionysus '69*, but the more important reason is how well he indicates how the occult/underground was adopted by academe in the years following World War ll. Just as Mick Jagger took Crowleyan satanism into the pop-culture mainstream, so Professor Schechner took the Dionysian orgy and made it into a three-credit course. At Goddard College, he got the co-eds to take off their clothes and do another version of the group grope that was becoming his theatrical specialty:

> While in residence at Goddard College in September 1970 I led a student workshop. I explained, as I usually do, that the work is done best in a minimum of clothes, and I recommended leotards for the women and shorts for the men. A student asked me if he could work naked. I said yes and about half the workshop of twenty people stripped. Frankly, I was shocked.[91]

Shocked was the professor—a bit, I suppose, like Claude Rains in *Casablanca* when he hears that gambling is going on at Rick's café. Schechner had been running the same sort of thing in *Dionysus '69* for years with the same sort of constituency. The avant-garde found a home at the universities without a ripple of protest, led by a cohort of fornicating, dope-smoking professors like Schechner. "I am a professor," he tells us at one point in *Public Domain*, and then adds in what has become almost a tautology: "I have a fine apartment, I enjoy the open pleasures of women and the more or less open pleasures of pot."[92] By the time Allan Bloom got around to writing his book on the fall of the universities in the late eighties, the Dionysian professorate had veto power over virtually the whole university apparatus from the tenure committees to grant-dispensing agencies such as the NEA and NEH. When Professor Schechner wrote about *Dionysus '69*, he fantasized a revolution of the political sort, complete with raging mobs who come to his Washington Square apartment and carry off—you guessed it—his stereo equipment. "I have had the fantasy of the revolution beginning, crowds storming across Washington Square and entering my apartment building, overpowering the doorman . . . ."[93]

That revolution never arrived; the other one, the cultural one, moved in the opposite direction. It was borne by Professor Schechner and his colleagues out of the apartments of Washington Square and into the classrooms of the universities across the country. That revolution was in many ways similar to AIDS, the disease it spawned, in that there was no violent overthrow, just a progressive weakening of the culture's immune system under the increasingly deleterious burden of uninhibited sexuality The institutions of culture did not get overthrown; they got AIDS as a result of excessive and perverse sexual activity and are now in a terminally weakened state, preliminary to death.

In order to give his vision of the three-credit, pan-cultural group grope an aura of respectability, Schechner has to go to the philosophical impetus that got the culture headed in that direction one hundred years before. Professor Schechner looks to Nietzsche as the ultimate legitimator of cultural revolution. He cites "the metaphysical solace" Nietzsche described in *The Birth of Tragedy*, the belief that "life is at bottom indestructibly joyful and powerful," which "was expressed most concretely in the choruses of the satyrs, nature beings who dwell behind all civilization and preserve their identity through every change of generations and historical movement."

"Everyone," Schechner goes on to tell us,

> has a sense of what Nietzsche is talking about: "The force that through the green fuse drives the flower." Underneath whatever repressive machinery civilization constructs to keep itself intact, a counterforce of great unifying celebratory, sexual and life-giving power continues to exert its overwhelming and joyful influence. At certain times in everyone's life and during certain periods of each society's history this counterforce is activated. It is perhaps improper to speak of it as a "counterforce" since it seems—when active—to be more authentic than the civilization— the specific social inhibitions—it opposes and frequently obliterates. Dionysus' presence can be beautiful or ugly or both. It seems quite clear that he is present in today's America—showing himself in the hippies in the "carnival spirit" of black insurrectionists, on campuses; and even in disguise on the patios and living rooms.[94]

Yet even so enthusiastic a proponent of Dionysiac revolution as Professor Schechner is not without his moments of ambivalence. During one of his group grope theater workshops, one of his female students was injured by an over-exuberant male participant. Although it was difficult to distinguish her cries of pain from the general Dionysian emoting going on at the time, Schechner eventually got the message and called an ambulance to have the young woman taken to a hospital.[95] The young lady could serve as a stand-in for all the people who died or were wounded to make the Dionysian age a reality. The incident was enough to make Schechner pause for a moment and reflect that he was not the only implementer of Nietzschean values during this century. A disaffected architecture student had attempted the same thing, and for a moment there is a glimmer of recognition that the "politics of ecstasy" creates casualties wherever it is implemented:

> But this same ecstasy, we know, can be unleashed in the Red Guards or horrifically channeled toward the Nuremberg rallies and Auschwitz. There, too, at the vast extermination camps, an ecstasy was acted out. The hidden fear I have about the new expression is that its forms come perilously close to ecstatic fascism.... Are we ready for the liberty we have grasped? Can we cope with Dionysus' dance and not end up—as Agave did—with our sons' heads on our dancing sticks?[96]

The image of "our sons' heads on our dancing sticks" is a haunting one. Schechner borrowed it from *The Bacchae*, of course, but it reminds one of a more recent image. The abortionist picking the head out of the dismembered limbs of a recently aborted fetus. The abortionist has to sort through the various body parts of the dismembered fetus to make sure nothing has been left in the womb. Both Schechner's reading of *The Bacchae* and the everyday carnage of the abortion industry indicate that all of the manifestations of Dionysian culture follow their rigid trajectory toward death. What begins in sexual liberation ends in death. Pornography leads to the snuff film when the quotient of violation is no longer satisfied with the usual venue of perversion. Gustav Aschenbach could see in his dream that sexual liberation led to bloodshed. Out of abortion came the ultimate snuff film of our generation, *The Silent Scream*. It was done by a doctor and showed on ultrasound the dismemberment of a fetus. The doctor who produced the film, Bernard Nathanson, has since become an opponent of abortion, but in the sixties, he felt that the *Zeitgeist* had handed him the permission slip he needed to overturn the law. In his book *Aborting America*, he describes the moral/intellectual climate in New York City in particular, where Schechner was staging his productions of *Dionysus '69*, and also in the country at large:

> There was talk of a new push for repeal in the legislature. The climate was right. The war protestors had securely captured the media. Male hair was coming down, grass was the white middle class party drug. All the women were on the Pill. The times, they were a-loosening.[97]

Both Aleister Crowley and the DeGrimsteds, who founded the Process Church of the Final Judgment, found Mexico a particularly congenial place for working magic because of the history of human sacrifice associated with the Aztec culture there. That same culture has found a home with us through the agency of rock music and Nietzschean philosophy. The major phenomena of our age—AIDS, drug abuse, terrorism, skepticism and the ruin of the universities, the destruction of high culture, especially music, the breakdown of the family, especially in the inner city—these are all epiphenomena of the Dionysian ecstasy, which is to say, the desire for sexual liberation from the constraints of the moral law that has been so avidly sought for more than a hundred years now. We as a culture desire sexual liberation yet are unwilling to admit the price we have to pay to get it. The satanists are only more consistent than the rest of us in this. They know that there can be no sexual liberation, no culture of Dionysian excess, without human sacrifice. We are loath to face this fact. MTV can regularly urge parricide, and yet there is always shock and consternation when someone gets hurt. Well, there is no sexual revolution without someone getting hurt. In fact, there is no sexual liberation without death. Maybe this connection is what Wagner had in mind when he wrote the *Liebestod* of *Tristan und Isolde*. Thomas Mann understood it, and Gustav Aschenbach was willing to pay the price. Charles Manson understood the same thing and was willing to pay the price. Bernard Nathanson understood it in an inchoate way when he felt moved by the spirit of the times to lobby for the overturn of abortion laws in New York in the late sixties. Aleister Crowley understood it, too, and was drawn to the ruins of the Aztec empire as a result. So were the DeGrimsteds. The author of the Book of Wisdom understood it, too, and condemned the ancient Canaanites for their "loathsome practices, their deeds of sorcery and unholy rites, hated as ruthless murderers of children, as eaters of entrails at feasts of human flesh, initiated while the bloody orgy goes on" (12:3-6). Euripides understood the same thing in the tragically ambivalent way that characterized his culture. Ecstasy led to death, and yet even the best, like Pentheus of Thebes, were drawn by their own prurient interests toward the flame of destruction. No army in the world was powerful enough to stop the god Dionysos. No leader in the world was above collaboration with this enemy.

It is time we learned the same lesson. No army is powerful enough to contain Dionysos. No government budget of any country or any combination of countries is rich enough to buy its way out of the damage that Dionysos can wreak when he calls and the women desert their homes "to perpetuate false Bacchic mysteries in the dark woods on the mountain." When Pentheus orders his soldiers to bind Dionysos, claiming "I'm the power here, not you," the god can only reply, "Your power is mortal, you don't know what you're doing: you don't even know who you are."

When Agave awakes from her Dionysiac intoxication, she does so gradually. At first she thinks she is carrying "a trophy for the palace," and she invites her father Cadmus to "take it in your hands" and "glory in my kill. Invite your friends to feast for you are blessed, blessed by our accomplishments." Cadmus, less blinded by the intoxication his daughter has sought so avidly, can see that the trophy Agave brags about is in reality the head of her son Pentheus. Under his tutelage she begins to see the enormity of what she has accomplished. In the pursuit of liberation from the natural, all she has accomplished is the murder of her own child. "Look carefully," Cadmus insists as he directs her attention to the still unrecognized head of Pentheus in Agave's lap. "Study it more closely."

His words could just as easy be addressed to our Dionysian culture as well. As we awake from the intoxication of the past hundred years, we, like Agave, begin to discern the true outline of the liberation we have sought so avidly and yet so blindly "I see horror," Agave answers as her sight gradually returns, "I see suffering. I see grief."

"Does it still look like a lion?" Cadmus asks.

"No, Pentheus: I am holding his head," Agave answers.

Even then Agave does not understand how it could happen that she would tear her own son limb from limb. "You were mad," Cadmus offers by way of explanation. "The city was possessed by Dionysos." Finally Agave understands the full consequences of her actions. "I see now," she says, "Dionysos has destroyed us."

As Professor Schechner might say, the parallels with our time are obvious. Agave wakes up after Woodstock, after Altamont, after twenty-some years of rock ritual and its various forms of intoxication, after twenty years of militant political feminist Bacchantism, complete with marches in Washington, to the sound of the vacuum suction curette and visions of her child dismembered and reassembled by the abortionist to avoid septicemia and a malpractice lawsuit. "Dionysos has destroyed us," as Agave says, but there is no indication that her sight has returned. There are signs here and there, but still no overwhelming evidence that this society is willing to choose the moral order over sexual liberation and death.

Euripides was in many ways a thoroughly modern man. He possessed that ambivalence which is the chief characteristic of Greek tragedy and civilization whereby you're damned if you do and damned if you don't. Pentheus is destroyed for not worshiping Dionysos: his mother is ruined for doing the exact opposite. That there was a way out of this dilemma was the intuition of the author of the Book of Wisdom and the message of hope suffusing the whole Judeo-Christian heritage. That that hope entailed the acceptance of an order—moral, social, even musical—which man could adopt but not create was an intolerable affront to a syphilitic philology professor from Basel. He aspired to a return to an age that antedated civilization and was its ecstatic antithesis. Unlike Euripides, it was impossible for him not to know better. His vision, unlike Agave's, was a deliberately chosen blindness. In the new dispensation, Dionysos could only be synonymous with the Antichrist. If there is to be any dispensation following that one, it can only be that of the Anti-Antichrist. Death—actual, physical, spiritual, cultural—is the only alternative.

Notes

1. Martin Vogel, *Schönberg und die Folgen: Die Irriwege der Neuen Musik* (Bonn: Verlag für systematischen Musikwissenschaft, 1984), p. 125.
2. Friedrich Nietzsche, *Werke in Drei Bänden* (Munich: Cart Hanser Verlag, 1954), vol. 2, p. 1152.
3. Nietzsche, vol. 1, p. 131.
4. Nietzsche, vol. 1, p. 131.
5. Nietzsche, vol. 1, p. 133.
6. Thomas Mann, *Doktor Faustus: Das Leben des deutschen Tonsetzers Adrian Leverkühn erzählt von einen Freunde*, in *Gesammelte Werke* (Frenkfurt am Main: S. Fischer Verlag, 1980), p. 699.
7. Mann, *Doktor Faustus*, p. 699.
8. Theodor W. Adorno, *Philosophy of Modern Music*, trans. Anne G. Mitchell and Wesley V. Blomster (New York: The Seabury Press, 1973), p. 40.
9. Adorno, p. 40.
10. Adorno, p. 40.
11. Vogel, p. 77.
12. Adorno, p. 59.
13. Adorno, p. 67.
14. Adorno, p. 66.
15. Adorno, p. 66.
16. Adorno, p. 68.
17. Thomas Mann, *Pro and Contra Wagner*, trans. Allen Blunden (Chicago: University of Chicago Press, 1985), p. 20.
18. Mann, *Pro and Contra*, p. 20.
19. Adorno, p. 77.
20. Adorno, p. 116.
21. Adorno, p. 69.

22. Vogel, p. 315.
23. Vogel, p. 315.
24. Vogel, p. 315.
25. Jost Hermand, *Kultur im Wiederaufbau: Die Bundesrepublik Deutschland, 1945-1965* (Munich: Nymphenburger Verlagshandlung, 1986), p. 404.
26. Hermand, p. 435.
27. Peter Jona Korn, *Musikalische Umweltverschmutzung: Polemische Variationen über ein erquickliches Thema* (Wiesbaden: Breitkopf & Härtel, 1981), p. 44.
28. Korn, p. 42.
29. Korn, p. 45.
30. Korn, p. 46.
31. Korn, p. 41.
32. Korn, p. 41.
33. Adorno, p. 69.
34. Hannah Tillich, *From Time to Time* (New York: Stein and Day, 1973), p. 101.
35. Tillich, p. 101.
36. Rollo May, *Paulus: Reminiscences of a Friendship* (New York: Harper and Row, 1973), pp. 88-89.
37. May, p. 45.
38. May, p. 99.
39. Tillich, p. 177.
40. C. G. Jung, *Memories, Dreams, and Reflections*, rec. and ed. Aniela Jaffe, translated from the German by Richard and Clara Winston (New York: Random House, 1989), p. 238.
41. E. Franklin Frazier, *The Negro Family in the United States* (Chicago and London: University of Chicago Press: 1966, original ed., 1939), p. 220.
42. A. E. Hotchner, *Blown Away: The Rolling Stones and the Death of the Sixties* (New York: Simon and Schuster, 1990), p. 64.
43. Hotchner, p. 70.
44. Aleister Crowley, *The Confessions of Aleister Crowley: An Autohagiography*, ed. John Symonds and Kenneth Grant (London: Arkana, 1979), p. 145.
45. Crowley, p. 539.
46. Crowley, p. 849.
47. Crowley, p. 746.
48. Crowley, p. 746.
49. James Webb, *The Occult Establishment* (LaSalle, Ill.: Open Court, 1976), p. 495.
50. Carl A. Raschke, *Painted Black: From Drug Killings to Heavy Metal—The Alarming True Story of How Satanism Is Terrorizing Our Communities* (San Francisco: Harper and Row, 1990), p. 94.
51. See Paul C. Vitz, *Sigmund Freud's Christian Unconscious* (New York: Guilford Press, 1988), pp. 101ff.

52. Raschke, p. 95.
53. Raschke, p. 96.
54. Philip Norman, *The Rolling Stones Story: Sympathy for the Devil* (New York: Linden Press/Simon and Schuster, 1984), p. 183.
55. Norman, p. 184.
56. Hotchner, p. 176.
57. Hotchner, p. 150.
58. Hotchner, 152.
59. Hotchner, p. 155.
60. Hotchner, p. 155.
61. Hotchner, p. 150.
62. Raschke, p. 100.
63. Kenneth Anger, *Hollywood Babylon* (Phoenix, AZ: Associated Professional Services, 1965).
64. Raschke, p. 100.
65. Norman, p. 269.
66. Norman, p. 269.
67. Hotchner, p. 183.
68. Norman, p. 269.
69. Raschke, pp. 109-10.
70. Norman, p. 233.
71. Norman, p. 233.
72. Norman, p. 238.
73. Norman, p. 268.
74. Vincent Bugliosi, *Helter Skelter: The True Story of the Manson Murders* (New York: Bantam Books, 1974), p. 640.
75. Bugliosi, p. 641.
76. Bugliosi, p. 239.
77. Bugliosi, p. 240.
78. Bugliosi, p. 241.
79. Norman, p. 329.
80. Norman, p. 333.
81. Tony Sanchez, *Up and Down with the Rolling Stones* (New York: William Morrow and Co., 1979), p. 184.
82. Norman, p. 335.
83. Hotchner, p. 214.
84. Norman, p. 316.
85. Raschke, p. 171.
86. Raschke, p. 172.
87. Raschke, p. 173.
88. Raschke, p. 103.
89. Raschke, p. 104.

90. Richard Schechner, *Public Domain: Essays on the Theater* (Indianapolis: Bobbs-Merrill, 1969), p. 107.
91. Richard Schechner, *Environmental Theater* (New York: Hawthorn Books, 1973), p. 95.
92. Schechner, *Public Domain*, p. 210.
93. Schechner, *Public Domain*, p. 211.
94. Schechner, *Public Domain*, p. 217.
95. Schechner, *Public Domain*, p. 222.
96. Schechner, *Public Domain*, p. 228.
97. Bernard Nathanson, M.D., with Richard N. Ostling, *Aborting America* (New York: Doubleday & Co., 1979), p. 63.

Bibliography

Adorno, Theodor W. *Philosophy of Modern Music.* Translated by Anne G. Mitchell and Wesley V. Blomster. New York: The Seabury Press, 1973.

Anger, Kenneth. *Hollywood Babylon.* Phoenix, Arizona: Associated Professional Services, 1965.

Aristotle. *Politics,* in *The Basic Works of Aristotle.* Edited with an introduction by Richard McKeon. New York: Random House, 1941.

Barzun, Jacques. *Darwin, Marx, Wagner: Critique of a Heritage.* Chicago and London: University of Chicago Press, 1981.

Bloom, Allan. *The Closing of the American Mind: How Higher Education Has Failed Democracy and Impoverished the Souls of Today's Students.* New York: Simon and Schuster, 1987.

Bugliosi, Vincent. *Helter Skelter: The True Story of the Manson Murders.* New York: Bantam Books, 1974.

Burbach, Hermann-Josef. *Studien zur Musikanschauung des Thomas von Aquin.* Regensburg: Gustav Bosse Verlag, 1966.

Chisholm, Anne. *Nancy Cunard: A Biography.* New York: Alfred A. Knopf, 1979.

Crowley, Aleister. *The Confessions of Aleister Crowley: An Autohagiography.* Edited by John Symonds and Kenneth Grant. London: Arkana, 1979.

Cunard, Nancy, ed. *Negro: An Anthology.* Edited and abridged. New York: Frederick Ungar Publishing Co., 1970.

Dalton, David. *The Rolling Stones: The First Twenty Years.* New York: Alfred A. Knopf, 1981.

Deathridge, John and Carl Dahlhaus. *The New Grove Wagner.* New York: W. W. Norton, 1984.

Derrida, Jacques. *Spurs: Nietzsche's Styles.* Chicago: University of Chicago Press, 1978.

Eastman, Max. *Love and Revolution.* New York: Random House, 1964.

Ebner, Ferdinand. *Schriften.* Munich: Kösel Verlag, 1963-1965. Vol. 2.

Euripides. *The Bacchae: A New Version.* Translated by C. K. Williams, with an introduction by Martha Nussbaum. New York: Farrar, Straus,Giroux, 1990.

Frazier, E. Franklin. *The Negro Family in the United States.* Chicago and London: University of Chicago Press, 1966, original ed. 1939.

Gregor-Dellin, Martin. *Richard Wagner: His Life, His Work, His Century.* Translated by J. Maxwell Brownjohn. San Diego and New York: Harcourt Brace Jovanovich, 1980.

Gustin, Molly. *Tonality.* New York: Philosophical Library, 1969.

Gutman, Robert W. *Richard Wagner: The Man, His Mind, and His Music.* New York: Harcourt, Brace & World, 1968.
Haimo, Ethan. *Schönberg's Serial Odyssey: The Evolution of His Twelve-Tone Method, 1914-1928.* Oxford: Clarendon Press, 1990.
Hayman, Ronald. *Nietzsche: A Critical Life.* New York: Oxford University Press, 1980.
Hermand, Jost. *Kultur im Wiederaufbau: Die Bundesrepublik Deutschland, 1945-1965.* Munich: Nymphenburger Verlagshandlung, 1986.
Hinrichs, Dr. Regina. "Tu was du willst soll das ganze Gesetz sein," *Theologisches* (January 1992), pp. 16-23.
Hotchner, A. E. *Blown Away: The Rolling Stones and the Death of the Sixties.* New York: Simon and Schuster, 1990.
Huggins, Nathan Irvin. *Harlem Renaissance.* New York: Oxford University Press, 1971.
Hughes, Langston. *The Big Sea: An Autobiography.* New York: Hill and Wang, 1940.
Jung, C. G. *Memories, Dreams, and Reflections.* Recorded and edited by Aniela Jaffe, translated from the German by Richard and Clara Winston. New York: Random House, 1989.
Kellner, Bruce. *Carl Van Vechten and the Irreverent Decades.* Norman, Okla.: University of Oklahoma Press, 1968.
King, Martin Luther, Jr. *A Comparison of the Conceptions of God in the Thinking of Paul Tillich and Henry Nelson Wieman.* Boston University, Ph.D. Dissertation, 1955.
Knight, G. Wilson. *The Shakespearian Tempest.* London: Oxford University Press, 1932.
Korn, Peter Jona. *Musikalische Umweltverschmutzung: Polemische Variationen über ein erquickliches Thema.* Weisbaden: Breitkopf und Härtel, 1981.
Lebrecht, Norman. *Mahler Remembered.* New York: W. W. Norton, 1987.
Mann, Thomas. *Doktor Faustus: Das Leben des deutschen Tonsetzers Adrian Leverkühn erzählt von einem Freunde*, in *Gesammelte Werke*. Frankfurt am Main: S. Fischer Verlag, 1980.
Mann, Thomas. *Pro and Contra Wagner.* Translated by Allan Blunden. Chicago: University of Chicago Press, 1985.
Mann, Thomas. *Tagebücher*, 1940-1943, 1944-1946, 1946-1948. Frankfurt am Main: S. Fischer Verlag, 1982.
Mann, Thomas. "Tristan," in *World Masterpieces Revised.* Maynard Mack, general editor. Vol. 2. *Literature of Western Culture since the Renaissance.* New York: W. W. Norton, 1965.

Bibliography

Mann, Thomas. *Der Tod in Venedig*. Text, Materialien und Kommentar mit den bisher unveröffentlichten Arbeitsnotizen [bearbeitet von] T. J. Reed. Munich: Carl Hanser Verlag, 1983.

May, Rollo. *Paulus: Reminiscences of a Friendship*. New York: Harper and Row, 1973.

Melichar, Alois. *Musik in der Zwangsjacke*. Vienna and Stuttgart: Eduard Wancura Verlag, 1958.

Melichar, Alois. *Schönberg und die Folgen*. Vienna and Stuttgart: Eduard Wancura Verlag, 1960.

Mellers, Wilfrid. *Caliban Reborn: Renewal in Twentieth-Century Music*. New York: Harper and Row, 1967.

Millington, Barry. *The Master Musicians: Wagner*. London and Melbourne: J. M. Dent and Sons, 1984.

Nathanson, Bernard, M.D., with Richard N. Ostling. *Aborting America*. New York: Doubleday, 1979.

Neumann, Erich. *Amor and Psyche: The Psychic Development of the Feminine, A Commentary on the Tale by Apuleius*. Princeton, N.J.: Princeton University Press, 1956.

Nietzsche, Friedrich. *Werke in Drei Bänden*. Munich: Carl Hanser Verlag, 1954.

Norman, Philip. *The Rolling Stones Story: Sympathy for the Devil*. New York: Linden Press/Simon and Schuster, 1984.

Oesterle, John A. "Toward an Evaluation of Music," *The Thomist*, 14 (1951), pp. 323-34.

Peyser, Joan. *The New Music: The Sense behind the Sound*. New York: Delacorte Press, 1971.

Raschke, Carl A. *Painted Black: From Drug Killings to Heavy Metal—The Alarming True Story of How Satanism Is Terrorizing Our Communities*. San Francisco: Harper and Row, 1990.

Robsjohn-Gibbings, T. H. *Mona Lisa's Moustache*. New York: Alfred A. Knopf, 1947.

Roman, Zoltan. *Gustav Mahler's American Years: 1907-1911*. Stuyvesant, N.Y.: Pendragon Press, 1989. A documentary history.

Sanchez, Tony. *Up and Down with the Rolling Stones*. New York: William Morrow and Co., 1979.

Sanders, Ed. *The Family: The Story of Charles Manson's Dune Buggy Attack Battalion*. New York: E. P. Dutton, 1971.

Schechner, Richard. *Environmental Theater*. New York: Hawthorn Books, 1973.

Schechner, Richard. *Public Domain: Essay's on the Theater*. Indianapolis: Bobbs-Merrill, 1969.

Schopenhauer, Arthur. *Die Welt als Wille und Vorstellung*. Zürich: Haffmans Verlag, 1888.
Smith, Joan Allen. *Schönberg and His Circle: A Viennese Portrait*. New York: Schirmer Books, 1986.
Spitzer, Leo. *Classical and Christian Ideas of World Harmony: Prolegomena to an Interpretation of the Word "Stimmung."* Baltimore: The Johns Hopkins Press, 1963.
Stössl, Otto. *Sonnenmelodie: Eine Lebensgeschichte*. Berlin and Leipzig: Deutsche Verlags Anstalt, 1923.
Stuckenschmidt, H. H. *Schönberg: His Life, World, and Work*. Translated from the German by Humphrey Searle. New York: Schirmer Books, 1977.
Szmolyan, Walter. *Josef Matthias Hauer.*Vienna: Verlag Elisabeth Lafite, 1965.
Tillich, Hannah. *From Time to Time*. New York: Stein and Day, 1973.
Ventura, Michael. "Hear That Long Snake Moan," *Whole Earth Review* (Spring 1987), pp. 28-43; (Summer 1987), pp. 82-92.
Vitz, Paul C. *Sigmund Freud's Christian Unconscious*. New York: Guilford Press, 1988.
Vogel, Martin. *Schönberg und die Folgen: Die Irrwege der Neuen Musik*. Bonn: Verlag für systematischen Musikwissenschaft, 1984.
Volz, Pia Daniela. *Nietzsche im Labyrinth seiner Krankheit: Eine, medizinisch-biographische Untersuchung*. Würzburg: Könighausen und Neumann, 1990.
Wagner, Richard. *Mein Leben*. Munich: Paul List Verlag, 1963.
Wagner, Richard. *Parsifal*. London: John Calder, 1986.
Wagner, Richard. *Richard Wagner's Prose Works*. Translated by William Ashton Ellis. Vol. I, *The Artwork of the Future*. Vol. 2, *Opera and Drama*. New York: Broude Brothers, 1966.
Wagner, Richard. *Richard Wagner to Mathilde Wesendonck*. Translated, prefaces, etc., by William Ashton Ellis. Second edition. New York: Vienna House, 1972.
Wagner, Richard. *Tannhäuser*. London: John Calder, 1988
Wagner, Richard. *Tristan und Isolde*. London: John Calder, 1981.
Webb, James. *The Occult Establishment*. LaSalle, Ill.: Open Court, 1976.
Werfel, Franz. *Verdi: Roman der Oper*. Berlin: Paul Zsolnay Verlag, 1926.

Index

Adorno, Theodor Wiesengrund, 139, 142
  on Hauer, 130-131
  influence on Mann, 107-108, 129-130, 133-134, 137
  Zur Philosophie der neuen Musik, 129, 133, 137, 138
  on Schönberg, 102, 107-108, 134, 137
  twelve-tone system, 134
    antidote to order, 130-132
    freedom and self-destruction, 133, 138
    rebellion against nature, 132, 133
  Weltanschauung, 134
Agoult, Marie-Catherine-Sophie d,' 47
Anger, Kenneth,
  films, 153, 159
    Inauguration, 150
    Invocation of My Demon Brother, 159
    Lucifer Rising, 149-151
  Hollywood Babylon, 149
  influence of Crowley on, 149, 150, 154
  occult interests, 149-151, 159-161
Antheil, George, 78, 81-82, 142
Apel, Theodor, 26
Apuleius, Lucius,
  Amor and Psyche, 24-25,
Aristotle, 20, 50
  on music, 31, 42
  Politics, 16, 82
Asquith, Margot, 80
Atkins, Susan, 154
Augustine, Saint,
  Confessions, 138-139
  tranquillitas ordinis, 15, 20

Baader, Andreas, 160
Bakunin, Mihail, 21, 114
  as anarchist, 9, 29, 31-32, 42
  on Beethoven, 9, 12, 131
  destruction as goal, 9-10, 12
  revolutionary beliefs, 11, 12-13
  suggestions for *Jesus of Nazareth*, 10
Balin, Marty, 158
Baudelaire, Charles-Pierre,
  Flowers of Evil, 139
Beardsley, Aubrey, 143
Beausoleil, Robert K., 151, 153-154
Beecham, Sir Thomas, 79, 80
Beethoven, Ludwig van, 32, 55, 56, 111
  and Bakunin 9, 12, 131
  Ninth Symphony 9, 12, 38
Belli, Melvin, 157

Berg, Alban, 119, 128, 133
  on Second Quartet, 102, 116
  student of Shönberg, 102, 105, 108
Bernadette Soubirous of Lourdes, Saint, 126
Berry Chuck, 142, 143
Biberstein, Robert Marschall von, 12
Bismarck, Otto Eduard Leopold von, 61
Bizet, Georges, 94
  Carmen, 68-69
Blavatsky, Helena Petrovna, 144
Bloom, Allan, 74, 163
Blunt, Anthony, 114
Boethius, Anicius Manlius Severinus, 16
Brockhaus, Luise, 48
Browne, Sir Thomas 19
Bugliosi, Vincent, 155-157
Bulgakov, Mikhail,
  The Master and Margarita, 153
Bülow, Hans von, 34, 56-57, 62
Burbach, Herman-Josef, 15-16
Burgess, Guy, 114
Buroughs William, 73

Cage, John, 70, 139, 142
  and African music, 115
  damage to music by, 102-103, 104
Carlyle, Thomas, 12
Cassady, Neal, 154
Chamberlain, Houston Stewart, 146
Cicero, 15-16
Clapton, Eric, 142, 143
Clemens, Samuel, 104
Cohn-Bandit, Daniel, 162
Copland, Aaron, 135
Crowder, Henry, 80
Crowley Aleister, 165
  Book of the Law, 145
  comparison to Hitler, 145
  Dionysian nature of rock concerts, 147, 161
  influence on Anger, 149, 151, 154
  influence of Nietzsche on, 144
  occult interests, 144, 146, 153, 161
Cunard, Lady Maud, 79, 80
Cunard, Nancy, 79-81, 115

Dahms, Walter, 102-103
Dalton, David, 149
Day, Doris, 155
DeGrimsted, Robert and Mary Ann, 165

Dehmel, Richard, 100
   influence on Schönberg, 96-99, 101-102, 116
   Welt und Weib, 96
Deussen, Paul, 51, 52
Duetschke, Rudi, 162
Dunbar, John, 143
Durell, Henry Edward, 83

Eastman, Max, 114-115
Ebner, Ferdinand, 109-111
Eliot, T. S.,
   The Waste Land, 79-80
Emmerson, Ralph Waldo, 54
Engels, Friedrich, 114
Ertegun, Ahmet, 142
Eugenie (Empress of France), 11
Euripides,
   The Bacchae, 152, 161
   influence on Nietzsche, 53, 83, 93, 148
   influence on Schechner, 162, 164
   liberation and death, 85-86, 165-167

Faithful, Marianne,
   and Anger, 149, 153
   drug use, 151, 160
   and Jagger, 143, 148, 152, 154
Feuerbach, Paul Johann Anselm von, 33, 61
   influence on Wagner, 13, 29, 67
   sensuality of, 67, 68
Förster, Bernard, 94
Freud, Sigmund, 58, 75, 108
   death, 125
   drug use, 73, 146
   and the Mahlers, 91, 101
   refusal of Christian conversion, 98
   and Salome, 91

Garbo, Greta, 127
Gast, Peter, 53, 66, 95,
Gautier, Judith, 54, 66
Gemelli, Bonaventura,
   Dionysus among the Muses, 53
George, Stephan, 102
Gersdorff, Carl von, 60, 61
Gershwin, George, 126
Gerstl, Richard, 101, 109, 119, 121
Ginsberg, Allen, 143
Gobineau, Joseph-Arthur de, 146
Goebbels, Joseph, 120, 126, 137
Goethe, Johann Wolfgang von, 15, 146
Goldman, Albert, 160-161

Gregor-Dellin Martin,
   on Heine and Laube, 25, 26
   on Nietzsche, 54, 66, 67
   on Wagner, 12, 54
      break with Nietzsche, 66, 67
      relationship with Minna, 27
Gropius, Walter,
   affair with Alma Mahler, 71, 101, 125
   emigration to U.S., 125, 139
   politics, 140, 143
Gutman, Robert W., 49

Haimo, Ethan
   Schönberg's Serial Odyssey: The Evolution of His Twelve-Tone Method, 1914-1928, 104-105, 108
Hanslick, Eduard, 21
Hardenberg, Friedrich Leopold von [pseud. Novalis], 20, 32
Harrison, George, 156
Hauer, Josef Matthias,
   and Adorno, 130-131
   comparison to Schönberg, 107-110, 113-114, 115-118
   marital troubles, 109, 115
   "Music and Drama," 112
   Nomos, 105, 110, 116, 119
   on *Tristan und Isolde*, 109-114
   twelve-tone system, 120
      diatonic scale, 111-112
      invention, 105-106, 115, 119
      as law of universe, 106, 117
      order without emotion, 105, 110-114, 121
      as spirituality in music, 106, 111-112
   as unbalanced person, 107, 109, 110, 111
Hayman, Ronald, 66-67
Hegel, Georg Wilhelm Friedrich, 12, 36, 98
Heine, Heinrich, 25
Heller, Erich, 132-133
Hemingway, Ernest Miller,
   A Farewell to Arms, 82
Henderson, Richard, 149
Hermand, Jost, 134, 136, 138
Herwegh, Georg, 29
Hess, Rudolf, 145
Heubner, Otto, 11, 12
Hindemith, Paul, 134, 136
Hinman, Gary, 153

Index

Hitler, Adolf, 104, 148
   comparison to Crowley, 145-146
   comparison to Manson, 155-156
   and Nietzsche, 95, 127-128, 156
   and occult avant-garde, 95, 128
Homer, 93-94
Hotchner, A. E., 153
Huggins, Nathan Irvin, 75-76, 77, 85
Hughes, Langston,
   The Big Sea: An Autobiography, 76-77
Hunter, Meredith, 159
Hurston, Zora Neale, 76
Huxley, Aldous,
   The Doors of Perception, 146-147
Huysman, Joris-Karl,
   La Bas, 139

Jagger, Mick, 74
   Beggar's Banquet, 153
   concert hysteria,
      Altamont, 157, 166, 85
      in Germany, 149
   drug use, 151-152
   Faithful as mistress, 143, 148, 149, 152, 153
   satanism and pop culture, 153, 162-163
   "Sympathy for the Devil," 153, 158-159
Jakobson, Gregg, 156
John Chrysostom, Saint, 15
Johnson, Robert, 85, 142, 143
Jones, Brian, 115
   and Anita Pallenberg, 149
   and the occult 149, 150
   drug use and death, 115, 152, 153
Joplin, Janis, 85, 157
Joplin, Scott,
   "Maple Leaf Rag," 70
Jung, Carl Gustav, 141

Kandinsky, Wassily, 120, 146
   On the Spiritual in Art, 117, 128
Kerouac, Jack, 73
   On the Road, 74
Kesey, Ken, 154
Kietz, Gustav, 13
King, Martin Luther, 142
Klein, Allen, 152, 153
Knight, G. Wilson, 7, 19
Kokoschka, Oskar, 125-126
Korn, Peter Jona, 136-138
Krenek, Ernst,
   Jonny Spielt Auf, 82, 142
Krug, Gustav, 49
Künzel, Marthe, 145

Lansbury, Angela, 154
Laube, Heinrich, 26, 27, 29
   Liebesbriefe, 27
Laussot, Eugene, 28-30
Laussot, Jessie, 28-29, 30, 47-48,
LaVey, Anton, 149, 150
Leary, Timothy, 146
Lenin, 94, 110, 114
Lewis, C. S.,
   The Abolition of Man, 131
Lewis, Jerry Lee, 85
Liszt, Franz, 11, 28, 47, 65
Little Richard, 85, 142, 143
Ludwig II (King of Bavaria), 48-49, 53, 57, 58
Lutherans
   Nietzsche, 51, 54-55, 56, 59, 62, 65
   Wagner 14, 54-55, 56, 62, 65
Luther, Martin, 23, 54-55

McCartney, Paul, 153
McKay, Claude, 76
Maclean, Donald, 114
Mahler, Alma, 71, 91-92, 96, 101, 125, 126
Mahler, Gustav 70-71, 77, 96, 98-99, 101, 102,
Mailer, Norman, 74, 141
   "The White Negro," 74, 141
Mann, Thomas, 42, 131, 132, 143
   Buddenbrooks, 33
   Death in Venice, 42, 127-128, 143-144, 148
   consequences of sexual liberation, 84, 165
   sexual liberation and order, 42, 71-73, 132, 142
   Doktor Faustus, 50, 127, 128, 129
   influence of Adorno on, 107-108, 129-130, 133-134, 137
   and Nietzsche's pact with the devil, 51-52, 60, 127
   sexual liberation for social revolution, 93, 148
   emigration to U.S., 50, 139, 142
   on Nietzsche,
      illness and madness, 69, 95
      musical heir to, 128-130
      pact with the devil, 51-52, 60, 132
   and Schönberg, 100, 134
      as heir to Nietzsche, 128-130
      meeting with, 126-127
      on *Pierrot Lunaire*, 127
"Tristan," 95

Mann, Thomas (*cont.*)
  on *Tristan und Isolde*, 42, 50, 77, 96, 100
Mansfield, Jayne, 149
Manson, Charles,
  comparison to Hitler, 155-156, 161
  murders by, 156-157
  occult and satanism, 155, 156
  and revolution, 155, 157, 160, 165
Marcuse, Herbert, 129, 139
Marx, Karl Heinrich, 12, 14, 29, 33, 61, 94, 114, 131, 162
Mason, Charlotte, 76, 77
May, Rollo, 139
Mazur, Kurt, 7
Meinhof, Ulrike, 160
Melcher, Terry, 155
Melichar, Alois, 115, 136
  Musik in der Zwangsjacke, 115
Mendelssohn, Peter de, 129
Metternich, Klemens Wenzel Nepomuk Lothar von, 31, 35
Meyerowitz, J., 97
Milton, John, 18, 131
Morrison, Jim, 64, 85, 125, 146-147
Mozart, Wolfgang Amadeus,
  The Magic Flute, 19, 20, 39, 41, 110

Nathanson, Bernard,
  Aborting America, 165
  The Silent Scream (film), 165
Neumann, Erich 24
Nietzsche, Elizabeth, 49, 66, 94, 95
Nietzsche, Friedrich Wilhelm, 55, 93-94
  and African eroticism, 69, 77-78, 141
  in new Dionysian music, 66-70, 86
  and revolution, 73-74, 86, 93-94
  The Birth of Tragedy, 53, 91, 129-130, 146
    and dissonance, 62, 63, 68, 70
    and revolution, 59-62, 63-64, 163
    and rock music, 64, 161, 162
    and role of reason, 55-57
  on *Carmen*, 68-69
  The Case of Wagner, 68, 69, 70
  Christianity, 53-54, 82-83
    defeat of culture, 60-61, 63, 74
    as negation of life, 21
    rejection of God, 91, 92, 93-94
  Ecce homo, 57, 63
    prediction for future, 60, 63, 127, 130-131, 133
    on *Tristan und Isolde*, 49
  Human, All-Too-Human, 91
  illness, 62, 66, 91
  brothel visits, 51-52, 67, 92, 94
  death, 65, 81, 95
  drug use, 73
  isolation, 62, 91
  madness, 53-52, 69, 92, 95
  influence on American bohemians, 73, 74, 75
  influence on Crowley, 144-145
  influence on Mann, 69, 95
  pact with the devil, 51-52, 60
  Schönberg as heir to Nietzsche, 128-129
  influence of *Tristan und Isolde* on, 49-50, 128
  revolution based on, 55-56, 61
  sexual liberation over reason, 52-54, 68, 69, 77, 78, 93
  influence of Wagner on, 47, 49-50, 62
    betrayal, 61, 65-69
    revolution, 33, 56-60, 83-84
  music,
    as Dionysian intoxication, 128, 155, 161-162
    and dissonance, 60-65, 129-130
    and reason, 53, 54-55, 57-58
    and new age revolutionaries, 59-60
  on *Parsifal*, 65-67, 68-69
  sexual liberation, 83-84, 92-94
  Thus Spake Zarathustra, 92, 139
  and transvaluation of values, 83, 85, 86, 93-94

Nitsch, Hermann, 162
Norman, Philip, 150, 152
Novalis, *see* Hardenberg, Friedrich Leopold von

Oehme, Herr, 8
Oesterle, John A., 35, 37
Overbeck, Franz, 66, 95

Page, Jimmy, 143
Pallenberg, Anita, 147-148, 149-150
Paul, Saint, 99
Perrone, Eduard, 113
Peyser, Joan,
  Schönberg's music as autobiographical, 100-101
  Schönberg's mystical beliefs, 116-117, 118, 119
Picasso, Pablo,
  "Les Demoiselles d' Avignon," 71
Pieau, Walter, 98

Index

Planer, Minna, *see* Wagner, Christine Wilhelmine (Minna) Planer
Plato, 17, 20, 31, 42, 50, 55
Podach, Erich, 127
Presley, Elvis, 70, 85, 142, 143
Proudhon, Pierre-Joseph, 13
Pythagoras, 15-16, 59, 138

Raschke, Carl A.
   on Anger, 149, 150
   rock music and satanism, 146, 160, 161
Rauschning, Hermann,
   Hitler Speaks, 145
Ree, Paul, 92
Rees-Mogg, William, 155-156, 161
Richards, Keith, 150, 151
Rilke, Rainer Maria, 91
Ritschl, Friedrich Wilhelm, 91
Röckel, August, 8, 12
Rohe, Mies van der, 134-135
Romundt, Heinrich, 65
Rosenberg, Alfred, 128
Rossini, Giacchino Antonio, 31-32

Salome, Lou, 91-92
Sanchez, Tony, 84, 150, 158, 159
Sanders, Ed, 151, 154
Sartre, Jean-Paul, 73
Schechner, Richard, 162-166
   Dionysus in '69, 162-163, 165
   Public Domain, 163
Schikaneder, Emanuel, 19-20
Schirach, Baldur von,
   Die Fahne der Verfolgten, 137
Schönberg, Arnold Franz Walter, 130-131, 143-144
   atonality,
     period, 102-103
     and sexual liberation, 102-103, 109, 115, 119
   betrayal by Nazis, 120-121
   Christianity,
     conversion, 98-99
     rejection, 120
   comparison to Hauer, 107-109, 113, 115-118
   death, 116-117
   destruction of classical music, 70, 121, 142
   drug use, 73
   emigration to California, 50, 103, 126, 139
   formalism and monotony, 134
   Harmonielehre, 117, 120, 128
   influence of Dehmel on, 96-99, 100-102, 109, 116
   influence on Mann, 100, 126, 128-130
   influence on Van Vechten, 77
   influence of Wagner, 95-96, 109
   Judaism,
     reconverted, 120
     renunciation, 98, 121
   marriage to Mathilde, 96, 98, 99
     marital troubles, 101-102, 109-110, 115 116, 119
   Moses und Aron, 136
     order and chaos, 110, 118-121
     revenge on West, 120-121
     and superstition, 116
   music,
     as confession, 100-101
     move into dissonance, 63-64, 71
     revenge on Christianity, 119-121
   and Nietzsche, 64, 96
   as painter, 96, 101, 105, 117
   Pierrot Lunaire, 127
   popularity after World War II, 103, 134 139
   Second String Quartet, 102, 116
   Style and Idea, 101
   as superstitious, 116-117, 119, 146
   "Three Pieces for Piano," 70, 102-103, 105
   twelve-tone system,
     claim of invention, 52, 103-104, 115-116, 119, 135
     as defeat of nature and God, 131-134
     as Hauer's invention, 105, 107, 115, 119
     movement of sexual disgust, 115, 119
     order without emotion, 105, 110-114, 121
   Verklärte Nacht, 69, 101, 110
     and Dehmel's poem, 98-100
     and *Tristan und Isolde*, 65, 80-81, 97, 109
   Von Heute auf Morgen, 81

Schönberg, Mathilde von Zemlinsky, 96
   affair with Gerstl, 101, 102
   marriage to Arnold, 98, 99, 102, 119
Schopenhauer, Arthur,
   influence on Nietzsche, 51, 59
   influence on Wagner, 31, 33, 41, 42, 132 133
   music as language of the will, 53, 54-55, 57
   Die Welt als Wille und Vorstellung, 31, 33
   world-as-will philosophy, 33, 42, 59

Shakespeare, William, 19, 20, 43, 102, 114
    Henry VI, 19
    Measure for Measure, 26
    The Merchant of Venice, 7, 17-18, 91, 128
    Troilus and Cressida, 16-17, 64, 128
Sixx, Nikki, 161
Slick, Grace, 158
Socrates, 53, 55, 56, 57, 59, 92
Spender, Stephen, 138
    The God That Failed, 114
Spitzer, Leo, 15
Stalin, Joseph, 110, 114, 115, 119
Stefan, Paul, 119
Steffens, Lincoln, 115
Steiner, Rudolf, 94-95, 117, 144, 146
Steuermann, Eduard, 126-127
Steuermann, Salome, 126
Stockhausen, Karl Heinz, 142-143
    and African music, 115
    damage to music by, 102, 104
Stössl, Otto,
    roman à clef, Sonnenmelodie, 107, 108
Strachey, Lytton, 114
Strauss, David,
    Das Leben Jesu für das Deutsche Volk bearbeitet, 51
Stravinsky, Igor Fyodorovich, 77, 78, 80, 81, 135
Strindberg, August, 92, 95
Strobel, Heinrich, 104, 136-137, 138
    Melos, 137
Stuckenschmidt, H. H.,
    on Schönberg's music, 136, 138
        inaccurate accounts, 95, 107, 137
        and influence of Dehmel, 96, 98, 104
Swaggart, Jimmy, 85
Sharon, Tate, 156

Taylor, Ann 28
Taylor, Mick, 159
Taylor, William Desmond, 149
Theophrastus, 15
Thomas Aquinas, Saint, 16, 17, 20
Tillich, Hannah, 139, 140-141
Tillich, Paul, 125, 139-141, 142
Twain, Mark, 104

Van Vechten, Carl, 75, 77, 81, 115
Ventura, Michael, 74, 83, 85
Viertel, Berthold, 126,
Viertel, Salka, 126-127

Vitz, Paul C., 146
Vogel, Martin,
    on atonality, 99-100
        as destructive, 133, 134
    and Schönberg, 96-97, 102
    on Hauer and twelve-tone system, 106, 107, 108
Volz, Pia Daniela, 52

Wagner, Christine Wilhelmine (Minna) Planer,
    marriage to Wagner, 26-29, 35, 39, 43, 47, 48
Wagner, Cosima von Bülow,
    affair with Wagner, 30, 47, 48
    divorce of Hans, 62
    marriage to Wagner, 56, 57, 58, 62
Wagner, Richard,
    affairs, 27-31
        Jessie Laussot, 28-29, 30, 47-48
        Mathilde Wesendonck, 30, 31, 39, 47-48, 132
    "Art and Revolution," 28, 53
    chromaticism, 99-100
    music organization, 103
    theories, 12-14, 21
    Christianity,
        and liberation of love, 21-26, 35-43
        rejection, 14-15, 53-54, 57-58
    exile from Germany, 10-11, 13, 28
    The Flying Dutchman, 12
    influence of Beethoven on, 9, 32, 38
    influence of Feuerbach on, 13, 29, 33, 67
    influence of Laube on, 26-27, 29
    influence on Nietzsche, 33, 50-54, 55-63, 128
        break up, 61, 65-70, 83,
        Tristan und Isolde, 37-43, 52-53, 55-56, 61-62
    influence of Schopenhauer on, 25, 31, 33, 41, 42, 132-133, 54-55
    Jesus of Nazareth, 10
    Das Liebesverbot, 26
    Lohengrin, 48
    Ludwig II as patron, 48-49, 53, 57, 58
    marriage to Cosima, 30, 47, 48, 56-58, 61, 62
        children, 39, 56
    marriage to Minna, 26-28, 40, 47, 48
        marital problems, 28, 29, 35, 39, 43,
    Meistersingers of Nuremberg, 48, 49-50

Index

Wagner, Richard (cont.)
music,
   harmony as order, 15-17
   liberated from text, 32-34, 36-39
   as representation of the will, 58-59
   as a woman, 32-33, 54
Oper und Drama, 31
Parsifal, 25
   ambivalence, 61, 65-66
   Christian overtones, 14, 54
   effect on Nietzsche, 65-68
   as repentance, 65, 66, 78, 79, 93
   return to tonality, 65-68, 100
revolutionary beliefs, 7-15, 21
and sexual liberation, 21-31, 79-81, 165-166
Siegfried, 49, 56-57
Tannhäuser, 48, 93, 100
   ambivalence, 34, 35, 39, 61, 65
   Christian overtones, 14, 22-26, 54
   and Minna, 27, 28
   Tristan und Isolde comparisons, 42-43, 65
Tristan und Isolde, 48-50, 78, 110, 162
   chromaticism, 34-38, 39, 42-43, 99-100, 120, 132
   emotion without order, 59, 62, 72, 114, 128
   Hauer's reactions, 108-113
   as musical adultery, 30, 37-40, 47-48, 111-114
   subjugation of reason to music, 56-59
   Tannhäuser comparisons, 39-43, 65
   and totalitarianism, 115, 116, 120, 132
   and *Verklärte Nacht*, 64-65, 80, 97-99

Waters, Muddy, 115, 143
Webb, James, 94, 117
Webern, Anton Friedrich Wilhelm von, 101, 105, 106, 108, 130
Wellesz, Egon, 107
Werfel, Franz, 125-126
   Verdi, 107
Wesendonck, Mathilde,
   platonic affair with Wagner, 31, 39, 47, 48, 132
Whitehouse, Mary, 152
Whitman, Walt,
   Leaves of Grass, 54
Wilde, Oscar, 143,
Wilson, Brian, 155
Wilson, Dennis, 154-155
Wolfe, Thomas, 139

Yates, Brian, 143

Zappa, Frank, 70
Zemlinsky, Alexander von, 96, 99, 101, 125-126
Zille, M.A. 19